Privacy AND THE POLITICS OF INTIMATE LIFE

Privacy

AND THE POLITICS OF INTIMATE LIFE

Patricia Boling

CORNELL UNIVERSITY PRESS

Ithaca and London

First published 1996 by Cornell University Press.

Printed in the United States of America

Library of Congress Cataloging-in-Publication Data

Boling, Patricia.
    Privacy and the politics of intimate life / Patricia Boling.
        p.   cm.
    Includes bibliographical references and index.
    ISBN 0-8014-3271-5 (cloth : alk. paper). — ISBN 0-8014-8351-4
(pbk. : alk. paper)
    1. Privacy, Right of.   2. Democracy.   3. Intimacy (Psychology)
    I. Title.
JC596.B65   1996
323.44'8—dc20   96-20609

This book is printed on Lyons Falls Turin Book,
a paper that is totally chlorine-free and acid-free.

For Mark

Contents

Preface

My reasons for becoming interested in the distinctions between public and private were personal and political as well as academic. During the time I was a graduate student, I was thinking about what kind of family I wanted to belong to, and entertaining in an immediate way issues such as the importance of choosing when and whether to have children, sharing responsibility for raising children, and the impact of having kids on primary parents' careers. At the same time that several issues close to home were leading me to think about the politicalness of various household and reproductive matters, I found myself and others subject to various forms of stereotyping and exclusion: "You can't be a feminist because you have children." "You can't be a serious academic because you're a mother." "Straight women aren't really as feminist as lesbians." "Bisexuals can't join the Gay-Lesbian Support Group." I felt insulted and angry, and began to feel a little contentious about the claim that "the personal is political." I also began to appreciate the richness of having different selves and displaying varying degrees of openness, intimacy, and self-exposure in different settings. I found myself drawn to thinking about public and private in ways that would do justice to the complexity of my experience of wanting to debunk the public-private distinction in its ideological mode, but also wanting to argue that some matters are no one else's business and ought not to be made public or political, by either one's opponents or one's allies. And of course all of this took place against a background of coming of age politically in Berkeley in the late 1970s, an atmosphere in which appreciation for and involvement in radical politics and the democratic politics of participation were deeply ingrained, and where feminism was taken for granted as part of the way an academic woman thought about the world.

Situating myself with respect to a complex set of issues begins to explain why I was drawn to certain issues and approaches. But I want to move beyond the genesis of my engagement with the politics of intimate life to the questions and thematic unities that animate the theoretical and political analyses I offer here. When I first started to work on the questions of "public" and "private" discussed in this book, I was convinced that certain practices and issues involving the family and intimate relationships needed to be understood as political. These include reproductive choice; the impact of pregnancy and child rearing on women's lives; joint responsibility for raising children; the psychoanalytic dynamic that makes the mother (and by extension all women) culpable for the frustrations of early infancy; and the privacy of gays, lesbians, and bisexuals. My interest in these issues has not abated in the dozen or so years since I began to study public-private distinctions, but I have become more skeptical of the position from which I started.

There has been a crucial shift in context for feminist arguments that the public-private distinction obscures oppression and disparities in power that occur in intimate-life settings. Ten or fifteen years ago such arguments were aimed at questioning the conventional wisdom that politics is a distinct realm of human experience, and that it is necessary to protect the political realm from "merely" private matters or perspectives. Now the feminist critique of a sharp public-private distinction has become the new conventional wisdom, part of the working assumptions of students, activists, and academics, drawing nods of recognition and agreement when presenters allude to it at conferences. Now, perversely, I find myself arguing against the feminist credo, "The personal is political."

Assuming that the personal is political is problematic on two grounds. First, some matters rooted in intimate life need to be hidden and protected from public exposure rather than being politicized. Often the personal is *not* political, is not public, and is not anyone else's business. Second, such an assumption sidesteps the difficult yet crucial process by which the experiences of intimate life are transformed into claims and perspectives that are politically negotiable, and the private sufferer or interest-seeker is transformed into a citizen. Feminist theorists, activists, and citizens need to think about how to "dress" issues housed in the intimate realm to go out in public, to explain how problems many perceive as personal are in fact rooted in structures of power that support and reinforce violence and inequality in intimate life. General in their consequences, these are properly matters for public awareness and discussion, and are open to change through collective political action.

Our bodies, sexualities, reproductive capacities, gender roles, and families continue to generate some of the most controversial issues in American public life today, as protests and violence at abortion clinics and debates about physician-assisted suicide, gay rights measures, and "outing" closeted gays and lesbians rage on. Despite its importance, there seems to be little agreement about the value of privacy or the role it plays in our public

life. The Supreme Court's decisions concerning the constitutional right to
privacy often fail to provide principled explanations for the weight accorded privacy in different areas, such as abortion, gay sex, and prosecutions for fetal abuse. Although there is much good work that deals with
public-private distinctions, it falls mainly into one of two camps: legal and
philosophical discussions that support privacy, and feminist approaches
that treat privacy as ideological because it hides power and oppression
from view. Curiously, feminist critiques of the public-private distinction
rarely pay close attention to debates about legal rights and principles; nor
do legal and philosophical discussions of privacy treat feminist arguments
as central.

I seek to bridge this divide by providing a new approach to public-
and-private matters and to thinking about our concepts of private, public,
and the political. I show how legal and philosophical defenses of and feminist attacks on privacy are both necessary to an adequate understanding of
these issues. I draw on ordinary language analysis as well as Hannah
Arendt's analyses of politics, private life, necessity, "the social," and parvenus and pariahs to remind us of something we often lose sight of: that
privacy is a double-edged sword. Sometimes it is good because it protects
us from scrutiny and interference. But sometimes it is bad because it shuts
off parts of our lives from public debate and prevents us from taking political action to improve those parts of our lives.

My approach provides insight into several issues on which much of the
legal, philosophical, and feminist work on public-private connections has
been confused. Noticing that *privacy* is connected etymologically both to
people and issues that are *deprived* of public significance or office and to
the notion of *protecting* private decision making has helped me understand
that privacy is an empowering concept which permits great latitude in
personal choices and actions. But it can also be a dangerously constraining
one when it prevents individuals from recognizing how social practices
and institutions such as gender and heterosexuality structure and limit
their choices and possibilities. Furthermore, treating the process of translating personal troubles into political claims as a central question refocuses
the debate. Conflating private and public, personal and political, keeps us
from tackling a crucial problem that deserves attention: How can issues,
practices, and perspectives located in intimate life be transformed into ones
that are politically recognizable and negotiable? Private activities must be
connected to the public life of politics and citizenship, so that power and
injustice in the private realms of familial sexual and economic relations

become actionable and sources of empowerment for would-be citizens instead of accepted as insurmountable givens.

The book is divided into two parts. Part I, "Theoretical Considerations" (Chapters 1–3), engages current debates in legal and feminist theory in order to bring clarity and insight to the political issues examined in Part II, "Contemporary Domains of the Public-Private Tension" (Chapters 4–6). Chapter 1, "Why the Personal Is Not Always Political," surveys the contributions of both feminist theory and legal and philosophical analysis to the question of privacy. The two approaches rarely acknowledge or address each other's insights, but instead seem to speak past each other. I argue that both perspectives are crucial if we are to understand private and public and see how they are connected.

In Chapter 2, "Privation and Privilege," I introduce ordinary language analysis and suggest conceptual distinctions based on common ways of talking about "public," "private" and "political" which pinpoint central problems in the way we think about public and private life.

Chapter 3, "Arendt on Political Approaches to Intimate-Life Issues," draws on Hannah Arendt's ambiguous attitude toward private life. I argue that there is a valuable distinction to be gained from Arendt's work on parvenus and pariahs between political and privative approaches to thinking and talking about issues rooted in intimate life.

Chapters 4–6 focus on contentious issues in contemporary American politics. In Chapter 4, "Problems with the Right to Privacy," I discuss using the privacy right to defend reproductive and sexual choice, focusing on contraception, abortion, consensual same-sex sodomy, and the maternal obligation to safeguard fetal health. This privacy-based strategy is problematic on many counts. It allows the courts to treat social inequalities as irrelevant to the exercise of fundamental constitutional rights. It often reinforces socially condoned gender, sexual, and familial roles and relationships. And it makes the impact of social practices difficult to recognize, so that the dilemmas raised by, for example, becoming pregnant or being gay are understood as individual and personal rather than shared and political. These problems notwithstanding, I conclude that the privacy right continues to be a useful if flawed tool.

Chapter 5, "The Democratic Potential of Mothering," engages the debate over maternal thinking and the ethic of care. I argue that maternal experience has the potential for helping women become engaged citizens, but only if it can be transformed from a private experience shared only with particular loved ones to a source of political activism and judgment.

Chapter 6, " 'The Personal Is Political': The Closet, Identity Politics, and Outing," addresses a number of issues related to gay and lesbian politics. These include the notion, once current among lesbian feminists, that membership and virtue derive from one's status as a lesbian; the belief that coming out of the closet is a core political act; and arguments in favor of outing closeted gays and lesbians. I argue that problems rooted in intimate life must undergo a transformation before they can be understood as political claims, and that intimate life sometimes needs protection from public scrutiny.

In the concluding chapter, "Privacy and Democratic Citizenship," I return to theorizing about private and public. I explain the practical political stakes involved in recognizing the distinction between private and public, and of explaining persuasively when and how they are connected. I argue that we need to reject black-and-white understandings of privacy, both those which envision it as merely an ideological barrier that keeps us from recognizing the political dimensions of oppressive relationships, and those which uncritically embrace privacy rights as empowering for people seeking control over their homes, bodies, and intimate relationships. I propose a more complex way of thinking about privacy, one that is cognizant of its "both/and" quality (*both* empowering *and* depriving), and that attends to the crucial task of connecting private, especially intimate-life, experience to political language, categories, and claims. I argue that respecting privacy when appropriate, making articulate connections between private experience and political arguments when engagement with unjust practices or institutions is called for, and knowing the difference between these two situations are all crucial to transforming ordinary people, suffering in the silence of their families, ghettos, homes, or closets, into citizens.

Many have helped sustain this project as it gradually progressed to its final form. I am happy to express my debts of gratitude to institutions that supported my research, and to numerous friends and colleagues who have helped me refine my thinking and encouraged me to carry on even when the project seemed endless and amorphous.

I have been fortunate in receiving institutional support in the form of an NEH summer stipend to write a draft of Chapter 2, a Purdue Research Foundation summer grant to write a draft of Chapter 6, and a semester off from teaching as a junior faculty leave at Purdue which enabled me to finish writing a draft of the entire manuscript.

I thank Berenice Carroll, Elizabeth Collins, Mary Dietz, Jack Donnelly, Terri Jennings, Robert Kagan, Helena Klumpp, Barbara Korbal, Constance Squires Meaney, Sandy Muir, Jennifer Ring, Ferdinand Schoeman,

Siobhan Somerville, Peter Steinberger, Leslie Vaughan, and Brian Weiner for their helpful readings of and comments on parts of this book in manuscript form and for their prodding questions and fruitful conversations at crucial stages of thinking and writing. Morris Kaplan, Molly Shanley, and an anonymous reviewer for the University of Michigan Press read the manuscript in its entirety and provided extremely helpful comments. Alison Shonkwiler at Cornell University Press has encouraged me to take away the "scaffolding" that belonged to earlier stages of writing, and to write more gracefully and economically. Her vision of this book has helped me through the tasks of rewriting and rethinking, and I thank her for her intelligent editorial guidance. I also thank my copy editor, Amanda Heller, for her painstaking work.

Hanna Pitkin set an intellectual example as my teacher and adviser at Berkeley which for a long time has inspired my efforts. Her willingness to read and engage my work, her insistence on thinking through various problems, her own lucid contributions to thinking about private and public, and her example of how to work on conceptual problems have influenced my approach to theoretical and political issues and my views about the centrality of connecting private, intimate life and the public life of citizenship.

My family, which has come into being, grown, and changed in the time it has taken me to write this book, has provided the balance between absorption in daily, homey tasks, intimacy, and renewal, and thinking and writing about abstract ideas which both kept me sane and shaped my thinking about privacy in very concrete ways. I especially thank Mark Tilton for his unstinting commitment to the joint project of raising our three children, for making time for me to do my work, for his ability to be good-humored when I was not, and for his insightful, probing questions that helped me refocus my thinking at crucial moments.

My thanks to you all; you have helped make my work better and clearer.

PATRICIA BOLING

West Lafayette, Indiana

Part I

THEORETICAL CONSIDERATIONS

One

Why the Personal
Is Not Always Political

WHY SHOULD WE THINK IN TERMS OF PUBLIC and private? The distinction between them is important at two levels: first, because privacy plays a key role in our law and our society, and second, because the value of privacy and the ways in which public and private life are connected are deeply contested. Appeals to privacy are understood and relied on by all of us. We do not barge into bathroom stalls, force open locked doors, peep at people while they are having sex, train binoculars on our neighbors, chastise our colleagues for being too fat, or address people we barely know as if they were familiars. Practices that reflect our awareness of and respect for privacy norms are part of our everyday life; they inform our social interactions in a variety of contexts, and help guard activities and places that we choose to protect from inappropriate intrusion. Yet many criticize respect for "the private" and sharp distinctions between public and private on the grounds that they obscure problems and perspectives that should be seen and acknowledged.

Why do critics of privacy give short shrift to the protective role privacy can perform? And why do defenders of privacy seldom acknowledge the ideological part privacy can play in hiding disparities in power and privilege, injustice and oppression? I explore these two positions—the skeptical feminist critique of privacy, and the legal-liberal defense of privacy as a value—with a view to discovering what is insightful and valuable, as well as flawed or problematic, in each. By using feminist theory and legal theory to interrogate each other, we can see more clearly what each approach has contributed to thinking about private and public, as well as the questions that have gone unanswered and the problems that remain unresolved. Exploring these complementary, even antagonistic, approaches is a crucial

3

first step toward developing a more adequate approach to thinking about public issues rooted in intimate-life venues and practices and the relationship between private, public, and political life.

The skeptical approach to privacy, often encapsulated in the slogan "The personal is political," questions whether there is anything distinct about relationships that occur in private and those that occur in public. On this view, both are marked by power, hierarchy, and oppression; privacy merely serves to obscure unjust practices, such as spouse battering, male domination, and homophobia, which would otherwise be understood as public and (often) political.

Analyses that treat the public-private distinction as problematic or even spurious point to the ways in which misplaced respect for the private sphere can *deprive* issues, perspectives, and people of public recognition. Such an approach helps us see how this distinction can compartmentalize human life into separate and opposed "spheres," and recognize the ideological function it plays in silencing voices that should be heard.

In contrast, from the liberal perspective privacy, whether as a value, a norm, or a legal or constitutional right, plays an important role in protecting various aspects of human life from inspection and control, and from social and political pressure from neighbors or majorities who would scrutinize and regulate matters that greatly affect our lives and identities.

We need to pay attention to both these discourses, because both tell us important things about the danger and value of thinking in terms of, and arguing on behalf of, privacy. We must think about why feminist theorists who attack public-private distinctions and legal and philosophical writers who defend them so rarely address one another's arguments; learn that it is possible, indeed crucial, for these two camps to stop talking past each other; and see how they contribute jointly to a nuanced and intelligent understanding of how private and public life are related.

The Skeptical Approach to Privacy: Feminist Critiques

Much of the contemporary work dealing with distinctions between public and private life argues for the connectedness or inseparability of private life and politics, or for recasting our notion of "the political" to take account of strengths and perspectives, such as nurturance, that are associated with women, as opposed to typically male qualities such as daring and aggression.[1] Jean Bethke Elshtain made an early contribution to the debate over how best to understand public and private by arguing that private life has been denigrated throughout the history of Western political thought; she attempted to validate the experiences and virtues of the "private realm" as politically redemptive.[2] Elshtain was joined by others who argued that women acquire a distinctive moral vision by being responsible for nurturing children, and that this vision should be valued and may be politically transformative.[3] None of these arguments, however, treats as problematic the gendered division of labor within the household which generally makes women responsible for nurturing work, nor do they suggest how the moral insights of the nurturing woman might be transformed into political values or perspectives, issues I explore in Chapter 4.

Wendy Brown has also questioned masculinist assumptions about political life. Although wary of embracing dichotomous categories or celebrating feminine virtues learned through experiences of subordination, Brown nonetheless suggests that child rearing might provide a model for transforming public life:

Drawing . . . dimensions of the work of childrearing toward our endeavors in public life is not, I think, impossible. We can engage with the environment and our bodies as if they were organic and sentient rather than passive matter awaiting our imposition of form. We can learn to develop new modes of life out of historically given ones, rather than staging coups or seizing history by force, impetuousness, or rape. We can find continuity in long labors of love in which we are truly invested and represented rather than in once-only deeds that record a performance rather than a person. We can prove and distinguish ourselves through our cares rather than by risking our deepest attachments or in an essentially superfluous space where performances witnessed by peers provide the only certainty that we are "real." We can achieve recognition for work rather than ownership, for devotion and not only daring, for ingenuity or imagination and not only audacity.[4]

In distinction to Elshtain, who celebrates private life and sees the separation of private from public as protective, Brown, like Carole Pateman, portrays the tradition of Western political theory as bracketing important political issues by writing off the concerns of the private realm as irrelevant.[5] Whereas Brown writes about Aristotle, Machiavelli, Weber, and Arendt, Pateman focuses on connections between the "sexual contract" and the "social contract." Pateman thinks that the latter has been viewed as a key development in Western political thought, whereas the former has been seen as irrelevant to the concerns of political theory. She argues that this "prepolitical" sexual contract, which gave men orderly access to women's bodies, is crucial to understanding why patriarchal power continues to define relationships within the family and household, as well as in the public world of work and law. In her view the marriage contract still carries an odor of slavery; housewives are expected to do household work without pay, and to provide sexual services to their husbands. Full-time workers outside the home are assumed to have wives who take care of their daily needs without receiving any pay for their services. Although women now have access to higher education in greater numbers than ever before, most are still relegated to low-paid jobs by the patriarchally ordered capitalist market.[6] Pateman views the sexual contract as explaining why formal, juridical equality exists alongside continued social inequality between women and men.[7] The separation of civil society into public and private spheres, and the continued existence of disparities in power which go unrecognized because they are merely "private," is a legacy of the mythic agreement giving men sexual access to women's bodies.[8]

For Pateman the feminist slogan "The personal is political" unmasks "the ideological character of liberal claims about the private and the public" by showing how intimate or familial relationships may be oppressive, and how private inequalities may affect women's ability to participate equally in public life. The ideological character of privacy is also evident in the comfortable assumption that "the writ of the state runs out at the gate to the family home," whereas in reality laws and policies support patriarchal relationships in intimate life.[9]

Much the same analysis of private-public distinctions informs Susan Moller Okin's work. She writes, for example: "The sharp dichotomization of public from private or domestic that characterizes virtually all of western political thought has to give way to the recognition that the two are, and always have been, inextricably connected. There are many reasons for this. Power (and therefore politics) exists in both domestic and non-domestic life. Moreover, the public world of government, law, and public opinion has always regulated and influenced what goes on and who dominates whom in the private sphere. . . . Our gendered selves as women or men are *constructed* primarily by our early experiences in the family."[10] I shall have more to say shortly about the way Okin equates power with politics here, as do many who are skeptical about public-private distinctions. Okin's distinctive contribution to thinking about how public and private life are connected rests in her arguments about how such gendered selves are constructed. She argues that the private, off-limits character of the family reinforces injustice, not only because of the different ways child rearing responsibilities affect the choices available to women and men about the occupations they pursue outside the home, but also because of the impact of the gendered division of labor within the household on the moral development of primary (that is, caretaking) parents and children.[11]

According to Okin, the family is a school of social justice because it is the first place where children see adults interact. Girls and boys who grow up in hierarchical families where sex roles are rigidly assigned have a hard time learning the capacity for empathy and developing a well-rounded moral psychology that will enable them to deliberate about justice as adults.[12] She also points to a deeper level at which the family is a school for human moral development, alluding to an argument more fully explored in the work of Nancy Chodorow and Dorothy Dinnerstein.[13] Dinnerstein argues that girls and boys who are reared primarily by women grow up thinking of the mother, and by extension women in general, as less than fully human, and end up feeling and expressing an alloy of intense love, anxiety, and hostility toward women, who are forever associated with the primordial comforter and enemy of infancy. The psychological imprint of female-dominated child rearing practices has profound consequences for the inability of adults to take women as seriously as men, to be as generous in overlooking women's faults as men's, and to view doing and making things in the world as women's work or nurturing children as men's work.

As several other theorists have also suggested, Okin thinks that under present gender-structured arrangements, women's experience of having been mothered as girls, and their responsibility as adults for being primary nurturers, leads them to develop a distinct approach to moral reasoning.[14] She believes that such differences in moral development are a stumbling block to creating an adequate theory of justice based on representative persons "whose psychological and moral development is in all essentials identical." Unless women and men come to share responsibility for child rearing, the only way to develop a just society will be for women and men to be equally represented in dialogues about justice.[15] By focusing on child rearing arrangements, Okin helps us see how decisions that most of us regard as personal and intimate in the context of our own relationships—who should work, who should stay home and raise the kids, who should make career sacrifices for the sake of the family—have a cumulative, general, public effect that is unjust. In this way she makes a significant and unique contribution to thinking about public and private.

My students often react to Okin's description of interactions within the family by criticizing her theory for assuming a privileged, middle-class, two-parent family, and failing to note the diversity of families in contemporary American society. Although this is an important criticism, I think that Okin's insights—about what children learn from watching the adults who raise them interact, about the moral sensibilities of primary parents, and about the constraints that domestic responsibilities place on one's ability to pursue a career or participate in public life in other ways—*are* applicable to a variety of family arrangements. For example, two lesbians raising children together, or a single mother interacting with friends or lovers, or a divorced and remarried parent still model egalitarian or not-so-egalitarian behaviors for their children.

Catharine MacKinnon's contributions to thinking about the public-private distinction are also original and important. Perhaps her most distinctive contribution to feminist theory is the notion that "the intimate degradation of women [is] the public order."[16] Although the ideological character of privacy is best articulated in her work on abortion, MacKinnon focuses on the disparities in power between women and men in intimate and social life throughout her work, whether she is addressing athletics, pornography, abortion, rape, or equality. Writing dramatically and often hyperbolically, MacKinnon frequently frames her analysis in terms of the appropriation of the female body or women's sexuality by men ("Sexuality is to feminism what work is to Marxism: that which is most one's own, yet most taken away").[17] Her writings focus on the tension between formal political or legal equality and actual social inequality, which undermines rights guaranteed under the law. Although sexist laws and policies provide the public, institutional frame for patriarchal power relations, MacKinnon argues that the real politics of women's oppression is rooted in the sphere of social relations, especially intimate relations with men.[18] Attacking overt, de jure legal discrimination touches only the tip of the iceberg, since many laws that appear to be neutral and fair on their face are premised on, and operate to reinforce, women's oppression by men.[19]

In her work on abortion, MacKinnon notes that although the right to privacy protects women from government intrusion into the decision to abort a pregnancy, it provides no conceptual basis for requiring the state to take positive steps to guarantee access to abortion for women who do not have the means to pay for one. Commenting on the abortion funding cases, MacKinnon writes:

The *McRae* result sustains the meaning of privacy in *Roe*: women are guaranteed by the public no more than what they can get in private—what they can extract through their intimate associations with men. Women with privileges, including class privileges, get rights.

Women were granted the abortion right as a private privilege, not as a public right. . . . It is not inconsistent, then, that, framed as a privacy right, a woman's decision to abort would have no claim on public support and would genuinely not be seen as burdened by that deprivation. . . . State intervention would have provided a choice women did not have in private.[20]

MacKinnon develops the conceptual limitations of the privacy right for addressing abortion funding into a broader argument about the ideological role privacy plays in reinforcing gender and class privilege. The conventional "liberal ideal of the private," she writes, "holds that, so long as the public does not interfere, autonomous individuals interact freely and equally. Privacy . . . means that which is inaccessible to, unaccountable to, unconstructed by, anything beyond itself. By definition, it is not part of or conditioned by anything systematic outside it. It is personal, intimate, autonomous, particular, individual, the original source and final outpost of the self, gender neutral. . . . In this scheme, intimacy is implicitly thought to guarantee symmetry of power. Injuries arise through violation of the private sphere, not within and by and because of it."[21]

MacKinnon relentlessly attacks the notion that private life is free from coercion and inequality. Attending to the context in which decisions about whether to have sex and use birth control are made, MacKinnon notes that most heterosexual encounters follow a male-defined script, with men as the initiators and intercourse as the outcome.[22] She argues that, when we begin to examine the context in which sex takes place, we notice that "who defines what is sexual, what sexuality therefore is, to whom what stimuli are erotic and why, and who defines the conditions under which sexuality is expressed . . . [are] issues [that] have not even been available for consideration." In a context where "socially, women's bodies have not been theirs [and] women have not controlled their meanings and destinies," protecting women's reproductive privacy has meant guaranteeing women sex on the same terms as men—that is, free from worry about pregnancy—which only increases women's heterosexual availability without increasing their pleasure in or control over sex.[23] Examining the social circumstances under which women engage in heterosexual intercourse reveals women's lack of social power and their inability to define and control one of the most intimate parts of their lives—sexual activity and expression.

Given the false assumption that privacy benefits all equally and promotes intimacy and mutuality, MacKinnon thinks that it is difficult "getting *anything* private to be perceived as coercive." She continues:

When what men do is private, their aggression is not seen at all, and women are seen to consent to it. . . . [Thus, f]or women the measure of the intimacy has been the measure of the oppression. This is why feminism has had to explode the private. This is why feminism has seen the personal as the political. The private is public for those for whom the personal is political. In this sense, for women there is no private, either normatively or empirically. Feminism confronts the fact that women have no privacy to lose or to guarantee. . . . To confront the fact that women have no privacy is to confront the intimate degradation of women as the public order.[24]

In sum, MacKinnon identifies the private, intimate realm as *the* realm of politics from women's point of view,[25] which is consistent with her view that sexual objectification is the normative way men treat women. Sex becomes politics, and privacy merely a tool for obscuring and protecting male power.

There are some characteristic problems with MacKinnon's work which undercut this ambitious theoretical project. For example, she posits a unitary women's experience and a unitary male way of treating women as objects for male pleasure. Her work is shot through with sweeping generalizations and harsh overstatements: "Man fucks woman; subject verb object." "Woman through male eyes is sex object." "A woman is a being who identifies and is identified as one whose sexuality exists for someone else, who is socially male."[26] One gets the impression that MacKinnon is more committed to eloquent, angry overstatements than to reflecting honestly on the diversity of male and female experiences and power relations. Although her work is frequently insightful, it often comes across as doctrinaire, dictatorial, and condescending, too inclined to tell us what our experience is and how we should feel about it. Also, her work often seems reductive: the problem boils down to sexuality, which is determined by male power. Other reasons for differences in power, such as class or race, are elided in this overarching analytic insight. Angela Harris's criticisms of MacKinnon for subsuming the experience of black women to generic (white) "women" are well taken.[27]

Yet another feminist theorist who has challenged the public-private distinction is Iris Young. Young's project in *Justice and the Politics of Difference* is the same one that inspired Okin's book *Gender, Justice, and the Family:* developing an adequate theory of justice. Central to Young's analysis is the idea that the experiences, voices, and interests of dominant groups are treated as normal, the measure against which other groups are compared and held to be different or deviant. This has led to the marginalization and exclusion of a variety of groups in our society, including women, blacks, ethnic minorities, and gays and lesbians.[28] Furthermore, this marginalization has been obscured by values central to our political and moral thinking: the ideal of impartiality in moral reasoning, the idea that there is something distinctive about the outlook of the citizen and the "civic public" characterized by such an outlook. Thus, "the ideal of impartiality legitimates hierarchical decisionmaking and allows the standpoint of the privileged to appear as universal. The combination of these functions often leads to concrete decisions that perpetuate the oppression and disadvantage of some groups and the privilege of others. . . . Based on assumptions and standards they claim as neutral and impartial, their authoritative decisions often silence, ignore, and render deviant the abilities, needs, and norms of others." Young believes that the ideal of impartial moral reason is reflected in the ideal of a public realm of politics which attains "the universality of a general will that leaves difference, particularity, and the body behind in the private realms of family and civil society."[29]

Since notions of impartiality and the civic public have worked to exclude or render invisible many groups, perspectives, and voices, Young urges us to abandon them as moral and political ideals. In her view, relegating personal feelings, desires, and commitments to the private realm does not eliminate them but merely drives them underground, where they become invisible and easy to ignore.[30] For Young, privacy and impartiality do not merely obscure oppressive practices.[31] Private life is also home to genuine differences in experience, interest, and perspective which we desperately try, in the name of impartiality and justice, to submerge, but which nevertheless continue to affect what we think and who we are, what interests we seek, and what our notions of justice are. Young has no use for "a unified public realm in which citizens leave behind their particular group affiliations, histories, and needs to discuss a mythical 'common good.' " Rather, she argues that "in a society differentiated by social groups, occupations, political positions, differences of privilege and oppression, regions, and so on, the perception of anything like a common good can only be an outcome of public interaction that *expresses* rather than submerges particularities. Those seeking the democratization of politics in our society, in my view, should reconceptualize the meaning of public and private and their relation, to break decisively with the tradition of Enlightenment republicanism."[32]

Young articulates new and powerful reasons for thinking that "the personal is political," focusing on differences that are usually depoliticized and shunted into the private sphere. She finds these differences crucial to a notion of justice that reflects genuine plurality. Thus she writes: "The feminist slogan 'the personal is political' expresses the principle that no social practices or activities should be excluded as improper subjects for public discussion, expression, or collective choice. The contemporary women's movement has made public issues out of many practices claimed to be too trivial or private for public discussion: the meaning of pronouns, domestic violence against women, the practice of men's opening doors for women, the sexual assault of women and children, the sexual division of house-work, and so on." Recognizing that what is private can be deprived of public status or significance and associated with shame, Young argues that no issue or person should be forced into privacy, and that "no social insti-tutions or practices should be excluded a priori from being a proper subject for public discussion and expression."[33]

At the same time, Young also argues that meaningful distinctions be-tween public and private are possible and may even be important. She believes that "there are good theoretical and practical reasons to maintain a distinction between public and private," although "the distinction should not be . . . a hierarchical opposition . . . between reason and feeling, mascu-line and feminine, universal and particular."[34] She argues for a notion of privacy which is empowering rather than impoverishing: "The private should be defined . . . as that aspect of his or her life that any person has a right to exclude others from."[35] Indeed, Young sees people, perhaps espe-cially people who are regarded as "deviant," as having and needing a right to exclude others from certain aspects of their lives. Where this right comes from and how it is to be negotiated and defined by Young's "heteroge-neous public" is an issue she does not address, though it is potentially problematic, given recent debates challenging the legitimacy of privacy claims within "outlier" communities, an issue I examine more closely in Chapter 6.

Young's argument that we should embrace and retain group identities rather than trying to overcome them,[36] and that justice requires admitting people into political life in all their particularity, is a dramatic reversal of the conventional wisdom that various differences are epiphenomenal and need to be ignored, compensated for, or eliminated if we want to attain justice. Her best insights have to do with cultural imperialism and the difficulty of appreciating and representing the position of people who, be-cause of race, gender, class, sexual orientation, or ethnicity, have very dif-ferent experiences of social life from one's own. Her analysis of the power of a conceptual framework based on impartiality and the separation be-tween public and private to validate certain kinds of reasoning and experi-ence and marginalize others offers a new way to think about the ideologi-cal power of privacy addressed by Pateman, MacKinnon, and others. When Young talks about public-private distinctions in terms of exclusion and silencing, she treats the problem as broader than gender subordina-tion, looking to all kinds of "otherness." She also proposes a way not just to talk about subordination and injustice, but to tap the potential for arriv-ing at more inclusive notions of justice, whereby repressed groups would be able to bring their own values, desires, emotions, and commitments to the political dialogue.

There are many lessons to take to heart in these skeptical feminist approaches to the public-private distinction. They tell us that we need to reconsider the values and content of politics, attending to what gets set apart in the private sphere of the family. Perhaps some of the values and practices of nurturing mothers may provide more worthy models for restructuring political life than either the heroic ideal or the technocratic bureaucracy, both of which have shaped the political realm until now. The tradition of Western political thought has treated the concerns of the private domain as irrelevant to political life. Privacy has played an ideological function, masking oppressive relations within the family, and obscuring the way state power has supported patriarchal relationships in intimate life. Questions of central importance to those historically excluded from participation in the political arena (women, slaves)—why they have had to bear the burdens of sustaining life; why their work has been trivialized and devalued; why they have been physically and sexually exploited; why they have been deprived of equality, citizenship, and rights—have been ignored, apparently regarded as "prepolitical" or rooted in natural inequalities.

Most Americans consider privacy an important right and value, protective of intimacy and mutuality, and available to all on equal terms. But respect for privacy undermines equality by obscuring and reinforcing a variety of social inequalities owing to gender, race, class, ethnicity, and sexuality. For women, intimate life is where they are most oppressed and unfree, most vulnerable to male sexual predations. Relations within the family have particular salience to the development of notions of justice. There children learn what is expected of adult men and women by watching their own parents' interactions. There boys and girls grow up thinking of the primary parent who meets, and frustrates, their earliest needs as not fully human. Responsibility for child rearing also affects women's chances for employment outside the home, and shapes women's moral development. Not only does respect for privacy obscure power, subordination, and inequality; private life is also home to desires, passions, embodied selves, commitments, and values that shape what we believe and who we are. Dismantling the public-private distinction is crucial to achieving justice by allowing these different desires, selves, and so on to emerge and inform people's ideas about justice.

Such a sketch conveys neither the richness of critiques of the public-private distinction nor their extraordinary impact on current feminist and political theorizing about the linkages among private, public, and political life. Feminist work has successfully called into question the old orthodoxy of treating private and public as distinct spheres, and viewing issues or groups located in the privacy of the home and intimate life as unworthy of serious political inquiry. This has been crucial in calling attention to and validating a variety of issues that in the past were not considered worthy of collective political attention or action. These include violence against women (spouse battering, rape, sexual harassment); sexual and reproductive decisions (birth control, abortion, choice of sexual or marital partners); civil rights for gays and lesbians; the impact of responsibility for child rearing on women's educational and employment opportunities; the development of distinctive male and female forms of moral reasoning; and the psychic roots of anxiety about female power and the disparagement of women.[37]

Some Criticisms of the Skeptics

Feminist political theorizing has made it impossible to ignore the private sphere and the ideological function played by public-private distinctions, generating a variety of analyses that attend to the play of power relations in private life and the intersections between private and public life. Yet such theorizing has been deeply problematic and one-sided. I turn now to a critique of the skeptical approaches to thinking about public and private just reviewed, and propose some alternative perspectives on how to think about public and private. In making such criticisms I strive not to be dismissive of theoretical insights that have revolutionized the way we think about public and private distinctions. Instead, I write as a sympathetic critic, nurtured and taught by theorists whose work has broken crucial theoretical and political ground.

Several of the theorists I have discussed make interesting equivocations about the value of privacy. For example, Carole Pateman writes that "feminist critiques of the dichotomy between private and public . . . do not necessarily suggest that no distinction can or should be drawn between the personal and political aspects of social life."[38] As we saw earlier, Iris Young echoes this view, as does Susan Okin, who writes: "Challenging the dichotomy does not necessarily mean denying the usefulness of a concept of privacy or the value of privacy itself in human life. Nor does it mean denying that there are *any* reasonable distinctions to be made between the public and domestic spheres."[39]

I take them to be suggesting that it is not privacy per se that is the problem but rather "the *ideological* character of liberal claims about the private and public,"[40] that is, privacy in the sense of *depriving* issues of public, political status or recognition. To put it another way, distinguishing between private and public is not a problem unless it leads us to treat everything that goes on in private as beyond the reach of public knowledge, critical reflection, or political debate and action. If we are careful not to make "public" and "private" into reified categories, their content fixed and immune to change or criticism, but see them instead as permeable realms of human life which change over time, making distinctions between private and public may be useful and liberating. Indeed, many theorists point out that our definitions of what is private and public do change over time, and are themselves open to political discussion, which raises the possibility of our developing notions of privacy that are protective without being oppressive.[41]

Although Pateman, Okin, Young, and others nod in the direction of acknowledging that privacy may be a useful concept, they nonetheless focus overwhelmingly on its role in depriving issues, people, and perspectives of public importance. Such an approach does little to further our thinking about the various roles privacy plays in contemporary political, legal, and social life. Of course we need to criticize privacy and public-private distinctions when they silence and obscure oppressive practices and arrangements. But we also need to recognize that privacy can play a protective, empowering role, and to think about what makes the distinction between public and private life important as well as what makes it oppressive.[42]

Neither our thinking nor our politics will be well served by ignoring complexities and tensions in private, public, and political modes of interaction or spheres of life. If we want to decide well about problems that straddle these different aspects of our lives, if we want to find ways to reinvigorate participation by ordinary people in political life by building bridges between issues that matter deeply to them and the public decision-making process, we must avoid the temptation to embrace only one aspect of the concept of privacy, be it the feminist disparagement of the private as privative, or the liberal-legal celebration of privacy as protective.

Students in my classes often voice the "essentialist" criticism of much feminist theory which proceeds from an undifferentiated subject, "women" in the abstract, who seem in fact to resemble the theorists themselves: to be white, middle class, and educated, and to live in two-parent, heterosexual families. Except for Iris Young, most of the feminist theorists of public and private whose work I have examined have little to say about the variety of women's experiences. In none of the theories is there sustained recognition that women may perceive male power differently depending on their class, race, sexuality, ethnicity, or personal experience.[43]

For example, MacKinnon never considers the possibility that women might seek or reach accommodation with men; that not all men are rapists or incest perpetrators; that some are even committed to sharing domestic work and mutuality in sexual pleasure. Sexual objectification is a universal phenomenon that affects all women in much the same way, to read Pateman's work on the sexual contract. Okin barely mentions single parents or same-sex households, or the financial constraints that fall on women and men who do not make much money when it comes to deciding who should stay home and raise the kids and who should work for a wage outside the home.

Several writers have begun to think about issues of class, race, and sexual and gender identity in relation to feminist theorizing, and even in relation to thinking about privacy. In an influential essay Angela Harris criticizes the homogenous "woman" of feminist theory, where the implicit assumption is that women are white and middle class. In reflecting on what privacy means to lesbians in a homophobic society, Shane Phelan is much more conflicted than Pateman and MacKinnon, and more appreciative of the ways privacy can protect minority groups from hostile majorities. Anita Allen argues that privacy protections have particular salience for women in terms of protecting them from the ever-present intrusions of family life. Dorothy Roberts argues that protecting privacy may be a way of promoting racial equality in the context of respecting the dignity of pregnant drug-addicted women of color. Addressing the meaning of privacy to women of color in the United States, Peggy Davis explains why privacy is highly valued by groups who traditionally did not have much privacy in making decisions about sexual intercourse or raising children.[44]

A third problem with the skeptical approach to thinking about public and private is that most of the writers rely on impoverished and often poorly articulated notions of politics. Earlier I remarked on Susan Okin's casual equation of politics and power. Defining politics in terms of power and conflict in fact seems to be commonly accepted, especially among writers making feminist arguments about the "politicalness" of interactions in intimate life.[45] Kate Millett, for example, has written that "all power is political so that, because men exercise power over women in a multitude of ways in personal life, it makes sense to talk of 'sexual politics' and 'sexual domin- ion.' "[46] Catharine MacKinnon verges at times on arguing that sex *is* poli- tics, since sex is always imbued with power relations. MacKinnon often uses "politics" to refer to the hidden power dynamics of practices that are not usually viewed as political, such as free speech advocates' defense of pornography.[47]

Collapsing power and politics in this way is troubling because it leaves no way to distinguish the collective action of citizens from corporate power plays or domestic abuse. Although systemic, oppressive relations of power, whether housed in formal political processes or in families, need to be addressed as political issues, not every relation predicated on power is by that token political. Young's criticisms of interest group pluralism helps clarify some of the difficulties with such stick-figure thinking about poli- tics. She writes:

The problem with interest-group pluralism is not that it is plural and particular, but that it is privatized. It institutionalizes and encourages an egoist, self-regarding view of the political process; each party enters the political competition for scarce goods and privileges only in order to maximize its own gain, and need not listen to or respond to the claims of others for their own sake. Thus interest-group plural- ism allows little space for claims that some parties have a responsibility to attend to the claims of others because they are needy or oppressed. The processes and often the outcomes of interest-group bargaining, moreover, take place largely in private; they are neither revealed nor discussed in a forum that genuinely includes all those potentially affected by the decisions.[48]

Young wants to move such political competition out into the open by giving the qualities and differences that are submerged in liberal politics public salience, and acknowledging them as the roots of situated knowl- edges and perspectives that shape people and their political values and in- terests. A question her theory raises, however, is how people can move from purely self-regarding pursuit of their own interests to listening and responding to the claims of others, and especially how they can come to feel responsible for others who are needy or oppressed.

Young's response to this question is sketchy. She quotes a passage from Hanna Pitkin, who argues that interest group competition draws us into politics because "we are forced to find or create a common language of purposes and aspirations. . . . We are forced . . . to transform 'I want' into 'I am entitled to,' a claim that becomes negotiable by public standards."

Young goes on, "In this move from an expression of desire to a claim of justice, dialogue participants do not bracket their particular situations and adopt a universal and shared standpoint. They only move from self-regarding need to recognition of the claims of others."[49]

But it is hard to see how Young's diverse groups of self-regarding interest-seekers will be transformed by their experience of public dialogue. For Pitkin, the appeal to common language and standards is crucial for transforming interest-seekers into citizens. In the process of making a claim to entitlement—figuring out how to explain one's interests in terms of an appeal to common values—one also begins to recognize the claims of others, and to have a stake in outcomes beyond one's immediate self-interest.[50] For Young, however, interest-seekers move from self-regarding need to recognition of the claims of others *without* adopting a "universal and shared standpoint." This happens, she claims, simply because everyone recognizes that if they do not listen to others, others will not listen to them. Young also says that "just norms are most likely to arise from the real interaction of people with different points of view who are drawn out of themselves by being forced to confront and listen to others."[51]

Although I understand why Young rejects the need for a universal and shared standpoint, I find that her theory raises other problems. How are people drawn out of themselves simply by being forced to confront and listen to others, especially others who are different from themselves, and are thus likely to be viewed with suspicion? Will interactions among people with different points of view *automatically* produce just norms? According to Pitkin, the appeal to common notions of justice is what produces such changes; Young posits justice as the outcome of the interactions themselves, and assumes that the interactions will be transformative, that people will listen to and learn from one another, even though she stipulates that people will not appeal to common language or values. In short, Young avoids a crucial problem of how to accomplish the transformation from the private pursuer of self-interest to the public citizen concerned with justice and the larger stakes of the decision-making process. But she has not considered whether there is something distinctive about political interactions. Instead she accepts a model of politics as unmediated competition among varied interests.

A related concern is that admitting all kinds of personal desires and needs into a "diverse" public sphere may not be appropriate, may even undermine political life. Young attacks the idea that "the impartiality and rationality of the state depend on containing need and desire in the private realm of the family,"[52] but I wonder if there are some desires and emotions that *need* to be prevented from entering political life. Hannah Arendt spoke of the rage unleashed among the poor by the French Revolution as an antipolitical passion.[53] One might consider bigotry, hedonism, greed, neurosis, sexual obsession, and incestuous desire as possible candidates for desires and outlooks that would be better off not introduced into political life. Furthermore, if justice is a matter not simply of applying fairness to the private sphere but of admitting all kinds of personal desires and needs into the "diverse" public sphere, will that sphere still be *political*? Or will the result be a babel of contending desires, affects, and passions? And on the other side, will feelings and commitments, the body and desires, lose a private character that protects them and allows them to flourish?

Having canvassed some of what we learn from feminist approaches to thinking about the public-private distinction, let us turn now to works on privacy by legal theorists and philosophers whose judgments about the centrality of privacy to human life are very different.

The Legal-Liberal Approach to Privacy

In "Feminism and the Public/Private Distinction," Ruth Gavison writes:

I believe feminists have succeeded in identifying and documenting real and danger-ous patterns. . . . However, if there are differences between private and public that must be maintained and invoked, the delegitimation of the distinction and the corresponding vocabulary will make meaningful communication and discourse more difficult. . . . [I]t is self-defeating to throw away important conceptual tools which are essential to clear thinking about these issues. . . . [F]ighting the verbal distinction between public and private, rather than fighting invalid arguments which invoke them, or the power structures which manipulate them in unjustifi-able ways, is as futile as seeking individual therapy for problems of social struc-ture.[54]

Like Gavison, I think the public-private distinction is vital for clarifying our thinking about issues that arise from our private, intimate life, but that have widespread or important public significance. Here I review two strands of arguments about the value of privacy: first, the attempts at legal justification which defend privacy for its role in fostering intimacy, equal-ity, political freedom, and the exercise of moral capacities for autonomy and self-determination; then broader philosophical and anthropological arguments about the centrality of privacy as a social practice to individual psychological development and diverse social relations.

Many writers who publish in law reviews and philosophical journals have puzzled over the question: What is it about privacy that makes it worthy of legal or constitutional protection? Judith Jarvis Thomson believes that there is nothing especially worthy of protection about privacy, that it is simply a label for a loose collection of values and interests that are really rooted in other practices and values, such as property ownership or liberty from government interference.[55] Others have suggested that the *real* value at stake is not privacy but autonomy, the freedom to act without interference from others or from the government.[56]

In my view, the argument that all of the interests and values expressed as privacy claims can be expressed as something else ignores or dismisses the family resemblance that unites such experiences of invasion or wrong, and does little to help us understand why such interests are important. Indeed, the argument that privacy is a derivative value has been countered by a variety of arguments for valuing and protecting privacy as a distinctive interest or right. Many argue that privacy and autonomy are closely intertwined concepts.[57] Others suggest that privacy plays a role in cultivating political freedoms, such as the First Amendment freedoms of association and discussion, and secrecy in jury deliberations and balloting; that privacy is essential to protecting intimacy; and that privacy can foster equality for groups who have a particular need for privacy or for protection from harassment.[58] Let us look more closely at two well-developed arguments, those dealing with autonomy and intimacy.

A number of writers see privacy as a social practice that enables people to develop autonomous selves, to be recognized by others as capable of independent decision making and worthy of being left alone.[59] David Richards, arguing that privacy is a deeply rooted value in the United States, believes that liberal constitutionalism protects the moral independence of individuals against the claims of majorities in questions of conscience and matters relating to intimate personal life.[60] Ruth Gavison suggests that our freedom is protected "by the fact that we enjoy privacy, either in the sense of being alone or intimate with others, to behave in ways that would be unlikely in public. . . . If we have to think that everything we do is observed and may be publicized, we shall have poorer lives. We also shall have less of a tendency to do the things that we are not sure about, fewer chances to experiment and acquire competence through trial and error, and fewer opportunities to experiment with behaving differently."[61]

In a well-known essay likening the attributes of a sovereign person to those of a sovereign territory or state, Joel Feinberg alludes to several different notions of autonomy, which he evidently regards as simply another way of talking about privacy: "The kernel of the idea of autonomy is the right to make choices and decisions—what to put into my body, what contacts with my body to permit, where and how to move my body through public space, how to use my chattels and physical property, what personal information to disclose to others, what information to conceal, and more. . . . My right to determine by my own choice what enters my experience is one of the various things meant by the 'right of privacy,' and so interpreted that right is one of the elements of my personal autonomy." Feinberg goes beyond the idea of controlling access to one's person or to information about oneself in his notion of privacy as autonomy to the idea of decisional privacy: "The most basic autonomy-right is the right to decide how one is to live one's life, in particular how to make the critical life-decisions."[62]

Feinberg points to a central tension that the legal privacy theorists run up against. For many, privacy in the most fundamental sense requires the ability to control access to one's person, at least at some times and in some places.[63] But how is the idea of privacy as controlled access connected to the idea of privacy as one's ability to make decisions that critically affect one's life, such as whether to continue a pregnancy? Feinberg suggests that both interests are connected to one's sovereignty as a person. The interest at stake is not just in excluding others from one's physical space, but in having a metaphoric zone "in which to be an individual" that one can carry into one's bedroom or into the street, where one can think one's own thoughts, have one's own secrets, live one's own life.[64] Anita Allen also thinks that the restricted access and decisional forms of privacy are connected, and sees infringement of either as offending values of personhood and "arous[ing] feelings of anguish, shame, fear, and anxiety."[65]

A core problem for the right-to-privacy jurisprudence has been deciding how much respect to accord privacy or autonomy concerns in situations where privacy is asserted against government interests. For example, by what standard does the Supreme Court decide that abortion is deserving of protection but consenting homosexual sex is not, when both involve choices of central importance to the individuals involved?[66] Feinberg suggests that "the boundary line . . . tends to follow, however erratically, the line of those liberties which are most fecund, those exercised in the pivotally central life decisions and thereby underlying and supporting all the others,"[67] but this is hardly adequate to explain the difference in treatment. So far, it appears that U.S. courts are more likely to protect those life choices that are closer to conventional gender and familial roles, and less likely to protect choices that are viewed by majorities as deviant or unacceptable, a matter I take up in more detail in Chapter 4, where I discuss the evolution of the U.S. Supreme Court's right-to-privacy decisions.

Others express doubts about defining privacy's value in terms of autonomy, arguing that the concept of privacy is diluted and loses credibility as a legal strategy when privacy is equated with autonomy. Thus, C. Keith Boone writes:

There is no instant formula for clearly marking the fuzzy boundaries of what we call the "private"; but there are sound theoretical and practical reasons for not conflating privacy with established public freedoms that are frequently associated with it. This could result in a conceptual bloat. . . . What the Court has found in those hazy penumbras of some constitutional amendments has sometimes to do with privacy, but other times merely with personal autonomy, personal sovereignty, or what the Court calls "personal liberty." In actual cases, personal autonomy may or may not involve a state of privacy. The Court has muddied its own waters by implying that the right to privacy embraces all cases of personal autonomy.[68]

Boone's point is well taken. Although we sometimes refer to decisions or activities as "private" because they are not subject to regulation or government control, usually the concept refers more specifically to private places, activities that take place in private, or information that is not available to all. Conflating privacy with autonomy or liberty does not help us see what is distinctive about privacy, or why it should be valued and protected.

Jeb Rubenfeld has also been critical of the "autonomy" approach to defining what is valuable about privacy, although he saves his best attacks for formulations that define the value of privacy in terms of "personhood." Since I understand "personhood" to convey the minimum requirements of what any self-respecting adult should expect by way of her ability to chart her own life course, control whom to come in contact with, and the like, I take Rubenfeld's criticisms of the "personhood" approach to apply to defenses of privacy as a vehicle for protecting autonomy.[69]

What bothers Rubenfeld about the personhood approach to explaining why privacy should be protected is the assumption that whatever is connected to sexuality is "more definitive of and more deeply rooted in who that person is than his neighbors' conduct can ever be."[70] Rubenfeld thinks that this hurts the cause of protecting the rights of women or homo-sexuals because it reinforces notions that women are defined by their iden-tity as potential mothers, or that homosexuals are defined by their sexual identity. He writes:

In the very concept of a homosexual identity there is something potentially disserv-ing—if not disrespectful—to the cause advocated. . . . Those who engage in homo-sexual sex may or may not perceive themselves as bearing a "homosexual identity." Their homosexual relations may be a pleasure they take or an intimacy they value without constituting . . . something definitive of their character. At the heart of personhood's analysis is the reliance upon a sharply demarcated "homosexual iden-tity" to which a person is immediately consigned at the moment he seeks to engage in homosexual sex. For personhood, that is, homosexual relations are to be pro-tected to the extent that they fundamentally define a species of person that is, by definition, to be strictly distinguished from the heterosexual. Persons may have homosexual sex only because they have elected to define themselves as "homosexu-als"—because homosexuality lies at "the heart of . . . what they are." Thus, even as it argues for homosexual rights, personhood becomes yet another turn of the screw that has pinned those who engage in homosexual sex into a fixed identity specified by the difference from "heterosexuals."[71]

Rather than defend privacy in terms of a notion of personhood that carries a dangerous accretion of identities that stigmatize and marginalize, Rubenfeld proposes that we look at the affirmative consequences of the laws that are challenged on privacy grounds, what it is they *produce*. He argues that anti-abortion laws create mothers out of women, and anti-sodomy laws channel homosexuals into heterosexual relationships (or bet-ter, I would say, into the *appearance* of heterosexuality).[72] Rubenfeld argues that laws against abortion, interracial marriage, private education, and sod-omy "all involve a peculiar form of obedience that reaches far beyond mere abstention from the particular proscribed act, . . . a form of obedience in which the life of the person forced to obey is thereafter substantially filled up and informed by the living, institutional consequences of obedience [with] profoundly formative effects on identity and character."[73] The problem is to avoid the reach of a progressively more normalizing, totaliz-ing state, which intrudes on life choices in profound ways, drafting women into motherhood, and children into public schools, preventing people from marrying across race lines or from having sex with people of their own sex. Rubenfeld sees privacy as a political tool which holds off the power of the state to mold people's lives "into standard, rigid, normalized roles." He writes: "The right to privacy is a political doctrine. It does not exist because individuals have a sphere of 'private' life with which the state has nothing to do. The state has everything to do with our private life; and the freedom that privacy protects equally extends, as we have seen, into 'public' as well as 'private' matters. The right to privacy exists because democracy must impose limits on the extent of control and direction that the state exercises over the day-to-day conduct of individual lives."[74]

To put it another way, Rubenfeld worries that defending privacy protections because of the importance of reproductive decisions or choice of sexual partner will lead defenders of choice to embrace essentialized identities—woman as mother, man (woman) who has sex with other men (women) as homosexual (lesbian). To avoid this problem and more clearly identify the danger against which privacy protects, he argues that privacy provides a way to curb an intrusive, normalizing state and protect democracy. One might of course respond that defending autonomy does not necessarily mean that one thinks about personhood or the self as having an essential core constituted by sexuality or gender. There may be many decisions or aspects of the self which shape a life, such as whether one gets to study music as a child or where one ends up moving for a job. Nor does pointing to choices about parenthood or sexual partners as bearing on autonomous personhood mean that these are the only or even the most important decisions we ought to protect.[75]

Ferdinand Schoeman proposes a very different approach to thinking about privacy from that of either privacy-as-autonomy theorists such as Feinberg or critics of autonomy such as Rubenfeld. Schoeman disagrees with the idea that privacy is nothing more than freedom from social and governmental interference with or regulation of self-regarding activities and decisions that do not harm anyone else. He believes that the fact that we seek protection from state and social intrusion or control is better understood in terms of privacy than autonomy because the point of being protected is to relate to people in various ways. In his view privacy suggests and nurtures involvement and intimacy, whereas autonomy suggests isolation, freedom from social intimidation or pressure. "That is to say," he writes, "privacy has two aspects: 'privacy from' and 'privacy for.' The 'privacy from' aspect suggests restrictions on others' access to a person. But typically there is this other dimension to the concept, the 'privacy for' dimension. For instance, I am accorded privacy from most others vis-à-vis my domestic life so that I may form deep and special relationships with family or friends."[76] Schoeman thinks that getting the contours of privacy right requires that we pay attention to the positive associational side of privacy, and not see it simply as a bar to interference or a guarantee of isolation. Privacy characteristically involves interpersonal or social affairs, not their absence. To take two examples, the decision to seek an abortion is made not in complete isolation but typically in consultation with one's partner, after consulting with one's doctor, receiving counseling, thinking about the impact on one's family, and so on. Freedom of thought and of conscience are nurtured by privacy, but again, their exercise implies interaction with others, not complete isolation. Privacy implies not the *absence* of social pressure, then, but its modulation through the individual's involvement in a variety of different associations, and the exercise of privacy norms within those associations.[77]

Schoeman suggests that membership in a variety of associations gives people a number of different venues where independent identities and values can be affirmed and supported, no one of which is monolithic in terms of being the source of identity or value. It is involvement in various associations, not abstention from all social contact or pressure, nor "thou shalt nots" to government interference, which Schoeman sees as providing protection from undue social pressure.[78]

The "privacy for"/"privacy from" distinction Schoeman uses to explain why social pressure is not always bad and constraining but rather can enable us to carry out certain roles and responsibilities can also help us think about privacy's role in fostering intimacy. Schoeman argues that there is not just one private and one public domain which are sharply opposed but many of each lying along a continuum. All of us move among various spheres of life, and each sphere is governed by its own rules about how to respect others' privacy, what sort of interactions are appropriate, and what constitutes moral behavior. Privacy plays an important role in helping maintain the integrity of different spheres of life.[79] For example, information that may be openly known in one realm may be completely inappropriate to reveal in another.

One of the things privacy is *for*, then, is preserving intimacy. Schoeman concludes *Privacy and Social Freedom* with a chapter on intimate life which suggests that intimate life is both especially valued and especially problematic in terms of maintaining relationships and exercising moral judgment. He writes: "Private life is more dynamic and involves subtler and more nuanced principles than does public life. . . . Managing private affairs requires much more feeling for detail and sensitivity to ambiguities. . . . In intimate spheres, we interact with specific others in the context of relationships, not with generic or fungible others as often typifies our public encounters and as defined by roles. Private morality aims at maintaining, restoring, or restructuring a balance in continuing relationships between the same parties that endure from episode to episode."[80] John Hardwig makes a similar argument about the morality that belongs to intimate relationships. He argues that if women think in terms of rights in their intimate love relationships, it is a warning signal that something is amiss in the relationship. The language and morality of rights, both Schoeman and Hardwig argue, is appropriate to the public sphere, where we deal with others at arm's length, but not for the more nuanced concern and care that belong to intimate relationships.[81] James Rachels also thinks that privacy is important in nurturing intimacy. He writes: "Consider the differences between the way that a husband and wife behave when they are alone and the way they behave in the company of third parties. Alone, they may be affectionate, sexually intimate, have their fights and quarrels, and so on; but with others, a more 'public' face is in order."[82]

To this point we have considered various arguments for valuing privacy: privacy allows us to do things we would not do in public, to experiment, to engage in self-reflection; it protects us from majoritarian pressures; it allows us to control who will have access to our selves and to information about ourselves, and to make decisions that critically affect our lives. Such arguments, however, provide no standards or criteria for weighing privacy or autonomy interests against competing public interests, nor do they tell us anything about what makes privacy a distinctive and important value, or what distinguishes privacy from autonomy. Furthermore, to the extent that privacy is defended because of its role in protecting personhood, sexuality or maternity may be read into the core of personhood, thus subtly undermining attempts to keep open sexual and procreative choices by essentializing homosexual or maternal identities. Schoeman's criticism is even more fundamental. He argues that it is a mistake to value privacy because it ensures autonomy or freedom from social or government interference. Privacy is meant not to secure isolation from social pressure but to facilitate social involvements and intimacy.

In these arguments one can see a shift from analysis that is rooted in legal discourse and concern about principled distinctions and the use of privacy rights to protect particular activities, to analysis that tries to understand privacy as a practice and a norm that grows out of and constitutes our various social relations. Because the latter approach—thinking philosophically and anthropologically about privacy—has been helpful to my thinking about what makes privacy an important value, I focus in the next section on the idea that privacy is a set of social practices that constitute our way of life.[83]

Ferdinand Schoeman believes that privacy is a culturally shared strategy that helps maintain a life in common, and he regards cultural values and traditions as things we are not entirely free to pick and choose, but which have authority for us.[84] Robert Post agrees. He writes: "We are . . . led to attempt to rationalize the value of privacy, to discover its functions and reasons, to dress it up in the philosophical language of autonomy, or to dress it down in the economic language of information costs. But this is to miss the plain fact that privacy is for us a living reality only because we enjoy a certain kind of communal existence."[85] What does this mean?

Suppose we take a simple example. Most of us recognize that there are places where we expect no one else to enter and observe us, such as the bathroom or the bedroom. We expect privacy in the home, and we act in ways that reflect this expectation: we lock the door, screen our phone calls, feel shocked and violated when awakened by obscene phone calls or observed by Peeping Toms.

We might expand on the spatial sense of private places, and think more metaphorically about the "territories of the self" we all carry around with us. Drawing on Erving Goffman, Post notes that a "territory" is "a 'field of things' or a 'preserve' to which an individual can claim 'entitlement to possess, control, use, or dispose of.' . . . Territories are defined by normative and social factors, as opposed to 'neutral' or 'objective' criteria [such as feet or inches]."[86] We can easily think of examples of ways we understand and respect these territories:

- I do not tell my secretary she is fat and should lose weight.
- Everyone on my hall hears a colleague's former wife berate him loudly and angrily in his office for being a terrible father and a disappointment in bed, but we say nothing to him about the incident. We pretend we did not hear because to do otherwise would be to violate the respect we owe him as our colleague.
- I become a volunteer soccer coach for my son's soccer team, and I am terrible. But my colleagues at work do not hold my deficiencies as a soccer coach against me: it has nothing to do with my ability to do my job.
- The dean of my school wants to know how many beers I drank when I went out on Saturday night, and where I went and with whom. I am appalled that he would ask, and try to pass his question off with a joke.[87]

Such examples suggest that we have clear, shared ideas about what kinds of information are none of our or someone else's business, and what kinds of remarks would be taken amiss.

James Rachels talks about respect for "territories of the self," using the example of how one acts and speaks differently in different social relationships. He elaborates on the way friends act together to convey that each sees the other as a friend. If I think of someone as a close friend, but she does not talk to me about her troubles or show me her poetry, although she does do this with others, then I conclude that we are not as close as I had thought. Rachels writes:

It is not merely accidental that we vary our behavior with different people according to the different social relationships that we have with them. Rather, the different patterns of behavior are (partly) what define the different realtionships; they are an important part of what makes the different relationships what they are. . . . [B]usinessman to employee, minister to congregant, doctor to patient, husband to wife, parent to child . . . the sort of relationship that people have to one another involves a conception of how it is appropriate for them to behave with each other, and what is more, a conception of the kind and degree of knowledge concerning one another which it is appropriate for them to have.

Rachels believes that we value privacy because it helps us control who has access to us and who knows what about us, and thus allows us to maintain the variety of relationships with others that we want to have.[88]

These examples suggest that we are privileged to talk to one another only about a range of acceptable topics, and in acceptable degrees of distance and intimacy. It strikes us as inappropriate to bring up topics that are none of our business, to accost a mere acquaintance as if he were an old friend, or to confide our deepest secrets in someone we do not know well. Although we may differ about where we perceive the lines to be, we understand that such lines exist, and we respect them in our relations with intimates, acquaintances, and strangers. Not only do we understand where the lines are, but also we value the norms of interaction that guide us to treat our colleagues, children, spouse, lovers, friends, and acquaintances differently and appropriately. We value cues about distance and intimacy because, as Rachels suggests, it is crucial to who we are to have different kinds of relationships because it enriches our lives to be able to be a different person in different contexts.

Furthermore, having others respect one's "territories" is an important way of learning who one is, and gaining self-respect. Jeffrey Reiman considers privacy a "complex social practice by means of which the social group recognizes—and communicates to the individual—that his existence is his own. And this is a precondition of personhood. To be a person, an individual must recognize not just his actual capacity to shape his destiny by his choices. He must also recognize that he has an exclusive moral right to shape his destiny."[89] Post echoes the point: "An individual's ability to press or to waive territorial claims, his ability to choose respect or intimacy, is deeply empowering for his sense of himself as an independent or autonomous person."[90] One might also consider how wounding the experience is of having another ignore or disrespect the space (literal and figurative) one takes up; for example, Patricia Williams describes how deeply humiliating it was to have someone look *through* her, as if she did not exist.[91]

In addition to thinking about what sorts of interactions are appropriate for various relationships, Post also identifies a concern with avoiding inappropriate disclosure of intimate facts. He writes: "Just as we feel violated when our bedrooms are invaded, so we experience the inappropriate disclosure of private information 'as *pollutions* or *defilements*.' . . . Information preserves, like spatial territories, provide a normative framework for the development of individual personality. . . . The civility rules which delineate information preserves must therefore be understood as forms of respect that are integral to both individual and social personality. They comprise an important part of the obligations that members of a community owe to each other."[92]

In a fascinating discussion, Schoeman suggests that gossip plays an important role in publicizing information that needs to be known without revealing the information in inappropriate ways. He uses the example of going around to each member of his department one by one and telling them that the department secretary has been engaging in a series of affairs. He argues that this way of making the information public is permissible, but announcing the same information at a faculty meeting to all of the assembled faculty members would not be. People need to know, but the secretary's affairs are not properly a matter that belongs on the official department agenda.[93]

Another interesting example Schoeman uses is that of Oliver Sipple, the man who knocked the gun from Sara Moore's hand and protected President Gerald Ford from an assassination attempt. Sipple was openly gay in his community in San Francisco, but he had not told his family back in Detroit that he was a homosexual. The national media described him as a gay activist, his family found out, and there was a deep estrangement between them. Some years later Sipple committed suicide. Schoeman thinks that the media should not have reported Sipple's sexuality because it was not germane to the story, and his family should not have learned about his sexual identity in this way. The "public right to know" violated

Sipple's right to privacy by publicizing information that did not belong to the sphere of the newsworthy.[94] Gay activists such as Michelangelo Signorile would argue that publicizing Sipple's homosexuality *is* valid because it helps break down heterosexist and homophobic assumptions. I discuss issues having to do with the closet and outing more fully in Chapter 6.

Naturally, in the information age the public's "right to know" all manner of information about public figures and events undercuts such civility rules. In Post's view such searching scrutiny is, like invasions of the "territories of the self," degrading and "utterly destructive of the conventions that give meaning to human dignity." It is not always easy to explain the public value of privacy, an irony that Post remarks: "If the value of privacy can be conceptualized only in personal or subjective terms, it should be no surprise that its value has not proved politically powerful." In his view privacy norms are extremely fragile in modern life, likely to be undermined by the prerogatives of public accountability and our desire to manage our social environment.[95]

The philosophical-anthropological approach to privacy offers a rich, densely contextual case for the role privacy plays in enabling us to interact with others on a variety of levels without causing offense or hurt, or intruding on one another's dignity. Arguments about privacy as a complex set of expectations and practices that guide various social interactions and (partly) constitute the sort of community in which one lives have strong appeal. Most of the time members of a community recognize and abide by these sorts of privacy norms. At this level, respect for privacy—for appropriate forms of distance and intimacy—is something most people in the United States intuitively and deeply understand, abide by, and value.

There are many ways to explain why privacy is important and ought to be protected: Because controlling access to one's self is central to human dignity, moral autonomy, the notion that one belongs to oneself; because we think it is important to be able to control decisions that centrally affect our life—whether to become pregnant or to carry a pregnancy to term, whom to choose for a sexual partner, whom to marry. Because people ought to be free to engage in actions and decisions so long as they have no adverse effect on others, in order to cultivate diversity and uniqueness, and to allow each person to experiment with his or her own notions of excellence and satisfaction. Because the state is increasingly able to intrude into the most intimate details of our lives, minutely examining and regulating, storing and sending information held in data banks, passing and enforcing laws that attempt to "normalize" us by pushing us into conventionally acceptable roles, for example, as mothers or heterosexuals. Because other bulwarks against state power—principally property—no longer work as they once did, whereas privacy seems to provide a legal and intellectual limit to state power. Because privacy structures our myriad personal and social relationships in ways we value, and facilitates our ability to move among a variety of public and private spheres and roles.

These arguments deal with different notions of privacy, which carry different weights. If Post, Schoeman, and others are right, privacy is compelling and useful when understood as a value that at a deep, unconscious level structures character and social interactions. But privacy as a particular kind of legal claim is much more contentious. So is privacy understood as a political value that shields certain aspects of social or family life from public scrutiny and interference. When privacy is asserted as a legal or political value in debates about contested moral and political issues, especially in situations that call into question conventional social values and gender norms, the value of privacy is much more open to attack and criticism.

As a legal or constitutional matter, it is not clear how much respect should be accorded to privacy, or how its value should be weighed against competing values, for example, in the free flow of public information, or in enforcing community morality. Without a clear sense of what grounds privacy as a value, the prospect of developing standards for assessing how much respect privacy deserves seems unlikely. Differences, variety, and diversity often go unacknowledged by writers who defend privacy, especially the different degrees to which poor and rich, nonwhite and white, immigrant and native, female and male, gay and straight are able to assert and defend their privacy.[96] Work on the cultural value of privacy subsumes or ignores such differences, frequently referring to a "community" which privacy is taken in part to define.

Connecting Skeptical and Sympathetic Treatments of Privacy

Where does this tour of feminist theoretical and legal-philosophical approaches to thinking about privacy leave us? Suppose we imagine a party where two separate conversations are going on in two different rooms of a large house. In the first room, most agree that it is futile to distinguish between political and private matters, since relations of conflict and power permeate social and private life as much as public and political life. It would be wrong to view private life as a distinctive part of human life which should be immune from public scrutiny or government regulation, since that would merely serve to cloak domination and inequality in social and family life in the rhetoric of choice and intimacy. Some insist that intimate life is particularly the realm of women's subordination to men; others argue that various forms of oppression—economic, racial, sexual, ethnic—occur in, and are veiled by, the privateness of social relations.

The group in the other room is talking about what makes privacy valuable and distinctive. Many view privacy as a crucial bulwark against a long list of threats, including data collectors, emerging computer technologies, drug and AIDS testing, gay activists, the religious right, and the media. Others talk about what privacy protections mean for particular groups, including women, gays and lesbians, and consumers of pornography. Several focus on the rising and falling fortunes of privacy protections in the courts, and argue for a clearer delineation of what makes privacy valuable, and for stronger legal protections for privacy. Curiously, hardly anyone wanders between the two rooms to participate in the other group's conversation.

Contemporary feminist and legal-philosophical work on privacy resembles this imaginary party. Theorists from these respective "rooms" do not have much to say to each other. They only rarely cite the other group's works and almost never address the concerns the other group takes to be central. Why is this so, and what can be done to link these two "conversations" about private and public life so that each group attends to and draws on the best insights developed by the other?

First, in honesty, it is not fair to say that these two sets of arguments ignore each other completely. Most feminist theorists leave open the possibility of valuing and protecting privacy when to do so would be empowering or would help defend reproductive or sexual choice, and many legal commentators are cognizant of and responsive to feminist arguments about the ideological power of privacy.[97] And a number of law review articles arguing that privacy should be protected take seriously feminist legal scholars' criticisms of privacy.[98] Still, academic specialization and the tendency to follow only the literature directly pertinent to one's community tends to result in law review commentary that ignores political theory and political theory that shows no acquaintance with legal theorizing.

But there is more to the lack of engagement among skeptical feminist critics and legal-liberal defenders of privacy than differing reading lists and publication outlets. Through the lens of the feminist critique, respect for privacy as a social and political value central to Western, especially liberal, politics is seen as a way to treat as politically irrelevant informal social differences in power owing to wealth, race, sexual orientation, and especially gender. Approaches to politics that treat economics, the body, and the household as private make them seem prepolitical, off-limits to public inquiry or action. Yet feminists have long analyzed how laws and institutions such as coverture and male-only suffrage supported "private" gender differences, and how informal gendered roles and divisions of labor support women's exclusion from and secondary status in the public world of paid work and governance. Attacking the public-private distinction was and is central to debunking the mythology of the private domestic sphere of unstrained affection and generosity, and showing how respect for "private" life makes oppressive relationships invisible and resistant to change.

Through the lens of legal theory, privacy can be seen to provide a strategy for protecting individuals from the oppressive power of the state and its ability to inquire into and regulate the details of daily life. Respect for privacy also offers a hedge against the power of oppressive social pressure to make individuals conform. Defining certain core activities or decisions and places or relationships as private is a way to prevent the state or legislative majorities from intruding on or attempting to regulate matters we want to set beyond their interference, such as freedom of conscience, religion, and association, and the individual's control over her body and intimate relationships, including consensual, nonabusive same-sex relationships with other adults.

Through the lens of philosophical-anthropological theorizing, we see privacy as part of a set of civility rules that govern the degree of distance or familiarity that is appropriate for different kinds of relationships, helping people to assert their own and respect others' dignity. The ability to reveal and hide different aspects of the self is crucial to the ability to interact at many levels. It also makes it possible for people to explore many kinds of relationships and roles and to develop multifaceted identities.

All of these ways of thinking about privacy are persuasive and relevant in different ways or in different contexts. Yet, as we have seen, it is hard to keep them all in focus at the same time, in part because the starting assumptions, methods of inquiry, and academic or political intent of these different projects are often dissimilar. But this is exactly what we need to do if we are to think clearly about the ways in which privacy can be both oppressive and empowering. Privacy is necessary for nurturing a broad range of socially and personally satisfying interactions, especially intimate relationships. But we also need to think about the ways privacy is folded together with privilege: What sorts of privacy are valued, and whose privacy? Some relationships, and some people, enjoy more privacy, understood as the ability to control access, than others. These differences need to be understood as historically produced and contingent, connected to power and to privileges of class, race, gender, and sexuality. Sometimes one person's privacy may be another person's injury or exploitation; for example, the right of consumers of pornography to view sadistic or object- ified images of women's or men's or even children's bodies may derogate the dignity of those who pose for such images. By the same token, some issues and perspectives are more likely to be regarded as *merely* private— unimportant, unworthy of public attention—than others, especially issues related to the abusive treatment of women and women's unpaid domestic work. Our notions of "the private" are thus framed and supported by pub- lic, sometimes formal, supports, such as women's historical lack of political representation and the continuing power of the double standard.

The development of parallel literatures and ways of thinking about public and private which for the most part talk past each other suggests the need for a vantage point that can help us gain some conceptual clarity about (1) what is valuable and worth protecting about privacy and private life; (2) what is dangerous and oppressive about hiding persons or prob- lems in private, depriving them of public significance; and (3) what is distinctive and worth pursuing about political life, and how issues rooted in private life can be made politically recognizable and actionable. In the chapters that follow I attempt to develop such a vantage point.

As we have seen, "private" and "public" are multifaceted concepts. Al- though privacy certainly *can* function ideologically, it does not necessarily do so. Tensions and inconsistencies in contemporary treatments of privacy are easier to understand when we distinguish between different senses in which something can be private. Thus, noting that *privacy* is connected etymologically both to *depriving* people and issues of public significance and to *privilege* can give us a more nuanced understanding of the roles privacy plays. Although it is a dangerously constraining concept when it prevents individuals from recognizing how social practices and institutions structure and limit their choices and possibilities, privacy can also be em- powering when it permits great latitude in personal choices and actions. In Chapter 2 I draw on what we say in our ordinary language about *pri- vate, public,* and *political,* as well as other forms and expressions that clarify these related concepts.

Another step might be to think of privacy is a particular kind of politi- cal tool used to protect (or suppress) certain interests or aspects of human life. On this view, treating intimate, especially familial, life and personal decision making as private—that is, as off-limits to public scrutiny and government interference—is a political decision,[99] visible in our social values, legal norms, and the fundamental law of our Constitution. Of course, we need to question who decides to value and protect privacy, and whose interests are served by doing so.[100] Some groups in American society continue to enjoy more privacy than others: for example, welfare mothers are more likely than middle-class parents to have their parenting and home-making skills held up to public scrutiny and government interference.

It may also help our thinking not to take public and private so literally as separate and opposed spaces or "spheres," but rather to see them as different approaches to thinking or talking about the *same* phenomena. We need to explore the difference between "political" and "privative" (personal, intimate, particular, therapeutic) ways of thinking and talking about issues.[101] This may be especially important in terms of issues such as housework, child rearing, and sexual orientation, which are "at home" in the intimate sphere, so we are especially inclined to think and talk about them in personal, particularistic terms. Indeed, the distinction may be a crucial one, given the temptations of what Arendt called "the social," or what Tocqueville characterized as the dangers of mass society: conformism, being wrapped up in one's personal life, relying on the immense tutelary power of benign bureaucratic government, losing our sense of the importance of political projects that pull us into collective engagements. All of these erode *political* approaches to thinking, talking about, and acting on issues of broad public concern. I develop the distinction between "political" and "privative" approaches in Chapter 3.

There are two related concerns which make no sense from the perspective of approaches that treat private life as already and intrinsically political, but which I think are crucial. The first has to do with translating private matters into political ones. If pressed to describe public and private in spatial terms (spheres), I would say that they encompass a variety of locations and relationships that vary in degree of intimacy, visibility, formality, and the extent to which they affect others, and that they overlap and intersect in a variety of ways. When privacy functions to deprive issues or persons of reality and recognition, how can we translate questions grounded in the private sphere of intimate life into politically recognizable ones? It will not help to show that public and private are identical, or to insist on preserving their fundamental separateness and distinctiveness if in fact public and private are different but connected parts of or approaches to human life.

We need to think about how practices or problems that are at home in the private sphere of familial or sexual relations but are of widespread general importance can be translated into political issues, that is, how to move between privative and political ways of thinking and talking about issues of general concern. It will not do to assume that everything that is personal or private *is* political, that the existence of power always and everywhere defines and delineates political life. The ability to articulate unjust power relationships as political issues cannot be taken as given; it is an endeavor that requires an appeal to common standards and shared notions of justice.[102] I address this problem of translation in Chapters 5 and 6, on maternal thinking and coming out of the closet.

Implicit in the idea of translation is the second concern: how to encourage and revitalize an aspiration toward active democratic citizenship, which presumes a degree of commonality as well as plurality and respect for differences. What does the political discussion and resolution of divisive lifestyle issues entail?[103] What kinds of debates and arguments are truly political? In my view some of the strategies engaged in by a variety of political groups—whether dismissing one's opponents as ideologues, expelling them from the community because their views are too divergent, or viewing any political compromise as conceding too much—suggest a dismissive attitude toward others' opinions and a standard of political purity that may undermine the possibility of democratic politics. At stake are the norms of discourse of a truly political community. These norms determine what kind of discussion is appropriate in a civic context; the degree of respect one owes one's opponents, as well as one's allies; the kinds of arguments and responses one needs to make to those with whom one disagrees; and the kinds of appeals one needs to make to build agreement and consensus. Erasing or ignoring differences between personal and political, private and public undermines active democratic citizenship in two ways. First, personal troubles or grievances may be taken as evidence of broader political problems without the sufferer's having to make claims based on shared standards of justice, equality, or liberty which may be crucial to developing the outlook of a citizen. And second, personal commitments or choices may be inappropriately held up to standards of public judgment. As I argue in my conclusion, respecting "politicalness" and respecting privacy are important parts of the process of nurturing democratic citizens.

Two

Privation and Privilege

P RIVACY TODAY IS AT STAKE IN A VARIETY OF
political contexts. We hear about a number of issues: privacy on the Internet and other forms of computer and
electronic media; privatization and the proper role of government; the
proper relation between government and business; the public's right to
know versus the privacy claims of newsworthy persons; and the need to
accommodate the domestic responsibilities of workers and citizens. When
we begin to probe our thinking, we realize that very different claims about
privacy and private life are at stake in these different contexts. A woman
asserting a "right to privacy" that allows her to have an abortion does not
mean the same thing by privacy as a public figure who objects to media
coverage of his personal affairs, and neither of these claims is much like
the notion of privacy at stake in privatizing public services or allowing
businesses to be free from pollution standards or workplace safety regulations. Furthermore, we have witnessed a blurring and confusion of public
and private as categories with the emergence of hybrid institutions (private
corporations that contract to carry out public functions, huge multina-
tional corporations that elude state regulation) and new issues that are
both private and public.[1]

The variety of claims for protecting privacy and the blurring and confusion of public and private characteristics in our institutions and practices
underline our uncertainty about what privacy means and how the private
and public spheres are differentiated and connected. For example, consider
a central tension in the way Americans think about privacy: liberals favor
regulating the economy and treating lifestyle decisions as private, while
conservatives would avoid interference with the private workings of the
market but regulate lifestyle decisions. The different value individuals accord the privacy of economic life and the privacy of intimate or familial

matters and matters of morality or conscience is a key source of political division in this country.

Two examples from the current public debate about abortion further illustrate how our thinking about public and private is rife with contradictions. Many have criticized pro-life activists on the grounds that their concern for human life extends only to the unborn: once babies are born into, say, poor, overburdened families, many advocates for the sanctity of unborn human life show little concern for ensuring that these children receive adequate nurture. Although most pro-life advocates believe that the choice to abort a pregnancy should be regulated or prohibited by government policy, most also believe that the means of raising healthy, bright, secure children is *not* rightly a matter of public policy, but must come from the resources of individual mothers or families.[2] Critics attack this as cynical posturing: human life is an appropriate public concern so long as it does not cost the taxpayers anything.

Many point to a similar problem in the pro-choice position. Relying on the rhetoric of privacy has made the decision how to resolve a difficult pregnancy into one that is entirely private, cut off from any claims on public support or assistance.[3] Advocates of reproductive choice who support both keeping the abortion decision private and making public Medicaid funding available for poor women seeking abortions get caught by the logic of their own arguments. On the one hand, in the absence of public funding, the ability to exercise one's "right to privacy" becomes a cruel hoax for poor women.[4] But on the other hand, the claim of entitlement to public funding is undercut by the demand that abortion opponents and government respect women's privacy. If the decision is protected from regulation and prohibition because it is *private,* that rationale subverts the claim that women must have a positive entitlement to public funding if they are to have a meaningful chance to exercise their right. Thus, both sets of partisans become tangled in conflicting views about the "privateness" of abortion, abortion funding, and child rearing.

It seems that there are deep and often unrecognized tensions and confusions in the everyday, ordinary ways we talk and think about privacy in American politics. Sometimes, for example, the claim that something is private insulates an action or decision from public scrutiny or control, even though it may affect large numbers of people (e.g., the management policies of a large corporation). Sometimes assertedly private lifestyle decisions (using certain drugs, for instance, or choosing a same-sex partner) are also part of the public discussion about what sorts of activities should be tolerated or forbidden. It is tempting to recognize only the private or public aspects of matters that are public and private at the same time, or to pursue the rhetoric of privacy or publicness even when it leads us into inconsistency or hypocrisy or undermines our political or personal aspirations. Developing a cure for one-sided thinking about privacy and publicness can help us see privacy as silencing but also empowering, oppressive but also essential for nurturing the many sides of a person's being.

We seek philosophical insight about privacy because it can help us understand tensions and confusions at the heart of our collective life and our political decisions and priorities. I believe that paying attention to language can clarify disputed and convoluted concepts and issues. It *matters* that we describe a variety of issues and practices as private, or argue that they deserve protection or respect because they are private, or alternatively that we say they are public and political *despite* their apparent privateness. It is not just a coincidence that we talk about "private property" and a "right to privacy," "privatization" of government services, and "privacy protections" for data stored in computer files. Despite the evident breadth and variety of the practices we designate "private," we do not simply decide at random to attach this label to different experiences and activities.

In this chapter we shall see how the way we use words related to privacy, publicness, and politics in ordinary American English can provide insight into patterns of thinking and acting that are troublesome or confusing. Figuring out how "private-" and "public-"related terms make sense is a step toward locating the areas of conceptual confusion in our contemporary political life. By looking at etymology and the language games in which the "private" and "public" families of words are used, we can begin to understand the values we place on private and public ways of being in the world, the manner in which these modes of being interact, and the source of some of the contradictory positions and passionate disagreements we hold on issues that are in various senses "private."

Why Ordinary Language Analysis?

What are the philosophical underpinnings of the approach I take here to thinking about the concept of privacy? Instead of looking only at how privacy-related issues have given rise to confusion, I propose to look at how we *talk* about privacy-related matters.[5] The idea is to look back and forth from language to the world, to gain insight into real-world problems as well as conceptual confusions.[6] J. L. Austin describes this connection between language and the world: "When we examine what we should say when, what words we should use in what situations, we are looking again not *merely* at words . . . but also at the realities we use the words to talk about: we are using a sharpened awareness of words to sharpen our perception of . . . the phenomena."[7] Hanna Pitkin suggests that studying language to gain conceptual clarity may be especially useful when other approaches do not help: "We may find that both theoretical and empirical work on some particular topic encounters persistent difficulty and confusion, as has been the case for instance in political science on the topic of power. Here again the investigators' concepts may require some attention; we may profitably stop looking at power phenomena in the world for a time, and back up to an examination of how we talk about 'power.' "[8] Political analysts who draw on ordinary language analysis have engaged in this kind of stepping back and examining language to clarify our thinking about a number of puzzling concepts, including representation, freedom, justice, neocolonialism, and human rights.[9]

By doing ordinary language analysis we can recognize regularities in our language and from them cull insights to help us resolve the conceptual confusion we face when we try to think about politically contested matters. These regularities, which Ludwig Wittgenstein referred to as the "grammar" of the language, go beyond the formal rules of syntax to the contexts in which it makes sense to say something.[10] As Pitkin puts it: "The appeal is not to the ordinary man, but to the regularities in our language, to the ordinary contexts in which a word or expression is at home, where it occurs naturally. That means both the verbal contexts in which the word is at home, . . . and the worldly context in which an expression might naturally be used."[11]

Appealing to the regularities in our language requires us to become adept at recognizing those regularities, often by finding examples and usages from the word family we are studying which illustrate a consistent, accepted usage, or which point to an anomalous one. The standard of proof for such an exercise is to produce convincing examples which make it clear that one word belongs rather than another. The process thus teaches us something about how we use the words and the concepts they help articulate.[12]

This enterprise is in marked contrast to the approach of imagining a counterintuitive hypothetical example in order to spur our thinking about the contours of a concept, as philosophers often do. One might think here of some of Judith Jarvis Thomson's well-known examples, such as the world-famous violinist who will die unless he is hooked up to another's body for nine months, or the special x-ray machine which allows one to look through the walls of another's safe and see the picture that is hidden there.[13] Choosing extreme cases or examples is tempting because we think that by doing so, we will be able to chart clearly the boundaries of the concept we are exploring. But the risk of such an approach is that it will lead us to speculate, in Pitkin's words, "abstractly about a concept apart from any context of speech, [to] use it without any of its usual contrasts; [and in doing so to] extrapolate the concept to infinity. But thereby we deprive it of the context, the contrasts, which normally complete its meaning."[14] We learn different lessons from attending to the contexts in which it makes sense to say something than we do from inventing extraordinary examples which we could scarcely imagine occurring.[15] Choosing counter-intuitive examples can show us language only when it is *not* doing its proper work, when it is divorced from the usual contexts in which, for example, we might make claims about our privacy. This will not do, for as Pitkin puts it: "Our concepts are fashioned in working use; they serve to differentiate some features of our world, our actions, our feelings, from others. They were not fashioned for speculating about the world as a whole, in general; for we would have no use for such concepts."[16] So instead of seeking to clarify and refine a concept by using examples that stretch it to absurdity, the ordinary language theorist looks to the messy, multifaceted ways we use the words related to the concept, bringing into focus the compass and variety, the inconsistency, as well as the family resemblances and commonalities of both the words and the concept itself.

Resorting to language analysis to remind ourselves of the "grammar" of our concept of privacy may strike some as bothersome and unhelpful, others as ahistorical and inattentive to the operations of power in language.[17] Suggesting that we can look back and forth between the way we use words and the world makes it sound as if language and social reality were distinct and separate rather than deeply interdependent and mutually constitutive. In resorting to ordinary language analysis, I wish neither to endorse nor to reinforce this kind of static view, nor do I wish to embrace uncritically the views of the powerful about privacy and public life. I am making only a modest claim: that we can use ordinary language analysis to get a snapshot of problems and tensions that exist in our thinking about public and private matters, including issues of power and privilege and the question who gets to define what counts as private and on what grounds. Ordinary language analysis can help us discover what privacy means, how it both empowers and deprives issues and people of reality. Conceptual confusion may arise when we take a part of the concept as the whole, and forget to incorporate other aspects of the concept into our thinking. According to Pitkin:

Wittgenstein says that conceptual puzzlement is like a disease, and its "main cause" is "a one-sided diet: one nourishes one's thinking with only one kind of example." We have a mental picture, and believe that it forces a particular generalization on us; but that belief merely reflects "the fact that only the one case and no other occurred to us." If we do notice other, conflicting cases, our conviction that there must be a single consistent rule leads us to dismiss them as confusing details. "A picture is conjured up which seems to fix the sense *unambiguously*. The actual use, compared with that suggested by the picture, seems like something muddied." So we cling to the picture, and to our generalization based on it.

As a consequence, when we are conceptually puzzled, *we need exactly what we do not want*. We want to escape the confusing encumbrance of detailed cases and proceed directly to the essence, the central core, of the puzzling concept. . . . The very craving for generality and clarity cuts us off from what would resolve our puzzlement: the messy, confused plurality of other valid examples of the word's use.[18]

Taking an ordinary language approach helps us avoid the trap of false coherence by forcing us to consider the possibility that a concept has crosscutting or contradictory implications. It makes it easier for us to view these implications not as a fault or a problem to be ironed out or clarified away, but as part of what the concept *means,* and thus part of what gives rise to our sense of conceptual puzzlement and paradox.[19]

Let us turn now to how we use *private, public, political,* and related words, beginning with their etymology. We will then consider the differences in meaning among different senses of *private,* the contrasts and oppositions that clarify conceptual distinctions, and the patterns that help us understand some of the grammar of this family of words. The aim is to sort out what we mean when we talk about private, public, and political matters so we can think clearly about practices and problems that reside at the intersections among private and public, private and political, and public and political life. Precisely because these practices and problems are contested, with many arguing that powerful interests and institutions shape the discourse about protecting and valuing privacy, it is useful to look to language for a record of where social contestation over meaning and power is at this point. By doing so we understand more clearly the stakes involved in the ongoing debates over meaning and politics. And we gain a better sense of whose interests in privacy, publicity, and politics have been articulated thus far, which ones are viewed as credible or dominant, and how divergent views are treated.

Etymology

Let us begin by examining some of the words and expressions that relate to "private," "public" and "politics."

Private

Private, adapted from Latin *privatus* (past participle of *privare,* to bereave, deprive, dispossess, rob), withdrawn from public life, deprived of office, peculiar to oneself.[20] The *Oxford English Dictionary* suggests some of the various ways we use the word *private.*

ADJECTIVE

Private (1)
   —A person who does not hold public office or have rank, distinction, or official position (1432), e.g., private soldier, an ordinary soldier soldier without rank or distinction of any kind (1579), private member, a member of the House of Commons who is not the member of any Ministry (1863), private trader, one who trades on his own account, as distinguished from an agent of a public company
   —that which pertains to a person in a nonofficial capacity (1613);
Private (2)
   —one who is withdrawn or separated from the public body (1380);
   —that which is kept or removed from public view or knowledge (1472);
   —by one's self, alone, without the presence of anyone else (1592);
   —a conversation or communication intended only for or confined to the person or persons directly concerned, confidential (1560);
   —a place which is unfrequented, secluded (1494);
   —a person who is retiring, secluded, secretive, or reticent (1585);
Private (3)
   —things or places which are not open to the public, but restricted or intended only for the use or enjoyment of particular and privileged persons (1398);
Private (4)
   —that which belongs to or is the property of a particular individual (1503);
Private (5)
   —that which pertains to or affects a person or small intimate body or group of persons apart from the general community (1526).

NOUN

Private (sb 1)

—(Obsolete) a private person, one who does not hold public office (1483);

—a private soldier (1781);

Private (sb 2)

—"the private," meaning private people, as opposed to "the public," or the people as a whole (1716);

Private (sb 3)

—retirement or privacy, used especially with *in,* for example, "in private," not publicly, in private company, in private life (1581); and

Private (sb 4)

—in its plural form ("the privates"), the private parts or genitalia.

Then there are related words, such as the verbs *deprive, privatize* and *reprivatize, keep private,* and *protect the privacy of . . .* ; the nouns *deprivation, privation* (1340), *privacy* (1450; 1598), and *privateness;* the adverb *privately* (1550); and kindred words and expressions, such as *privilege* (1154, from *privi + legium,* private law), privy, confidential, in confidence, secret, retired, reserved, secluded, guarded, discreet.

When we group the different meanings and senses of *private* that derive from these definitions, interesting patterns emerge. Several, such as *deprive, privation,* and *private* in sense 1 and sb 1, tap into the word's ancient Latin root, *privare,* to bereave, deprive, rob, isolate, or make solitary. The contemporary English words *deprive, privation* and *deprivation* bring to mind the condition of lacking basic physical and human necessities such as food, clothing, sleep, housing, and emotional nurture. Although the original sense of the word *privatus* clearly supposes participation in public life to be part of a fully human existence,[21] for contemporary English speakers the lack of public participation or recognition does not seem as serious as a "deprivation." A private matter may be lacking in public status or recognition, but private life also has its attractions, and may provide a welcome respite from the burdens, responsibilities, and constant intrusions of being a public figure or holding public office.

In contrast to the sense of *private* as lacking in public significance, sense 2 suggests a quality of protection or confidentiality. It is used to describe people or places that are hidden or secluded, or to refer to pursuits or actions that either are hidden from view or take place among intimates, often within the family or at home. This protective quality is accentuated when *private* is used to justify limiting access to a person or a place, as in sense 3; here the core value is one's ability to exclude unwanted others.[22]

Sense 4 suggests possession or control, in the sense of "private property" or "private house." This meaning is connected to sense 3. It is in this sense too that we speak of "private enterprise," of businesses or companies as "privately owned" or "privately run," and of "privatization," the move from public to private ownership and control, especially of essential services.

Sense 5 designates actions or decisions that have limited impact, in contrast with events, acts, or decisions that affect the general community.[23]

From this overview we can articulate various dimensions of privateness: lack of (or sometimes freedom from) public or political office, involvement, or significance; intimacy; exclusivity, including the ability to control information about oneself and contact with the world; ownership; and objective impact. Sometimes these differing dimensions of privateness sort together, sometimes not. For example, a large corporation may decide to close down a plant and lay off thousands of employees, thus combining enormous public impact with private ownership and management.

Public

Public, adapted from Latin *publicus,* from Latin *poplicus,* from *poplus,* later *populus,* people (changed to *publicus* under the influence of Latin *pubes,* adult male population).

ADJECTIVE

Public (1)

> Of or pertaining to the people as a whole; that which belongs to, affects, or concerns the community or nation; common, national, popular (1513). Used in phrases such as "public good," "public weal," *res publica,* "public state" (1436); used now to modify act, bill, statute (as opposed to private acts of Parliament), opinion (the opinion of the mass of the community).

Public (2)

> Done or made on behalf of the community as a whole; authorized by, acting for, or representing the community (1560).

Public (3)

> Open to or shared by all members of the community; generally accessible or available, not restricted to the private use of any person or group; generally levied (as in a tax or rate) (1542).

Public (4)
> Open to general observation, sight, or cognizance; existing, done, or made in public; manifest, not concealed (1548).

Public (5)
> Of, pertaining to, or engaged in the affairs or service of the community (1571); or to a person in his capacity in which he comes in contact with the community, his official or professional capacity as opposed to his private capacity (1538).

Public (6)
> Devoted or directed to the promotion of the public welfare; public-spirited (1607).

NOUN

Public (sb 1)
> The community or people as an organized body; the nation, state, or commonwealth; the interest or well-being of the community (1612). Or, the community as an aggregate, but not in its organized capacity; the members of the community (1665).

Public (sb 2)
> A particular section, group, or portion of a community or of mankind, especially used as a plural (1709).

Public (sb 3)
> In a place, situation, condition, or state open to public view or access; openly, publicly, *in public,* as opposed to *in private;* also, in a published form or in print (1450).

Related words include *publish, publicize, make public, publicity, publicness, publican, pub, popular, populace,* and a number of expressions using *public* ("public record," "housing," "forum," "enemy," "good," "nuisance," "address system," "relations," etc.).

Again, when we step back, we can see several distinct ways we use the word *public:* to refer to events, policies, or decisions that have widespread or general impact or importance (sense 1); to refer to authority or governance (senses 2, 5, 6, and sb 1); to indicate open access to both places and information ("publicity," senses 3, 4, sb 3); and to refer to identifiable, more or less attentive interest groups or audiences or "publics" (sense sb 2).[24]

As with *private,* different senses of *public* do not always sort together.

For example, the pursuit of interests by various "publics" (sense sb 2) may subvert the larger common good of "the public" (sense 1).[25] Decisions about policy or consultation about foreign affairs may take place behind closed doors, in secret. Many things that are publicized or widely known are not matters for public decision making or government action.

Political

Politic, adopted from French *politique,* adaptation of Latin *politicus,* adopted from Greek *politikos* (from *polis,* city, state), pertaining to citizens, civic, civil, political. Now superseded by *political.*

ADJECTIVE

Political (1)
> Of, belonging, or pertaining to the state or body of citizens, its government and policy; public, civil; of or pertaining to the science or art of politics (1551).

Political (2)
> Belonging to or taking a side in politics or in connection with the party system of government; in a bad sense, partisan, factious (1769).

Political (3)
> Of persons, apt at pursuing a policy; sagacious, prudent, shrewd; of actions or things, judicious, expedient, skillfully contrived (1430). In a sinister sense, scheming, crafty, cunning; diplomatic, artfully contriving or contrived (1580).

Political (4)
> Used in phrases such as "political geography," "economy," "prisoner" to differentiate from other kinds of maps, economic statistics, or prisoners (1682).

SUBSTANTIVE

Politics (sb 1)
> The science or art of government; the science dealing with the form, organization, and administration of a state or part of one, and with the regulation of its relations with other states (1529).

Politics (sb 2)
> Political actions or practice; policy (1644). Political affairs or business; political life (1693).

Politics (sb 3)
>   The political convictions, principles, opinions, or sympathies of a
>   person or party (1769).

Politics (sb 4)
>   Conduct of private affairs; politic management, scheming, planning
>   (1693).

Other words and expressions in this family include *politicize, politicized, make political, politically, polity;* a variety of words that form compounds with *politics* ("office politics," "electoral," "departmental," "company," "boardroom," "sexual"); and a variety of expressions that use *political* as a modifier ("political in-fighting," "cartoon," "agenda," "cronies," "activism," "debate," "deals," etc.).

Political and *politics* can refer to affairs of state, matters that concern or belong to the citizenry, matters related to government and governance (senses 1, sb 1). *Political* also refers to partisanship and factiousness (sense 2); to sagacious, prudent skill in pursuing a policy; or to devious craft, cunning, and diplomacy (senses 3, sb 4). When we talk about a person's "politics," we mean the principles and beliefs she or he holds (sense sb 3; also sense 2). Or *political* may be used as to designate a manner of doing something or a specific field of inquiry.

As with *private* and *public,* different senses of *political* and *politics* do not necessarily sort together. Citizens may lobby, educate, or protest to get an issue recognized as a matter for public recognition and debate without necessarily intending to effect government action or public policy; or they may struggle for recognition and government action for a long time before legislatures finally enact policies, courts rule on cases, departments or agencies issue directives identifying actionable grievances or requiring compliance from regulated industries, or presidents pull out troops. Political activists, citizens, and politicians may hold passionate convictions without knowing how to pursue them in a politic fashion. Conversely, many are adept when it comes to the ins and outs of office or departmental politics, but such maneuvering often has nothing to do with political convictions or matters of concern to the city, state, country, or citizenry.

Paying Attention to Ordinary Language

Having surveyed some of the various meanings of *private, public,* and *political,* we turn to the question, How are these words used in ordinary

English? Can these words give us some clues about our concepts of private, public, and politics? Can they help us think about practices and problems that straddle the boundaries between public and private, or combine qualities of being private *and* public, intimate *and* political?

When we first begin to consider the word *private,* we are drawn to think in terms of binary contrasts: private as opposed to public, inner to outer, personal to political, small-scale and idiosyncratic to large-scale and broadly shared, hidden and secret to visible and widely known. This can lead us to assume that just because *private* generally contrasts with *public,* every sense of *private* must have a corresponding sense of *public* with which it contrasts, and that if something is private in one respect, it must be private in *all* respects. Especially when we talk about "the private" versus "the public," or "the private sphere" versus the "the public sphere," we are likely to think of public and private as mutually exclusive worlds and qualities.

But it is misleading to think this way. "In general," Austin writes, "it will pay us to take nothing for granted or as obvious about negations and opposites. It does not pay to assume that a word must have an opposite, or one opposite."[26] For example, we commonly find that practices or institutions, such as the closing of large plants or gender relations within the family, are private in some respects, public in others. We need to be alert to differing meanings and senses of private and public, and conscious of the temptation to cut the world into two dichotomized spaces.

I have already pointed out the division in the meanings of *private* between those that suggest that something or someone is lacking in public office, status, or importance, and those that suggest a degree of exclusivity, control, or privilege. Senses 1 and sb 1 belong to the first category, and senses 3 and 4 to the second, as does the word *privilege,* a term that was well established in English before *private* made its first appearances. Recall that various relationships are regarded as *privileged* (lawyer-client, priest-penitent, doctor-patient, husband-wife), which means that one cannot be legally compelled to reveal the content of conversations because of the value accorded confidentiality in such relationships. Here, *privilege* is clearly related to *privacy* and the notion of being "privy" to secret information. Senses 2, sb 2, and sb 3 are more ambiguous: sometimes these suggest control over access, the attempt to preserve solitude or confidentiality from unwanted scrutiny or intrusion, and sometimes they have a resonance of being "merely" private, being too withdrawn or unimportant to attract notice or to matter to anyone else. Let us examine the privileged and privative senses of *private* in turn.

In contemporary American English *private* is used most often in the senses of exclusivity and ownership, to talk about places or events one cannot visit or attend without an invitation, information or personal decisions that are nobody else's business, or property that is owned and managed in the interests of the owner. Although other uses of *private* are also common—"the privates" meaning sexual organs, a private in the army, or private in the sense of personal (e.g., "in my private opinion")—they are often swallowed up in the protective, "privileged" sense of *private* in contemporary discourse.[27] It is almost as if, in a society that enshrines individualism and property rights, we easily forget that private can also imply a sense of being de*prived* of public significance. Yet the fact that *private* and its cousins—words such as *deprive* and *privation* as well as *privy* and *privilege*—originate from the ancient Latin *privare* suggests that they always carry some residue or resonance of lacking public significance.[28]

But, as we saw in Chapter 1, many feminists argue that the privateness of the "private realm" of domestic relations and the family masks political relations of power, inequality, and oppression. Indeed, many argue that it is precisely privacy, in the sense of a perquisite or privilege, which is at the root of privacy in the sense of being deprived of public significance: that is, those who hold power, privilege, and property have constructed the public-private distinction in order to place a variety of arrangements off-limits to inquiry and criticism. Thus, the division of domestic responsibilities between women and men has been viewed not as a significant political issue but as natural, private, and prepolitical.[29] When *private* is used to mean "deprived of public significance" in feminist discourse about the public-private distinction, it is not because feminists do not recognize or understand the protective quality of privacy; it is because they want to insist on the connection between power relations and the privatization of domestic life.

Many matters may strike us as private in terms of their objective impact (sense 5): they do not affect very many people; they lack broad significance or importance; or they seem trivial, caught up in relationships with intimates and the ordinary, repetitive concerns of domestic life, such as preparing food and caring for children. This kind of thinking can be a self-fulfilling prophecy. Practices and issues connected to intimate family life, sexuality, and the body have long been seen as having no public significance, are hence shielded from public scrutiny, and are thus unlikely to fuel attempts to reorient public policies, even though they exert a tremendous impact on people's lives.

What ought we to conclude from these ways of thinking about privacy? One possibility is that being protected from public exposure or regulation also carries an implication of not being a matter fit for public recognition, of not being available to public scrutiny and action. That is, privacy in the sense of privilege, control, and exclusivity may also imply privacy in the sense of lacking public status. Some things that are private in terms of being located in the intimate spheres of the family, household, or sexual relations may thus be trivialized and personalized, and thereby deprived of public significance when they ought not to be.

Alternatively, matters that are private in the sense of lacking public office or impact may also be private in the privileged, empowering sense. For example, while the privateness of sexuality and "the privates" deprives sexual practices and arrangements of public importance, it also provides protection and entitlement to pursue sexual practices that the majority might otherwise prohibit. Intimate life may sometimes be home to the cruelty and denigration of spousal battering, rape, incest, and exploitation, but it is also home to trust, openness, confidentiality, and affection. Losing sight of the protective, nurturing quality of private life can lead to theorizing that ignores an important part of the way privacy functions in our common life, and to advocacy that sounds shrill and inaccurate.

Much of the time our thinking does indeed seem to be nurtured by one-sided examples that get at only some aspects of the concept of privacy. Specialists (both feminist scholars and legal and philosophical scholars who write about privacy) and ordinary English speakers alike often draw on only one sense in which something can be private and ignore all the others. Reminding ourselves of the etymology of the *private* family of words and of the range of their ordinary usage prods us to be more careful and nuanced—more attentive to their both/and quality—when we theorize or make policy about matters housed in private life which have important public consequences.

Reminding ourselves that the senses of privacy as "privilege" and "privation" share a joint ancestry can help us see why privacy claims often seem double-edged: privileging while also depriving of public status, or removing from the public agenda activities or practices that perhaps *should* be matters of public concern. Thus, the other side of protecting the intimacy of the family and domestic life is our society's continuing inability to recognize women's responsibility for child rearing and domestic work, with all it entails for women's chances at education, good jobs, and leisure, for children's early attitudes toward women, and so on as a bona fide public issue, deserving of public recognition and remedy. In American society, protecting the "privacy" of decisions such as abortion or choice of sexual partner or practices such as child rearing appears to undermine public demands for policies that support maternal and infant health care, provide for the nurture of young children, meet the needs of working parents, or accommodate alternative intimate relationships through employee and survivor's benefits.

There are several verbs that connect to the *private-public-political* family of words: to "keep something private," "privatize," "make something public," "go public,"[30] "publish," "publicize," "make something political," "politicize." I begin by exploring the differences in meaning and use between the expressions in the following pairs: "make public" and "publicize," "keep private" and "privatize," and "make political" and "politicize."

Starting with the "public" verbs: whereas we say (for example) that Bill Clinton *made public* the letter he wrote to his ROTC colonel when he was in college, we would say that the press and the media *publicized* that letter in news stories and editorials. When certain members of the Senate Judiciary Committee had knowledge of Anita Hill's allegations concerning Judge Clarence Thomas's use of sexual innuendo in the workplace, and that news was leaked to a few members of the press, the journalists had to decide whether to *go public* with their stories. Although movie stars and presidential candidates try to *stay in the public eye,* we do not usually speak of *keeping* (something, someone, a news story) *public.*

Publicize differs from *make public* in its suggestion of making something known in a particular way. *Publicize* is connected to publicity, publication, publishing, public relations, public address systems, in short, to making things public through the agency of the mass media. *Make public,* by contrast, can be used in more familiar, small-scale contexts: one can *make public* the fact that one is pregnant, or any number of facts that are not generally known and are of interest only to one's friends and acquaintances, not to the general public.

When we turn to verbs related to *private,* we see some interesting differences. There is no parallel to the expression "make something public": we do not speak of "making something private," perhaps because once something has become a matter of public knowledge, it is impossible to make it private again. This difference helps us understand something about our concepts of public and private. When we *make* a matter public, our language suggests that we are able to call it to public attention through our intentional efforts. The fact that we do not speak of *keeping* something public suggests that whereas *bringing* a matter to public attention is open to volition and effort, *keeping* public attention focused on it depends less on one's efforts to reignite or engender interest than on its perceived importance to most people.[31]

By contrast, the expression to "keep something private" has a protective quality, which we also see in related expressions such as to "keep secrets," "keep it to yourself," and "keep things quiet." These expressions suggest that we protect (hide, shield, guard) something that will suffer from exposure to the harsh light of public scrutiny or curiosity. Once we let the cat out of the bag, tell the secret, make the story public, we cannot make it private again. We cannot recapture the hidden, safe quality our language suggests when we talk about *keeping* something private.

Thus, "making things public" and "keeping things private" suggest different ways in which public and private are privileged statuses or conditions. When we make a problem or issue public, we call it to the attention of our fellow citizens; we invite or demand public discussion and perhaps action. Either the issue commands interest and public action, or it withers away. When we keep something private, we guard or protect information or news that we do not wish others to know. This frees us from attention, scrutiny, curiosity, or publicity that we would find invasive or unwelcome.

What about other contrasts between public and private? If we look at the differences in meaning between the expressions "make public" and "publicize" and "keep private" and "privatize," we find very different relationships or contrasts at work within and between the two pairs. Whereas "keeping private" has to do with protecting information or people from public knowledge or scrutiny, "privatize" has nothing to do with stories or people who are the focus of public attention. Instead, one hears calls to privatize services or forms of assistance that are now publicly provided, but which one thinks should be provided privately—for example, by privately owned companies or through the agency of private charity—rather than by government action. Examples that are frequently discussed include transportation systems, utilities, schools, and assistance for the needy.[32] Thus, the gulf between "keep private" and "privatize" is much wider than that between "make public" and "publicize," since the former tap into completely different meanings of *private* (private in the sense of limited access as opposed to private in the sense of not being provided by the government or funded at taxpayer expense), whereas "make public" and "publicize" are at least both related to disseminating information. We can see this distinction clearly when we think about the words we use as contrasts or opposites to *privatize*. When we talk about government providing a service or fulfilling a function that previously has been provided privately, we use words such as *nationalize* or *socialize* (e.g., to nationalize the railroads or to socialize medicine.) *Privatize* and *publicize* are not opposites, or even remotely connected; *publicize* has to do with using the media to make something widely known, and contrasts with the idea of keeping something private.

We can make sense of these apparent inconsistencies or tensions by noting that the different verbs we have been considering go along with different senses of private and public. *Publicize, make public,* and *keep private* work at the level of knowledge, awareness, and publicity, whereas *privatize, nationalize,* and *socialize* work at the level of governance, ownership, and control. The governance dimension is also apparent in the Supreme Court's decisions declaring and defining the contours of the constitutional right to privacy. Although *privacy* has been used to articulate a range of activities and decisions with which government cannot interfere, a variety of limitations and interferences with privacy have also been permitted, making the right-to-privacy jurisprudence an extremely controversial field. We shall return to these controversies in Chapter 4, where I use linguistic distinctions between these different dimensions of privacy to clarify our troubled public discussions and policy-making about abortion, sodomy, and "fetal abuse."

A last pair of interest is *make political* and *politicize*. To "make something political," or "make a political issue" out of something, means to press for recognition of a claim or an issue. For example, a student body might wish to make tuition increases into a political issue, or the citizens of a town might try to make political the sale of land to be used as a garbage dump for waste from distant cities. In such instances, "making political" decisions that are ordinarily viewed as uncontroversial, as matters over which university administrators or urban planners or sanitary engineers have the last say, means that they are put forward as deserving of broader discussion and debate, especially the consultation and participation of those affected. Normally, "make political" has a rather civic-minded flavor, a sense of proposing for public debate issues that deserve public attention and resolution.

Politicize is also used to talk about an issue or a process that is ordinarily handled without incident or controversy, but for some reason has created larger political divisions, questions, or controversies. In contrast to the civic-minded flavor of "making something political," to "politicize" something has a seamy connotation, redolent of power politics, special interests, untoward use of "pull" or influence, of an issue being made partisan when it should not have been. We often use the construction *to be* or *become* plus *politicized* rather than *politicize* on its own, as in the example, "Unfortunately, the selection process has become politicized." Use of the passive voice focuses one's attention on the state or condition of being politicized rather than the actors or groups who argued to make the issue political, or the substance of their arguments.

Stepping back from the pairs *make public–publicize, keep private–privatize,* and *make political–politicize,* we notice that the verbs made by adding *-ize* to *public, private,* and *politic* draw on narrower, more specific sense of public, private, and political than the verbs formed with auxiliaries: "make public," "keep private," "make political." Adding *-ize* to these words has the effect of making the matter public, political, or private in a particular, instrumental, almost technical sense,[33] whereas using the auxiliary *to make* or *keep* (public, political, private) taps into older, broader, and richer senses of these words.

Building on the contrasting meanings of verbs formed with auxiliaries and verbs formed by adding *-ize,* let us examine how we use the word *politically*. One often hears "politically" combined with adjectives or past participles of verbs: "politically astute observation," "politically sensitive issue," "politically motivated decision," "politically honed instincts." Another way in which *politically* is used is to indicate the frame of reference for a judgment. For example, sentences such as the following make sense in contemporary English: "It was a politically astute decision to broker peace between Israel and the PLO"; "Hillary Clinton's comment about staying home and baking cookies was politically costly"; "How does this play out politically?" In all of these examples *politically* is used to indicate a particular ground for judgment or evaluation. We could simply have talked about "an astute decision"; adding *politically* makes it clear that we are referring to more specific kinds of astuteness or sensitivity.

We also use *politically* to mean in a political fashion or manner, so as to invite participation, according to the rules of parliamentary procedure, democratically, and the like. We can imagine a variety of expressions that use the term in this sense: "Let's decide the matter politically," or "They're trying to talk about it politically." Although one can imagine such sentences, they sound rather strange, as though we are trying to suggest that cunning, artifice, or stratagem is at work. If we mean to allude to participatory forms of decision making, it would be more common to say, "Let's decide democratically," or "Let's put it to a vote," or "Let's invite all those who are interested to participate."

Why is *politically* used more frequently to designate a specialized turf or area of judgment than to modify verbs that have to do with actions taken by citizens or political leaders or bodies? Perhaps the word is not very exact; we are not sure exactly what it means to decide or deliberate about something "politically," so we use other expressions, such as "democratically," "put it to a vote," or "invite participation," which are clearer and more precise. Or perhaps the scheming, crafty, infighting sense of the term has taken the place of the participatory sense, so that we seldom combine *politically* with active verbs that have to do with ordinary people's involvement in discussion, judgment, and decision making.

How do the nouns *publicity* and *publicness* differ in meaning and usage? Anyone responsible for planning a large event—a teach-in, a protest march, a brown bag series—has had to arrange for publicity for the event. *Publicity* means the media coverage, the advertisements and posters, the blurbs on local radio programs, and so on that publicize the event, as well as the media coverage and widespread knowledge which the event itself generates.

In contrast, *publicness* means the quality that makes something public, and therefore encompasses more than *publicity*. Something can be public because of its widespread or severe impact; because it affects all or most of us; because it is a focus of public attention or widely known; because it is a matter for public organizing and activism; or because policies, laws, or decisions are made about it by government bodies. *Publicness* is an odd, academic-sounding word that rarely occurs in ordinary conversation, whereas publicity is something even seven-year-olds understand. Like the contrasts between "make public" and "publicize," and so on, the pair suggests that a narrow, technical understanding of public is competing with, and perhaps undercutting, an older, richer one.

Working with Language

Thinking about language and how we use it is a way to get a fresh vantage point for understanding concepts that are richer and more complicated than we usually realize. Working with language can give us the kind of distance and focus that put the familiar in a new frame of reference, helping us notice things we have heard so many times that we scarcely hear them anymore. We have seen how etymology, language games, and the grammar of *private, public,* and *political* can help illuminate some of the values and practices that are central to our common life as contemporary English speakers in a society where these words are understood and used in predictable, regular ways. We nod in recognition when such regularities are identified; we depend on them to be understood by and to help us understand others. Thinking critically about the regularities in our language can give us insight into private, public, and political life and help us consider what roles privacy, publicness, and politics play.

The dual character of *private* as both privative and protective is visible in the etymology and usage of the *private* and *public* families of words: we "keep things private," but we "make things public." Privacy can be protective and concealing. It can be a bar to official intrusion or interference, a way to articulate to nosy neighbors or to government officials that something is none of their business. We do things in private we would never do if people we did not know well were present: swear, voice our opinions candidly, express affection, flout convention.

And yet privacy can conceal *too* much. The private life of home, family, and sexuality houses more than loving intimates. It also houses a gendered division of labor and power, and treating intimate life as a sacrosanct, hands-off sphere—respecting its privacy—can conceal many injustices. To the extent that one's sexuality is private, one can expect to be left alone in the privacy of one's home (although even this is questionable).[34] But daring to present oneself publicly as gay, bisexual, or lesbian invites a homophobic response: "I don't care what they do in private, just don't shove it in my face." Don't ask, don't tell. Here, most obviously, privacy is double-edged: it privileges, but it also deprives intimate issues of public legitimacy.

There is a crucial insight here: both these pictures of privacy have important things to say about the way privacy functions in our lives. Privacy is not solely a protective, empowering ground for claiming autonomy and personal freedom, nor is it just an oppressive prison. Both of these are aspects of how privacy functions for us, and theorists make a mistake when they take one account or the other for the whole picture. Part of the task of this book is to identify these mistakes, and to offer more complete, nuanced understandings of the value and peril of private life and of relying on privacy as a political strategy. If "the personal is political," as the slogan asserts, the personal is *also* private, and this privateness must be respected. We need to figure out how to talk about and understand the political character of issues or problems rooted in intimate life without jeopardizing what is valuable and humanly important about their intimate and private character. I object to the unqualified equation of public and private, personal and political, in much current academic and activist work. Making connections between politics and private life takes hard work—the work of recognizing and respecting what is valuable and worth protecting about private life and of understanding and negotiating one another's political claims. We "keep something private" or we "make something political," but this distinction overlooks a crucial question: How do we go about "making political" issues that are housed in intimate life? How do we call them to public attention, make them recognizable as political issues? And how do we do this while respecting ways in which privacy is protective and in need of preservation?

When we think about the typical, ordinary ways of using words relating to "politics" and "public," several of the minor patterns and regularities we have noted suggest that there is a tendency to think about public and political life in terms of techniques, strategy, or acumen, in terms of power plays within workplace- or identity-based groups and organizations or personal relationships, to the neglect of notions of the political that have to do with matters of the broadest public concern.

The ubiquitous references in ordinary English to organizational variants of "politics," from "office to politics" to "sexual politics," suggest that we are less likely to think of politics in terms of how the generalized "we" of the community or polity should act about matters of broad public concern than we are to see politics as denoting power or skill at understanding and maneuvering the structures that affect us as "political players" in groups or organizations. Similarly, the use of "politically" to modify "astute" and "motivated" deepens our impression that politics is about gamesmanship, about being politically savvy on the job or in an organization. Even those whom one would expect to have the most at stake in recapturing both the notion and the practice of democratic politics—groups marginalized from the political life of collective decision making, such as women, gays, racial minorities—often draw on images of politics that emphasize cunning and partisan uses of power structures rather than uses that emphasize citizen participation and encompassing organizations or coalitions.

The impression of an erosion of the civic sense of *public* and *political* and a growth in senses that have to do with shrewdness and cunning, with partisan conflict and pursuing one's particular agenda or interests, is borne out by the way *politicize* and *publicize* differ from *make political* and *make public,* and the way *publicity* differs from *publicness*. When we make something political, we explain and argue for its political significance; but when an issue becomes politicized, considerations such as partisan politics and special interests are paramount. Of course, there can be an overlap between making something political and politicizing it, but the expressions have different flavors. There is a similar tension between *publicness,* which refers to the quality of being public, and *publicity,* which refers to the efforts taken to publicize something. If we consider the frequency with which we use these different senses of *public* and *political* in everyday speech, we might conclude that the politicalness and publicness of events and issues has become a second-order concern. We are more likely to hear how a controversy has become politicized than of its political significance, more likely to speak of its publicity than its publicness.

I take seriously the hints we get from language games involving *public* and *politics* which suggest that we are much more inclined to think and talk about politics in terms of cutting deals and pursuing partisanship than in terms of collective, civic involvements in matters of broad public concern. These hints emphasize the loss of "the political" as a source of "public happiness," which political theorists have long decried.[35] In my view, revitalizing democratic politics is not passé or impossible, but a goal anyone who values justice must work toward. The erosion of such an ideal is evident not only in our language but all around us, as politics has come to seem the province of pollsters, "spin doctors," news analysts, and talk show hosts, and as ordinary citizens grow more cynical and disaffected.

We cannot nurture democratic politics, where ordinary citizens participate in making important decisions that affect their lives, unless we learn to translate problems or troubles rooted in the private, intimate sphere of our lives into political issues. Their privateness notwithstanding, sometimes injustice and power experienced in private must be addressed and rectified politically. Addressing the various forms that oppression takes in private life—economic exploitation, racism, sexism, homophobia—is crucial for invigorating political life, for making citizens out of private sufferers. But to do so, we need to be able to explain what difference these injustices make to our common, shared life, how resolving them is crucial to notions of justice that we all care about, that we want to preserve for our sons and daughters. At the same time, we need to respect and value privacy when it is not a veil concealing unfair power and privilege, but rather a shield protecting intimacy and diversity. In the next chapter I begin to develop the relationship between recognizing the injustices located in private life, respecting the protective role of privacy, and nurturing democratic politics as I interrogate and develop some of Hannah Arendt's ideas about private life, politics, and "the social."

Three

Arendt on Political Approaches to Intimate-Life Issues

I N DIFFERENT WAYS CHAPTERS 1 AND 2 ADDRESSED the problem of one-sided thinking about privacy. In this chapter I take up a different theroretical problem. In contrast to scholars and activists who regard the politicalness of intimate-life issues as self-evident, I argue that the public character of issues connected to sex, the body, gender roles, and families cannot be asserted or assumed, but has to be explained and justified through a process of translating private matters into political issues.

This is a two-part argument. The first part concerns how issues rooted in intimate life can also be public. Something—omnipresent images of female bodies, let's say—can be "public" in a variety of senses: because it is widely seen or known, is a focus of public attention, has widespread or general impact, is a reflection or source of cultural values, is subject to state regulation or policy-making, or is a topic of public debate.[1] Not all of these ways of being public are the same, of course. Although virtually all of us are exposed to images of bodies, only a few academics, feminists, and advertising executives focus on the impact those images have, think about how such images reflect and reinforce cultural values, debate the stance we should take toward them as a matter of policy, or treat them as a focus of public interest. For most people in the United States today, images of bodies exercise power over us of which we are largely unaware. In this sense they are public but not political. Issues do not become political simply because we *say* they do; they must be transformed from the way we ordinarily understand and talk about them in private into politically negotiable claims or perspectives. *We,* the public, must be transformed from passive consumers to aware, critical activists.

The second part of the argument concerns the need to retain the home as the place where many important human relationships and practices belong. Sometimes the personal is not political but private, and should remain so. Intimate life is shrouded in privacy for good reason; even when we *do* perceive injustice hiding behind privacy, we still need to respect the fragility of private life. We need to take care when we expose the political character of practices such as child rearing or being in the closet to phrase and shape our demands for change without utterly destroying the possibility of living a life in private. In brief, we can think critically and politically about practices that take place in private without thereby accepting the view that privacy is always and only ideological, a form and reflection of illicit power and privilege.[2]

I turn for help with this project to the work of Hannah Arendt and scholars who have followed her complex and problematic approach to thinking about public and private.[3] For Arendt, the foremost theorist of the public-private distinction, the phrase "intimate-life political issues" would have been a non sequitur; issues related to the household were to her simply not admissible in politics because "politics is never for the sake of life." The assumption in much recent feminist political theorizing that household concerns are eminently political would simply have confirmed Arendt's fear that the modern age has lost the ability to appreciate the distinctiveness of the public and private spheres as "the social" takes over our public space.[4] She thought and wrote in terms of abstract categories ("the private," "the public," "the social," "the public realm," "the private sphere") and stark, rigid contrasts. To contemporary readers, Hannah Arendt seems more concerned with isolating and separating public and private than with connecting them.

But even if we reject her conclusions, which point toward excluding private matters from public life, we recognize that Arendt was troubled by much that should be troubling to us, too: the modern erosion of genuine political life, the possibility that household matters may enter public life in the wrong spirit, and the need to appreciate and protect private life in a world where intimacy and the personal have become matters of public inquiry. A dialogue with Arendt can be productive because working through her objections to treating household matters as public issues can help us find the right approach or vocabulary for politicizing them. In light of the new orthodoxy which takes for granted that "public" and "private" are ideological, oppressive categories, a reexamination is overdue of the arguments and evidence Arendt used to support her fundamental insight that there are and should be distinctions between public and private life.

I begin with Arendt's treatment of these distinctions in *The Human Condition,* expand on what she meant by her oppositions between "the social" and "the political" by looking at some of her earlier writings, examine some competing feminist interpretations of Arendt, then use my reading of her work to reflect on problems in contemporary identity politics.

Notions of Public and Private in *The Human Condition*

Hannah Arendt's thinking about public and private is complex. She nearly always opposes what is "merely" private—connected to necessity, animal life, labor—to what is public—connected to action, words, glory, and new beginnings. Arendt admired the polis, especialy the practice of sequestering household, bodily, and economic concerns from public life. But she also thought that labor was crucial to a "specifically human life," and criticized the Greeks for sacrificing so much of private life to the public realm.[5] I attend to both these strands in Arendt's thought, for it seems to me that they are often incompatible, inconsistent. Arendt both loved the polis and the ideal of political life it represented, *and* found insupportable the injustice on which the life of the polis was founded; she both attacked the introduction of private matters into public life and the centrality of labor in modern society, *and* believed that the private realm of the household and the activity of laboring deserve to be honored as integral parts of the human condition.

There is no denying that Hannah Arendt believed the Greeks were correct in excluding from public life matters pertaining to the household—housework, household economy, the labor of women in giving birth to children and of slaves in producing the necessities of life. She contrasted the communal concerns—freedom, equality among citizens, action, and speech—of Greek political life with the individual concerns—enslavement to the needs of the body, inequality, violence, and domination—of the family.[6] For the Greeks, household life was a necessary precondition for politics, but household matters were never permitted to enter the public realm.[7]

She admired the Greeks for having a clear sense of the distinctiveness of public and private pursuits, a distinction she thought we moderns had a hard time making because the growth of "the social" has made it difficult for us to "understand the decisive division between the public and private realms, between the sphere of the *polis* and the sphere of household and family, and finally, between activities related to a common world and those related to the maintenance of life, a division upon which all ancient political thought rested as self-evident and axiomatic." Arendt's distress at the rise of "the social" is connected to her perception that the widening of the social sphere has given public significance to matters that formerly and properly belonged in private. She calls society "that curious hybrid realm where private interests assume public significance." For her the social realm includes "all things connected with the necessity of the life process itself, which prior to the modern age comprehended all activities serving the subsistence of the individual and the survival of the species."[8] Sometimes Arendt's attacks on "the social" sound shocking to contemporary ears, as when she criticizes the liberation of women and workers because it has led to "an abandonment and betrayal in the case of the children."[9] Surely, we want to say to her, there are ways to ensure a secure private life for children without relegating whole classes of people to living exclusively within the four walls of the household.

Yet for all her evident admiration for the Greeks' ability to banish "merely" private matters from public life, Arendt also valued private life, and had interesting and complicated things to say about the relation between private matters and the public realm of citizenship. Even in the texts that defend strict distinctions between public and private most wholeheartedly, Arendt expresses reservations about the way the Greeks totally subsumed the latter to the former.[10] She is also uneasy about their oppression of women and slaves. Thus, she writes in *The Human Condition*: "The price for the elimination of life's burden from the shoulders of all citizens was enormous and by no means consisted only in the violent injustice of forcing one part of humanity into the darkness of pain and necessity." Furthermore, the equality of the *polis* "presupposed the existence of 'unequals' who, as a matter of fact, were always the majority of the population of the city-state."[11] Among forceful passages in *On Revolution* that demonstrate how the entry of enraged masses of miserable poor people into public life led to the failure of the French Revolution to bring about political freedom are sprinkled comments that indicate Arendt's own sensitivity to poverty and exploitation: "The absence of the social question from the American scene was . . . quite deceptive. . . . Abject and degrading misery was present everywhere in the form of slavery and Negro labor"; "[We have to] ask ourselves if the goodness of the poor white man's country did not depend to a considerable degree upon black labor and black misery." Arendt also recognizes the brutality of the conquest of North America.[12] Despite her trenchant criticisms of a revolution aimed at solving the problem of poverty, Arendt clearly sees the poverty and misery of eighteenth-

and nineteenth-century Europe: "To avert one's eyes from the misery and unhappiness of the mass of humankind was no more possible in eighteenth-century Paris, or in nineteenth-century London . . . than it is today in some European, most Latin American, and nearly all Asian and African countries."[13]

These occasional understated glimpses of Arendt's attitudes toward poverty, misery, oppression, and the need to value and protect private life suggest that she was not proposing that citizens of modern nation-states make the same tradeoffs the ancient Greeks made in enabling a few to be full-time citizens by banishing most to the private life of the household. Nor did she simply denigrate the private sphere and its preoccupation with the needs of the body. Because Arendt was at pains to defend our ability to make and control the world against an intense preoccupation with the "mere life" of the body, it is easy to think that she despised bodily life (the private) as opposed to worldliness (the public), when in fact she respected both. Many passages in *The Human Condition* suggest that she valued the physical necessity and intimacy of private life as a coequal part of human experience. She believed that being human meant both living in a humanly made world, with enduring structures, objects, institutions, and meanings, and leading a human life tied to the body, nature, and Mother Earth.[14]

In contrast to the implicit scorn of her discussion of private life in the polis, Arendt occasionally talks about physical need as a crucial spur. Only necessity "possesses a driving force whose urgency" makes it "first among man's needs and worries," and "prevent[s] the apathy and disappearance of initiative which so obviously threatens all overly wealthy communities. Necessity and life are so intimately related and connected that life itself is threatened where necessity is altogether eliminated." Foisting onto someone else the "toil and trouble" of labor does not automatically make citizens more human by freeing them for higher activities, since we cannot eliminate the pain and effort of labor without depriving "the specifically human life of its very liveliness and vitality. The human condition is such that pain and effort are not just symptoms which can be removed without changing life itself; they are rather modes in which life itself, together with the necessity to which it is bound, makes itself felt. For mortals, the 'easy life of the gods' would be a lifeless life." Arendt repeatedly describes labor as an integral and positive part of the human condition: "the 'blessing or the joy' of labor is the human way to experience the sheer bliss of being alive which we share with all living creatures, and it is even the only way, men, too, can remain and swing contentedly in nature's prescribed cycle." "The blessing of life as a whole" is "inherent in labor," and the "blessing of labor is that effort and gratification follow each other as closely as pro-ducing and consuming the means of subsistence."[15]

Furthermore, Arendt obviously appreciated the enormous gulf that lies between ancient and modern perceptions of private life, as one can see in this passage:

Not only would we not agree with the Greeks that a life spent in the privacy of "one's own" (*idion*), outside the world of the common, is "idiotic" by definition, or with the Romans to whom privacy offered but a temporary refuge from the business of the *res publica;* we call private today a sphere of intimacy whose begin-nings we may be able to trace back to late Roman, though hardly to any period of Greek antiquity, but whose peculiar manifoldness and variety were certainly un-known to any period prior to the modern age.

This is not merely a matter of shifted emphasis. In ancient feeling the privative trait of privacy . . . was all-important. . . . A man who lived only a private life . . . was not fully human. We no longer think primarily of deprivation when we use the word "privacy," and this is partly due to the enormous enrichment of the private sphere through modern individualism.[16]

Arendt writes approvingly about private property, which she views as the only efficient way to ensure "a tangible, worldly place of one's own" which can "guarantee the darkness of what needs to be hidden against the light of publicity."[17] The private realm is the proper location for human activi-ties that cannot survive in the "bright light" of public life, including myste-rious, sacred matters and forces that are central to human life.[18] We need privacy as a "reliable hiding place from the common public world, not only from everything that goes on in it but also from its very publicity, from being seen and being heard. A life spent entirely in public, in the presence of others, becomes . . . shallow. While it retains its visibility, it loses the quality of rising into sight from some darker ground which must remain hidden if it is not to lose its depth in a very real, non-subjective sense."[19]

Such passages caution us against reading Arendt as simply denigrating privacy or private life; she obviously appreciated both the privative and nonprivative senses of *private* that I discussed in Chapter 2. Arendt clearly believed that the human condition consists both in having a body subject to the rhythms and cycles of nature and physical need, *and* in inhabiting a public space of political participation in decisions of real and lasting impor-tance. Where, then, does the animus against labor, necessity, and the body in Arendt's thought come from? The fact that we have made labor our central public activity meant, she believed, that we have taken the human condition in the mode of incessantly producing and consuming the necesities of life and given it the place of honor at the center of our public life. She feared that the metabolic processes of biological life and of laboring had transformed the nature of public life: now we endlessly produce and consume more and more products, even converting objects such as chairs and tables into consumer goods to be used up and thrown away. We have forgotten what higher pursuits might fill our leisure time, so that now the "spare time [left to] the *animal laborans* is never spent in anything but consumption, and the more time left to him, the greedier and more craving his appetites."[20]

The division of labor, which Arendt associates with the preeminence of laboring as a public activity, had made us infinitely more productive. But in her view it has also unleashed a process of production and consumption which is out of control, and which along with the unthinking, process-oriented attitude of *animal laborans* threatens our ability to make sense of the world we have created. Scientific and technical knowledge increase faster than our ability to attach human meaning to these accomplishments. Thus, *animal laborans* has been "permitted to occupy the public realm; and yet, as long as the *animal laborans* remains in possession of it, there can be no true public realm, but only private activities displayed in the open."[21]

One begins to understand why Arendt turned to the ancient Greeks: she was trying to recapture an ideal of public life grown strange and remote to modern sensibilities, and to make vivid the mode of public action connected to collective responsibility for the world, to citizenship and political action. We need the images of shining glory, immortality, great striving, and commitment of Greek political life because our experience of the substantive publicness of political life—the sense of public that has to do with accountability, citizen participation, and political activism—has been almost nil. For us moderns, public life has nearly been taken over by the activity of labor and its concomitant preoccupation with "making a living."[22] Public space for collective deliberation and debate has been transformed into the distinctively modern public space where, in Jennifer Ring's words, "nothing truly public has ever transpired. . . . Side by side, but not collectively, people . . . purchase consumer items for their private dwelling and their private bodily needs. Neither speech nor reasoning takes place at a shopping mall."[23]

If Arendt's intent in holding up to us the glory of the Greek polis is to defend this older sense of public life against the onslaught of "the social"—if what she really cares about is protecting politics, not forbidding the entry of private matters per se—then what we need to think about are the real dangers to public life. Surely Arendt herself believed that we are better off when, like the Greeks, we ban private matters from the public arena. The problems of the modern age are the result of importing into public life the process-based thinking of the laborer, who performs a repetitive, monotonous chore in a mindless fashion.[24] But we need to make an important analytic distinction, one that Arendt herself did not make very clearly. Perhaps it is not the fact that something emerges from the mysterious, dark ground of household life that makes it threatening to the political life of active citizenship and participation. Perhaps it is instead the fact that an issue such as housework or poverty is likely to emerge from its "home" in the private world in a form or spirit that makes it unfit for public accountability, deliberation, and control.[25] There is a difference between saying that problems rooted in private "household" life—for example, the misery of the poor or the oppression of slaves or women—cannot be admitted into public life at all, and saying that they cannot be admitted in their privative attitudes of preoccupation with an empty belly or unthinking task orientation, but must first be transformed into politically recognizable language and demands. Arendt is apt to be read as taking the first of these positions, but the important lesson her thought suggests to us is found in the second formulation.[26]

Can Arendt help us think about the "spirit" or attitude appropriate to different activities or realms? Is it *always* possible or useful to translate a private matter into a public issue? What does such a translation entail? One way to start addressing these questions is to take seriously the positive things Arendt has to say about the private sphere. Private life is a place to recoup one's forces so that one can go back to the active and draining participation of a citizen in public life. Like the anthropological philosophers I discussed in Chapter 1, Arendt recognized that the private world of the household, family, and intimate relationships is home to activities that are crucial to human existence, and cannot take place anywhere else. Thus, she writes, "there are very relevant matters which can survive only in the realm of the private. For instance, love, in distinction from friendships, is kills, or rather extinguished, the moment it is displayed in public." For Arendt, the point of distinguishing between public and private, "the most elementary meaning of the two realms," is "that there are things that need to be hidden and others that need to be displayed publicly, if they are to exist at all. If we look at these things, . . . we shall see that *each human activity points to its proper location in the world.*[27]

In other words, the public-private distinction is not just about physical location but also about distinct human activities which require publicness or privateness. Acting and speaking, which require courage, a firm sense of reality, and memory, must be seen and heard by many pairs of eyes and ears, from many different perspectives, yet all attending to the same actions and words.[28] Loving a particular other, interactions that are of interest to only one or a few (the mundane trivia of daily life), mysteries such as birth and death, the raising of children—these are activities that need to be protected from the public glare if they are to be done well, or at all. The distinction is a crucial but problematic one. Citizens need a public space in which to appear if they are to speak and act. Other qualities, activities, and relationships need to be hidden from strangers and from public scrutiny or pressure. These include care and love for children, intimates, the dying, even providing the ordinary small comforts that lend savor to human life.[29] Both kinds of activities are important, and both need to be valued and nurtured. But what happens to this distinction when "the private" and "the public" give way to "the social"? What if practices and relationships that require privacy to flourish are also public in one or more ways, for example, because they have broad impact, or because they are unjust or oppressive? What if issues whose proper home is in the private sphere become a source of political activism? These are important questions for thinking about what I have called "intimate-life political issues." I attempt to resolve them by working on Arendt's notion of "the social" and developing the insight that the designations "public," "private," "social," and "political" have less to do with physical location in the world than with the approach one takes to thinking and talking about a particular issue.

Parvenus and Pariahs

Instead of thinking of public and private in terms of the spatial metaphors that resonate throughout *The Human Condition,* perhaps we should think of them as shorthand ways of referring to the different kinds of meanings and relationships human beings construct in their impersonal, collective mode as citizens and their intimate mode as friends, lovers, or family members, as writers such as Ferdinand Schoeman and Robert Post suggest.[30] Or they may refer to the attitudes with which we approach civic engagements, as opposed to practices related to producing life's necessities, or those rooted in familial, sexual, or other intimate relations. In other words, perhaps the distinction is not between activities or pursuits that characteristically take place in different locations but between political versus nonpolitical, or "social," approaches to talking and thinking about certain actions, wherever and with whomever they usually occur.[31] For example, one might have an intimate personal conversation about abortion (maybe one's own experience of abortion), but one could also talk in more general, impersonal ways about abortion as a political issue. It is not the subject matter or the existential site of the practice of abortion that makes the issue either personal or political; rather, it is the attitude or approach one takes—whether positioning the issue as a dilemma for a particular woman or family, or framing it in more systemic, institutional terms—that is decisive.

Hannah Arendt is also a useful source of insight for this more metaphoric way of thinking about public and private.[32] One historical and political problem Arendt struggled to come to grips with was the catastrophic event of her day, the destruction of European Jewry, a life-and-death issue for her as a German Jew who emigrated to France in 1933 and to the United States in 1941. Arendt's interest in the issue of Jewish identity and political responsibility is plain in her biography of Rahel Varnhagen, her essays collected in *The Jew as Pariah,* and her book on the trial of Adolph Eichmann, sources that are especially useful for understanding what Arendt means by "the social," a category that looms large but is illdefined in *The Human Condition.*[33]

Arendt writes in *The Origins of Totalitarianism* and *Rahel Varnhagen* of a period at the end of the eighteenth century when Jews in Prussia were allowed to assimilate into society. Jews who succeeded in being accepted into high society, into its salons and intellectual and social life, were viewed by both Gentiles and themselves as "exceptions," different from the masses of primitive, uncultured Jews to the east, not fitting the anti-Semitic stereotypes and assumptions that remained prevalent.[34] She dissects the desire to assimilate and the mechanics of assimilation during this period in her biography of Rahel Varnhagen, a woman who ran a successful salon in Berlin in the late eighteenth century, and who spent her life trying to overcome what she regarded as the key misfortune of her life, having been born a Jew. Although Rahel eventually married a German officer, was baptized, and changed her name, she was never able to avoid the slights and slurs of a society that always saw her as a Jew and a social climber. Arendt's biography leads us through the slow, brooding, introspective history of Rahel's relationships, to her recognition late in life that the price of assimilation was too high. She writes:

The parvenu could never admit . . . that he was gnawed by a multitude of things which he did not even really want, but which he could not bear to be refused; that he had to adapt his tastes, his life, his desires to these things; that in nothing and not for a single minute did he dare to be himself any longer. . . . As a Jew Rahel had always stood outside, had been a pariah, and discovered at last, most unwillingly and unhappily, that entrance into society was possible only at the price of lying, of a far more generalized lie than simply hypocrisy. She discovered that it was necessary for the parvenu . . . to sacrifice every natural impulse, to conceal all truth, to misuse all love, not only to suppress all passion, but worse still, to convert it into a means for social climbing.[35]

Although Rahel never understood assimilation in political terms, never moved beyond the confines of her own personal misfortune to think about anti-Semitism more generally, Arendt claims that she ended her life as a conscious pariah, having accepted that she did not fit into society.[36]

Arendt again reflects on the "politics of the personal," as we might put it today, in essays she wrote in the early 1940s about the experience of German Jewish immigrants in the United States. The type who buries his own tastes and desires in order to fit in and be accepted emerges again in her story of "Mr. Cohn," who with the rise of Nazism flees Germany, first to Czechoslovakia, then to France, each time molting and becoming the model Czech, the perfect Frenchman. Arendt describes the politics of daily life for refugees: "Once we could buy our food and ride in the subway without being told we were undesirable. We have become a little hysterical since newspapermen started . . . telling us publicly to stop being disagreeable when shopping for milk and bread. We wonder how it can be done; we already are so damnably careful in every moment of our daily lives to avoid anybody guessing who we are, what kind of passport we have. . . . We try the best we can to fit into a world where you have to be sort of politically minded when you buy your food."[37] The deeper current in her stories about "fitting in" is the mortal danger that in struggling to assimilate, Jews failed to understand the changing political situation that fed anti-Semitism. Assuming that their genuine lack of political ambition would be recognized, Jews did not assume a responsible role in public affairs, which Arendt thinks set them up for being led to the slaughter. She contrasts the assimilationist tradition of the parvenu with one based on conscious pariahdom, showing that people such as Heinrich Heine, Franz Kafka, and Bernard Lazare were rebels who translated their status into political terms, sought solidarity with other Jews, and tried to "come to grips with the world of men and women."[38]

Arendt's comments about parvenus and pariahs take on special significance in light of her own struggle to think politically about a private matter turned political: What happens when one's religion or ethnicity becomes deadly? For Arendt, the heroes are not the ones who grovel to shed their identity and win acceptance within the rules of the dominant anti-Semitic society, never thinking beyond their own personal predicament. Instead her heroes are the loners, the rebels who embrace their unpopularity and attack the anti-Semities who oppress and victimize them. As Jennifer Ring puts it:

If political action in Arendt's more general sense excludes concerns with the private aspects of life, conscious pariahdom invites the mingling of public and private concerns. Indeed, what Arendt seeks is the making public of aspects of the outsider's private life. Parvenus, the social climbers who deny their historical identity and seek to "pass" as insiders or members of the dominant culture, take the blame for their exclusion on themselves. Pariahs, on the other hand, recognize that even their private lives are defined by politics. The parvenu sees that he is excluded and asks of himself: "What have I done wrong? How can I be more acceptable to the insiders?" In contrast, the pariah knows that his outsider status is not of his own making, yet recognizes that he has some choices about and indeed some responsibility for what he does with it.[39]

The contrast between the pariah and the parvenu is important not only because it addresses the intersection between private life and politics, but also because it gives us a way to think about the difference between political and nonpolitical ways to address private matters turned political. It gives us insight into what Arendt meant by "the social," where private issues take on public significance and political action is practically forgotten, where people find their primary satisfactions in their intimate lives and at the shopping mall.

When Arendt addresses "the social" in *The Human Condition,* she describes it in a variety of ways: it gives a public character to the activities of private life and privatizes the political realm; it is associated with the vast growth in productivity, as work moves outside the household to factories and the division of labor increases; and it gives the activities involved in satisfying the needs of the body central importance. "The social" is also associated with increased conformity, with large-scale organization, with the advent of the behavioral sciences and statistics, with the replacement of radically new "action" by rule-governed, predictable "behavior." She pictures society as a giant family with a unity of interests; with the rise of "the social," we see "mass society" and "mass hysteria," as plurality evaporates and everyone thinks what his neighbor thinks. The welfare state takes as government's central political concern the satisfaction of physical needs, caring for society as if it were a family or a household.

The image of the parvenu gives an edge to these characterizations. Like

Jennifer Ring, Hanna Pitkin sees "the social" as associated with the attempt to win acceptance into society, even when that means internalizing the standards of those to whom one would assimilate—standards by which the likes of oneself are worthless. It means separating from one's pariah group to join and support those who condemn them; converting one's identity as a Jew into a character trait or personal defect which effort and discipline might overcome; being on guard against personal or spontaneous impulses that might betray one; craving things one does not really want. It means no longer daring to be oneself in anything, sacrificing truth, managing impressions, becoming incapable of autonomous judgment or action, remaining an isolated and unhappy victim.[40]

The monstrousness of "the social" becomes even more glaring in Arendt's account of masses of decent people obeying lawful orders to carry out the Final Solution or acquiescing in the policy of exterminating the Jews, having lost the ability to judge evil for themselves. Few decent people resisted the horror of the camps.[41] Hitler's Germany illustrates conditions of mass society under which, in Arendt's words, "we see all people suddenly behave as though they were members of one family, each multiplying and prolonging the perspective of his neighbor."[42] For Arendt, Adolph Eichmann—the thoughtless, banal engineer of the Final Solution, the competent bureaucrat who made the trains to the camps run on time—represented the triumph of process thinking, the thinking of a laborer performing his job in a mindless, repetitive fashion, over political judgment. Nor was Eichmann unique: his perspective was multiplied thousands of times by a population cowed into going along with mass murder because they had lost the diversity of viewpoints that might have caused them to think about what they were doing and encouraged them to resist wrongdoing. Genocide, the attack on the essential plurality of human life, thus became state policy in the ultimate triumph of "the social"—society as one family, one voice—over "the political."

"The Social" and Making the Personal Political

I understand "the social" and "the political" in Hannah Arendt's theorizing as two different ways something can be public. "The social" is a category of phenomena that are public in their impact, perhaps even in terms of our awareness of them, but not in terms of our willingness to engage them as political issues (for instance, omnipresent images of perfect female bodies, the example at the beginning of this chapter). More broadly, I take "the social" to be a metaphor for a variety of ways of refusing to take responsibility for the world: by treating a variety of matters as too complicated for ordinary people to decide about, deferring to experts and technicians, and allowing political choices to be treated as though they were nothing more than bureaucratic or administrative decisions.[43] These attitudes result in conformity, process thinking, thoughtlessness; absorption in our private affairs and interests; behaving in ways that can be predicted and quantified by social scientists rather than acting in essentially new and unpredictable ways; treating social power as given and unchangeable; "passing," fitting in, accepting and internalizing values that undermine one's personhood and self-respect.[44]

"The political," by contrast, refers to practices or issues that are actively contested, the focus of activism, education, persuasion, and appeals to shared values and principles. Pariahdom is one way to respond politically to a social condition in which one's group is denigrated and subject to racism, prejudice, or discrimination. Being a pariah means choosing to be an outcast in order to engage with practices, values, and institutions that are unjust. It means refusing to assimilate or to curry favor with one's oppressors; criticizing cultural and political practices that threaten one's group or society; pointing out the larger stakes for the entire community of perpetuating various injustices; and showing the connections between forms of institutional and cultural power and problems that appear to be merely private, particular, or pathological.

The image of the pariah embodies one possible way to understand the kind of political attitude for which Arendt argued, especially given her own distaste for following intellectual fashions. But being a pariah is not the only model for how one might respond politically to practices or interactions centered on private life. The larger lesson of Arendt's thought is the need to respect the distinctiveness of *both* the private and public realms of life, to avoid making private-life matters public in a way that will simply colonize the public realm for "the social," and to protect private life from the disruptions and harsh glare of public scrutiny.[45]

Hanna Pitkin has argued that appealing to shared notions of justice is central to transforming private misfortunes or grievances into claims that are politically negotiable, and to transforming the "privative" attitude of one whose problems arise from the "private" life of the home or the market—the bitter housewife, the outraged poor—into a broader concern for the community in its attempt to deal justly with a variety of claims. Such an appeal to political principle is crucial, not just for getting others to take seriously issues they might otherwise regard as trivial or particularistic, but also for helping members of the aggrieved group feel that they have a stake in the political process, transforming them from victims or interest-seekers into citizens with a stake in the political process and the standards the community articulates there.[46] Recasting Pitkin's argument that it is not a particular subject matter or set of issues that needs to be excluded from politics but attitudes that make the housewife or the laborer, driven by necessity, adopt a process-oriented outlook, Bonnie Honig suggests that politics needs to be protected from "a variety of sensibilities, attitudes, dispositions, and approaches, all of which constitute *all* selves and subjects to some extent, all of which engage in a struggle for dominion over the self, and all of which are incompatible with the understanding(s) of action that Arendt valorizes."[47]

Once we pose the problem in terms of finding appropriately political language and sensibilities with which to address issues housed in private life rather than walling off private-life concerns from politics, several tightly latched intellectual doors swing open. If the point is to "dress" matters rooted in the private life of the body, home, or economic need to go out in public, then politics does not have to be just about war and diplomacy. It can address a variety of topics. We can talk about ways of making the sustained work of nurturing human life a valued, respected activity, and ways to express such respect in our public life.[48] We can address domestic violence and oppressive gender arrangements. We can discuss homophobia and its manifestations in our laws, regulations, and social lives. We can treat as political many practices and arrangements that have been accepted as part of the prepolitical realm of violence and necessity, locked away in the darkness of the household. Instead of seeing everything connected to our bodies and physical needs as beyond the reach of politics, we can begin to engage the private forms of power that govern our sexual, gender, and familial arrangements.[49] Recognizing injustice—the sense of outrage and wrong, the feeling that "no one should be treated this way"—becomes a key to articulating personal problems or grievances as political claims, a way to let people be drawn by their daily experiences into acting politically.[50]

In addition to appealing to justice as a means of moving from a "social" to a "political" mindset, there are several other ways to think about connecting private life and politics. Seyla Benhabib suggests a slightly different way of introducing private-life issues into politics with her notion of a "procedural" rather than a substantive concept of public space. She argues that "what is important . . . is not so much *what* public discourse is about as the *way* in which this discourse takes place. . . . From the standpoint of this procedural model, neither the distinction between the social and the political nor the distinction between work, labor or action are that relevant. At stake is the reflexive questioning of issues by all those affected by their foreseeable consequences and the recognition of their right to do so." But her contrast between administrative, clientelistic responses to private issues turned public (such as child rearing, reproductive freedoms, domestic violence, and the constitution of sexual identities) and *democratic* responses which make such issues "accessible to debate, reflection, action and moral-political transformation" sounds very similar to the contrast between social and political responses to issues rooted in private life discussed earlier.[51]

Bonnie Honig develops the public-private distinction suggested by Arendt's thought very differently. She rejects privileging the public, civic, or institutional space of politics in favor of proliferating "sites of action beyond the single public realm to explore a broader range of spaces of potential power and resistance . . . sites of critical leverage within the ruptures, inadequacies, and ill-fittednesses of existing identities." Having suggested that identity, gender, race, ethnicity, and the body may be sites for performative resistance and action in the private realm, Honig hastens to add that under this formulation "not everything is political . . . ; it is simply the case that nothing is ontologically protected from politicization, that nothing is necessarily or naturally or ontologically *not* political." She does not jettison the distinction between public and private but sees it as "the performative product of political struggle, hard-won and always temporary." Benhabib's procedural notion of public space, like Pitkin's and Arendt's, is concerned with the kind of discourse that takes place in public gatherings of various kinds. By contrast, Honig suggests that the colonization of public life by the social has proceeded to such a point that "routinized, bureaucratic, and administrative regimes" have displaced politics, forcing feminist politics to "go underground, looking to locate itself in the rifts and fractures of identities, both personal and institutional, and doing so performatively, agonistically, and creatively, with the hope of establishing new relations and realities." Honig's is an important reformulation of the public-private distinction, founded on her criticism of Arendt for so emptying the public realm of content and erecting such a "nonnegotiable public/private distinction" that Arendt herself may have contributed more "to the loss or occlusion of action than any rise of the social." But the performative productions, struggles, resistances and challenges Honig advocates seem radically individualized, not to say privatized, and she is unduly pessimistic about the possibility of appealing to commonly shared values or collective action.[52]

Art and storytelling are also ways of giving intimate experiences a public reality they would otherwise lack. Arendt tells us that "even the greatest forces of intimate life—the passions of the heart, the thoughts of the mind, the delights of the senses—lead an uncertain, shadowy kind of existence unless and until they are transformed, deprivatized and deindividualized . . . into a shape to fit them for public appearance . . . [either] in storytelling . . . [or] in artistic transposition of individual experiences."[53] Storytelling can transform the individual's life story, moving from detail and particularity to the broader meaning of the problems one confronts and the ways one deals with them. Consider Paul Monette's autobiography, *Becoming a Man,* a personal story about growing up gay and coming of age as a gay man.[54] Of course, the story helps us understand Monette's experiences; but we also feel that we have learned something about the larger forces that gay children and adults must deal with, the pain their sexuality causes them in a heterosexist society, and the ways the closet deforms their lives. Storytelling does not simply make intimate life public; it also helps us to recognize and think about common, characteristic problems or experiences that are rooted in intimate life. We begin to see them as connected to deeper and broader forces than the biographical circumstances of their protagonists' particular life stories.

Morris Kaplan suggests another way to connect private life to politics in his use of Arendt to develop a democratic theory of sexual politics. Kaplan reads Arendt's careful historical analysis of anti-Semitism in a variety of works—*The Origins of Totalitarianism, Rahel Varnhagen, Eichmann in Jerusalem*—as a genealogy, a historically contextualized account of how a private or social characteristic, once viewed simply as exotic, came to be racialized and pathologized.[55] Focusing on Arendt's historically situated thinking about Jewishness, he notes her best teachings come from attending to politics and private arrangements—marriages, families, social circles— not in generic or idealized terms but as practices we can understand only by taking into account the specific historical, cultural, and institutional settings of anti-Semitism. Kaplan thinks about "public" and "private" as historically situated practices and shows how the arrangements of private life (gender, homophobia, passing) can be understood only in terms of specific historical constellations of power and interest. He uses Arendt's analysis as a model for his own historically grounded reading of the rise of homophobia, building on her insights about parvenus and pariahs to understand passing and coming out in a homophobic society.

In sum, there are a variety of arguments about how best to bring private matters into public life, all of them except Honig's compatible with the reading I offer of translating private-life matters into politically negotiable claims by adopting the attitude of a parvenu or appealing to justice. But what are we to do about the other half of the public-private tension, which has to do with safeguarding the private realm from the harsh glare of public life?

Let us return to Arendt's insight that "there are things that need to be hidden and others that need to be displayed publicly, if they are to exist at all." Benhabib argues that this "phenomenological essentialism" is indefensible, and that it leads Arendt "to limit her concept of public space in ways which are not compatible with her own associative model" of politics. She argues that "different action-types, like work and labor, can become the locus of 'public space' if they are reflexively challenged and placed into question from the standpoint of the asymmetrical power relations governing them."[56]

Although I agree with the idea that activities or practices whose existential home is in private life can be challenged politically, I do not think this argument discredits the notion that some activities need to be protected from public scrutiny (or exposed to it) if they are to exist at all. Arendt's insight about the protective, nurturing quality of private life is borne out both by our language, where we frequently use *private* in senses having to do with limiting access to oneself and to certain places and interactions, and by the philosophical work on the centrality of privacy as a social practice by Schoeman, Post, and others, which I reviewed in Chapter 1. If coming to political life in the "right spirit" is a way of protecting *political* life from inappropriately narrow or process-oriented ways of thinking, how do we protect the *privacy* that allows a variety of social and intimate activities and interactions to flourish and gives people a "reliable hiding place" from the demands of public life? If some private matters should be and are open to political challenge, are there some that are *not*? How do we decide when it is inappropriate to politicize private, especially personal or intimate, matters?

Benhabib herself offers one way of answering such questions when she suggests that Arendt's notion of a home, the four walls of one's private property, provides a crucial shelter in which to unfold capacities, dreams, and memories, to nurse the wounds of the ego, and to lend depth of feeling, something like Virginia Woolf's "room of one's own." She writes, "With Arendt's concept of the home, we reach the most significant sense of 'privacy' in her theory, and which feminist theorists must not only share but also cultivate."[57] I think that the privateness of the "home," conceived of as a space where relationships based on intimacy and trust might develop, is what Arendt and Benhabib and the anthropological philosophers discussed in Chapter 1 are describing, and ought generally to be respected. Of course, this privateness should not be an impermeable shield: when practices that "belong" in private turn unjust or exploitative, then we have to find ways to talk about them politically, translate the perspective of private sufferers into that of citizens, and transform personal griefs or problems into politically negotiable claims.

And yet sometimes we inappropriately politicize private matters. Perhaps it is not surprising that some identity-based political movements have been insistent both about attacking the validity of public-private distinctions and about defining membership in terms of intimate affiliations. I am troubled by the kind of identity politics that anxiously focuses on defining the community, sorting out "us" from "them" and finding criteria for one's politics in one's intimate behavior. (Notice that "politics" is used here in the sense of a set of convictions, principles, opinions, and sympathies of a person or party, not in the sense of pertaining or belonging to the state or civic life.) Such a politics of community or group solidarity often has difficulty recognizing, appreciating, or tolerating diversities of experience or reaching out to or persuading others who are not like "us."[58] When membership is based on intimate-life decisions or practices— whether one is gay or straight, a "marriage resister" or married, in or out of the closet—then the politics of community or identity undermines privacy in ways I find dangerous. It is crucial to distinguish between translating oppressive social practices into political issues and making the individual's choices about her family life or sexual practices the basis for judging her political commitments.[59] We need to be able to do the former without justifying the latter.

There are several reasons to respect the privacy of a person's decisions about her sexual partners and practices or her familial and child rearing arrangements. One is the interest in protecting the spontaneity, openness, and trust that nurture intimate and loving relationships. This interest is central to the argument for protecting intimate "forms of life" made by philosophers such as David Rachels, Ferdinand Schoeman, and Robert Post, and to Arendt's argument that some precious human practices and values are extinguished when they are exposed to the glare of public life and the judgment of strangers.

A second is the specter of "Big Brother" in the bedroom or the home, policing the details of one's physical and emotional relationships with one's lovers, spouse, friends, or children. Such intrusion is no more welcome or justifiable when the motives are to encourage egalitarian relationships than it would be if the motive were to enforce heterosexuality, prohibit miscegenation, or encourage women to stay home and nurture their children. As Cindy Halpern puts it, "The point is not to institute cadres of diaper-changing and dishwashing police, but to empower women to insist on their own equal importance and value in the allocation of daily tasks and the making of family decisions."[60]

A third reason to respect the individual's privacy about intimate-life decisions has to do with the need to value and respect diversity. Scrutinizing an individual's intimate practices and demanding conformity to an implicit standard promotes homogeneity and undercuts and devalues differences. Assuming an essentialized identity based on intimate affiliations or decisions likewise renders the diversity of people's experiences invisible and places normalizing pressure on different or dissenting group members.

Obviously there are times when groups form out of a need for community, or a desire for safety and openness that people cannot find in their day-to-day lives as minority members of mainstream society. But the politics of groups that impose new orthodoxies, create new homogeneities, or ignore the diversity of members' experiences of relationships, class, ethnicity, and so on is antithetical to the irreducible plurality of political life. In my view, genuinely *political* responses to social power have to look beyond the safety of one's allies and cohorts, and address large, diverse collectivities. As political individuals we argue with and try to persuade people with whom we disagree, form coalitions, compromise, and build support for the positions we believe in. Group or identity politics may be a necessary precursor to such political action, but it is not the same thing.

For many feminist theorists Hannah Arendt is a problematic thinker, seeming often to spurn the concerns of the body and household life and to glorify an image of politics centered on masculine values and activities: display, disputatiousness, the quest for glory and immortality. So why draw on her theorizing to distinguish between "social" and "political" approaches to public issues housed in intimate life?

There are several reasons to do so. Arendt helps us think about what public and private *are,* and how they might be connected. She worried about the danger of private concerns and attitudes taking over public life and destroying the political realm. She feared that we would forget how to interact as citizens, remaining content in our roles as intimates, consumers, and producers. She argued powerfully that we must take responsibility for shaping our collective life, and evoked the polity as a crucial human achievement. But she also appreciated both the privative and protective qualities of private life. She acknowledged and wrestled with the dual or mixed character of privacy and the distinctiveness and connectedness of private and public life. Arendt clearly valued private life as well as political life, and thought that eliminating privacy would make human life shallow.

Arendt's care and concern for the distinctiveness and value of both private and political life, and her concern about the erosion of active democratic politics by "the social," are congenial to my own thinking. Combining these concerns with the feminist insight that the private life of the household, the body, and sexuality often gives rise to injustices which must be addressed politically has led me to connect some of Arendt's profoundest insights with feminist moves to politicize private, especially intimate, life. Drawing on Arendt's contrast between pariahs and parvenus rather than the dichotomous spatial imagery of *The Human Condition,* I conceive of "the social" and "the political" not as physical locations but as different modes or spirits in which people approach problems or issues. "The social," a mode in which we passively defer to experts, allowing political choices to be treated as though they were merely administrative decisions, undermines our self-respect as we are transformed from private sufferers to clients of the welfare state. "The political," a mode in which we actively contest practices or issues and appeal to shared values and principles, transforms private issues into political ones, thus engaging us in debates and drawing us into deciding as citizens which standards will constitute our common life.

There is no longer any question about whether private-life issues should enter our public life; they have done and will continue to do so wholesale. The problem is not how to wall off the concerns and preoccupations of private life from politics but, as Hanna Pitkin has argued, how to *connect* them. We need to get the connection right between private and public life because our many commitments and activities, frustrations and sufferings, insights and injustices, can provide an impetus for involvement in democratic politics. Or they can simply fuel the immense tutelary power of the state to minister to ever more of our needs.

The other reason for worrying about how we translate private-life concerns into public issues has to do with respecting privacy as a value that facilitates manifold social interactions and allows us to experiment as we develop intimate relationships. One could take this for an attempt to rejuvenate the liberal valuing of private life, but I think it is more than that. Arendt's thought points us toward more fundamental reasons for valuing the life lived in private, reasons that have to do with what it means to be a person with one's own perspective rising from the dark, hidden ground of the life lived behind four walls, where we experience what cannot be experienced in public. Arendt would protect this kind of privacy from the disputatious life of a citizen. Her aim in doing so was to defend the existential ground of human being.

The point for feminist theory, which has often demonized the private and argued that public-private distinctions are nothing more than an ideological construct for rationalizing the privileges of the powerful, is of critical importance. Feminist theory needs to move beyond this sort of ideological critique. This move is important, but it is not enough. Sometimes privacy is valuable and needs to be protected. Feminists need to work on distinguishing more clearly between times when private life hides injustice and times when it shelters difference and intimacy, for it surely does both. No political movement for justice can enlist the allegiance of thoughtful and diverse constituencies unless it recognizes that private life has to be valued and protected—not in an uncritical way, but by drawing careful and thoughtful distinctions.

My discussion now shifts gears. The next three chapters focus on particular areas of controversy in contemporary political life in a kind of political theorist's version of case studies. Chapter 4 deals with abortion and emerging reproductive issues, Chapter 5 with mothering and maternal thinking, and Chapter 6 with issues related to coming out of the closet, identity politics, and outing. The arguments of Part 1 are meant to illuminate, and to be illuminated by, the more applied inquiries of Part 2, in which I take up particularly divisive and unstable debates about political and policy issues facing courts, legislatures, activists, and citizens.

Part II

CONTEMPORARY
DOMAINS
OF THE PUBLIC-PRIVATE
TENSION

Four

Problems with the
Right to Privacy

THE U.S. SUPREME COURT'S PRIVACY JURISPRU-
dence has become deeply problematic for addressing several reproductive and sexual choice issues, including homosexual sex, abortion funding, requirements of parental notification or
consent for minors seeking abortions, and charges of fetal abuse against
pregnant women. Beginning with *Griswold v. Connecticut,* we can see how
the Supreme Court has developed a dominant reading of privacy which
is deeply conservative and conceptually vexed, although more politically
empowering understandings are also possible.

The Right to Privacy from *Griswold* to *Roe*

As we saw in Chapter 2, when people talk about "private," they can
mean a variety of things: first, private in the sense of lacking public office;
second, activities that are usually carried out "in private," including most
forms of physical, sexual, or emotional intimacy; third, places or things to
which access is limited; fourth, individual ownership of property; and fifth,
having limited impact rather than wide-scale or general effects.

The courts also recognize a variety of privacy interests. In tort law the
individual can assert a right to control the access of others to her solitude
or personal affairs, or to potentially embarrassing information about her
private life.[1] Fourth Amendment protections against unreasonable
searches and seizures safeguard the home and similar places where one can
be confident of being free from surveillance or intrusion, and able to control access to one's innermost activities and relationships. Protection for
private property is a central concern of American law,[2] and possession of

85

or control over property, whether a domicile or financial resources, is often crucial for being able to assert one's legal and constitutional rights effectively. Let us look more closely at how privacy figures in constitutional right-to-privacy decisions since 1965.

The Supreme Court first declared constitutional protection for the right of privacy in *Griswold v. Connecticut* 381 U.S. 479 (1965) in an opinion written by Justice Douglas, who rooted the right of privacy in values that he thought underpinned protections set out in the Bill of Rights. The First, Third, Fourth, Fifth, and Ninth Amendments include guarantees of freedom of religion and association; the right not to have soldiers quartered in one's home; "the right of the people to be secure in their persons, houses, papers, and effects, against unreasonable searches and seizures"; protection against compulsory self-incrimination; and the provision that the enumeration of certain rights in the Constitution does not "deny or disparage others retained by the people." Douglas also drew on existing case law to help establish support for the idea of constitutional protection for a privacy right not enumerated in the Constitution, including *Pierce v. Society of Sisters* 268 U.S. 510 (1925), *Meyer v. Nebraska* 262 U.S. 390 (1923), *NAACP v. Alabama* 357 U.S. 449 (1958), *NAACP v. Button* 371 U.S. 415 (1962), and *Skinner v. Oklahoma* 316 U.S. 535 (1942). *Pierce* and *Meyer* declared constitutional protection for the right of parents to control their children's education, while *NAACP v. Alabama* and *NAACP v. Button* protected the freedom to associate and the privacy of one's associations. *Skinner* overturned an Oklahoma law that mandated sterilization for certain classes of recidivists, declaring a fundamental interest in controlling one's ability to procreate.

The privacy interest Justice Douglas describes in *Griswold* is not merely a negative bar to state interference with individual decision making; it also protects a "positive capacity to form certain kinds of associations with others."[3] But for many the associational interests at stake in protecting privacy seem overshadowed by the language Douglas used to describe the intimacy of the marital relationship: "Marriage is a coming together for better or for worse, hopefully enduring, and intimate to the degree of being sacred. It is an association that promotes a way of life, not causes; a harmony in living, not political faiths; a bilateral loyalty, not commercial or social projects. Yet it is an association for as noble a purpose as any involved in our prior decisions." At least part of the force of the opinion striking down Connecticut's law forbidding the use of contraceptives by married couples came from the perception that its enforcement would have "a maximum destructive impact upon that relationship."[4]

The rationale for protecting the decision allowing the use of contraceptives shifted from *Griswold* in 1965 to *Eisenstadt v. Baird* 405 U.S. 438 in 1972. Whereas Justice Douglas's *Griswold* opinion focused on the intimacy of the marital relationship and the importance of protecting the marital bedroom from police searches, Justice Brennan's decision for the Court in *Eisenstadt* said nothing about intimate relationships, married or otherwise, or the privacy of places like the bedroom or home. Instead, Brennan stressed the importance of procreative decisions to the individual: "If the right of privacy means anything, it is the right of the *individual,* married or single, to be free from unwanted governmental intrusions into matters so fundamentally affecting a person as the decision whether to bear or beget a child."[5]

This shift allowed the Court to extend privacy protections beyond the married couple to any person wishing to use contraceptives. Since *Eisenstadt* and *Carey v. Population Services* 431 U.S. 678 (1977) concerned the distribution and the sale of contraceptives, respectively, there was no concern in these cases with protecting private, intimate places from searches for evidence of the use of contraceptives, as there was in *Griswold*. Thus, in the later contraception decisions, the focus of privacy protections shifts from controlling access to the home or bedroom and protecting the intimacy of marriage, to protecting the individual's right to decide free from government interference about matters that affect one's future as drastically as conceiving a child.

Roe v. Wade 410 U.S. 113 (1973) also makes the fundamental importance for one's future of the decision to bear a child the basis of its argument for protecting privacy. There, as in *Eisenstadt* and *Carey,* Justice Blackmun's majority opinion speaks very little about the nature of privacy or what is "private" about the decision to abort, focusing instead on the gravity of the decision to bear a child as the justification for preventing the state from interfering with a woman's decision to abort.[6]

Significantly, the reasons for protecting privacy in *Eisenstadt, Carey,* and *Roe* are different from those in *Griswold,* where the Court argued that the decision to use contraceptives should be protected from state interference because of the intimacy of the marital relationship and the outrageousness of permitting searches of the marital bedroom to turn up evidence of contraceptive use (the second and third senses of privacy discussed earlier). In the later decisions the justification for protecting privacy is rooted in respect for decisions that fundamentally affect a person's life. The language that recurs in these opinions—"the right of the individual . . . to be free of unwanted governmental intrusions," "the Constitution protects individual decisions . . . from unjustified intrusion by the State," "the detriment that the State would impose . . . by denying this choice"—draws on the first sense of privacy as autonomy, not subject to government regulation.

The virtue of this shift in argument is that it turns our attention from a notion of privacy based on respect for a conventional relationship—marriage—to a broader notion of respect for intimate decisions which can encompass a variety of relationships. But it is a problematic shift as well. First, the shift in meaning is not acknowledged. "Privacy" continues to be used in the later decisions as if it explained what is important about the decisions at stake, as if matters were still being described as private because they are connected to places or activities where intrusion or interference would seem outrageous, rather than being private in the sense that there are no laws to regulate them. Although *Griswold* is cited as establishing the right of privacy, the lines of analysis and justification taken there have narrowed and shifted in the later cases. In *Eisenstadt, Carey,* and *Roe,* procreative choice is private (constitutionally protected from state interference) because it is of "fundamental importance," not, as in *Griswold,* fundamentally important (and hence constitutionally protected) because it is private. The concept of privacy is burdened with an unspoken freight of justification which it does not carry in the post-*Griswold* cases. Saying that certain matters are (or should be) "private" in the sense of being free from state interference does not explain *why* those matters are of such fundamental importance that they deserve constitutional protection. *That* explanation would require a fully reasoned defense of the moral autonomy of the individual.[7]

Second, Justice Douglas's opinion in *Griswold* is powerful in part because of the clarity with which the right of privacy is connected to offensive intrusion into places, relationships, and practices we usually expect to be hidden and protected. Because we commonly think that marital and sexual decisions deserve respect and should be shielded from prying or intrusion, it is easy to see how the statute at issue in *Griswold* offended against the sense of privacy that pertains to intimate matters and activities that normally go on "in private."

In contrast, the Court opinions that defend privacy because of the fundamental importance of reproductive decisions to the individual fail to explain what makes such choices *private*. We must demonstrate something more than the importance of a given choice to the individual in order to explain why it should be left to the individual, or is private in some other sense, since one can easily imagine decisions that matter greatly to the individual, and normally are made in private, but are neither defensible nor private, such as the choice to commit incest, child abuse, rape, or spouse battering. Simply asserting that because the decision is of fundamental importance to the individual it should be treated as private is not enough. If the right to privacy is the correct strategy to use in defneding reproductive choices, we must be clear about what makes such decisions private.

Third, defending abortion rights in terms of privacy makes it hard to see abortion as a *public* issue that stems from the experience women share as a group. There are costs attached to classifying a matter as private, and thus denying it public status. For example, a woman is likely to view an accidental pregnancy as a private problem, something shameful, her fault, rather than thinking about the issue in terms of the larger social pattern of sexual encounters taking place on male terms, which needs to be understood and addressed systemically. Furthermore, protecting abortion rights in terms of privacy has made it harder to legitimize *public* responsibilities for and solutions to the problems of childbearing and child rearing in the United States. In contrast to the social policy of most other advanced industrialized countries, U.S. policy and legal options seldom extend to subsidizing families or restructuring school, jobs, and career tracks to accommodate pregnancy and child rearing, or to providing inexpensive, high-quality day care facilities.[8] A woman facing an ill-timed or unwanted pregnancy is given the option of raising a child with inadequate support or aborting it and perhaps becoming pregnant again later, when her personal resources are greater.

In sum, in the post-*Griswold* right-of-privacy decisions, the Court does not persuasively argue why reproductive decisions are private except in the general sense of privacy as lacking official significance or not being regulated by government, which is not a reason for keeping them that way at all. Furthermore, as a rhetorical strategy, appeals to privacy are costly because they make it harder to talk about the systemic structuring of child rearing arrangements, the workplace, sexual encounters, or public responsibilities for supporting women's decisions about pregnancy.

One could make better arguments for the privateness of reproductive decisions, for example, by showing that even outside of marriage, procreative decisions are private in various senses besides that of autonomy. Courts could argue that decisions about the body and medical treatment are generally left to the individual and protected from public interference; that abortion and contraception present moral dilemmas best resolved by the persons immediately involved; and that physical and sexual intimacy permeate procreative decision making. Courts could also combine protections for privacy with an explicit concern for equality, which would meet

objections several critics have raised about privacy's being useful for protecting only the privileged. Or one could offer a persuasive explanation of
how moral autonomy is connected to privacy, as Justice Blackmun did in
his dissenting opinion in *Bowers v. Hardwick,* which I examine in this chapter. Thus, respect for what goes on "in private" might yet provide a foundation for respecting decisions of this sort.

But even a well-crafted argument for privacy may not be the best strategy for providing constitutional protection for decisions about reproduction and sexuality, for two reasons. First, arguing that decisions are "private" provides no basis for making positive claims to entitlement which
may be crucial if poor women are to have access to abortion or other
reproductive services. And second, thus far the courts have recognized and
treated competing senses of privacy very differently. The privacy connected to autonomy in decisions about reproduction and choice of sexual
partner is often accorded less respect and protection than the privacy connected to familial relationships such as those between spouses or between
parents and children. We now turn to an analysis of privacy protections in
reproductive decisions after *Roe,* the emerging "fetal abuse" cases, and the
area of sexual choice.

After *Roe:* Privacy as Familial Attachment versus Privacy as Autonomy

Even in *Roe v. Wade* itself there is a clear recognition that a woman's
right to abort does not deserve the same protection as privacy interests
recognized in earlier decisions: "The pregnant woman cannot be isolated
in her privacy. She carries an embryo and, later, a fetus. . . . The situation
therefore is inherently different from marital intimacy, or bedroom possession of obscene material, or marriage, or procreation, or education, with
which *Eisenstadt, Griswold, Stanley, Loving, Skinner, Pierce,* and *Meyer* were
respectively concerned."[9] This situation is inherently different from married couples' deciding to use contraceptives or parents' deciding how their
children should be educated because a woman's decision to abort means
that the state's interests in protecting potential human life are extinguished. As a pregnancy progresses, the woman's rights are confronted by
an increasing concern with protecting fetal life.

The hint that privacy rights in *Roe* are not to be accorded the same
respect as the privacy rights of parents to control their children's education
or of marriage partners to use contraceptives has developed into four
strands of decisions which limit the notion of a right to privacy as individ-

ual autonomy: (1) cases restricting adults' access to abortion, including the abortion funding decisions; (2) the decisions dealing with parental consent and notification; (3) cases involving legally mandated interventions in pregnancy and so-called fetal abuse by pregnant substance abusers;[10] and (4) the refusal to extend privacy protections to homosexual behavior. Let us look more closely at how privacy protections fare in these different areas.

Restricting Access to Abortion

In the abortion funding cases, *Maher v. Roe* 432 U.S. 464 (1977) and *Harris v. McRae* 448 U.S. 297 (1980), the Supreme Court held that the right to privacy imposed no obligation on the state or federal government to guarantee access to abortion by providing funding under the Medicaid program to women who could not afford to pay for their abortions.[11] Funding schemes like the one at issue in *Maher* which paid for the costs associated with childbirth but not those of abortion were deemed a permissible way to use financial incentives to encourage women to choose childbirth over abortion, despite dissenters' objections that such policies were coercive and aimed at a particularly vulnerable population. The majorities' defense of this position was that such coercion exists in society, and that it is not incumbent on the courts or legislatures to provide any (or any particular) medical services.[12] The abortion funding decisions establish limits to the fundamental right to privacy set out in *Roe*. There is a fundamental right to seek an abortion free from criminal sanction, but nothing more. The right to privacy is not one that compels the state to eliminate other kinds of interferences with access to abortion, be they social, economic, or legislative.

In my view this niggardly approach to abortion funding was possible because the constitutional basis for protecting the decision to abort a pregnancy rests on privacy. Under the privacy approach, a woman has a right to be free from overt state interference (i.e., criminalization), but having won that freedom, she has no grounds for claiming a right to the resources that would enable her to exercise her right. In essence the Court said, "We grant that there is a right to privacy which permits woman to decide on her own how to resolve her pregnancy. But when we say the decision is 'private,' we mean it is hers to make without any assistance from the state. While we will make sure that the state does not bar abortions outright, we will not override policies—legislative decisions—to discourage or otherwise burden the abortion decision." If "privacy" in the sense of autonomy means freedom from government prohibition, that is *all* it means. The state has no affirmative obligation to ensure poor women a meaningful opportunity to exercise their privacy rights. They are simply free to seek on their own the means to exercise their rights.

The Court's decisions restricting access to abortions in *Webster v. Reproductive Health Services* 492 U.S. 490 (1989) and *Planned Parenthood of Southeastern Pennsylvania v. Casey* 120 L. Ed. 2d 674 (1992) build on the principle established in the abortion funding cases that the state is not obliged to remove barriers to exercising abortion, and may in fact encourage women to choose childbirth over abortion. Chief Justice Rehnquist's plurality opinion in *Webster v. Reproductive Health Services* (1989) relies on the "no obstacle that would not have been there anyway" approach to explain why Missouri's law prohibiting the use of public facilities and staff to perform abortions did not run afoul of the Constitution: "Just as Congress' refusal to fund abortions in *McRae* left 'an indigent woman with at least the same range of choice in deciding whether to obtain a medically necessary abortion as she would have had if Congress had chosen to subsidize no health care costs at all,' Missouri's refusal to allow public employees to perform abortions in public hospitals leaves a pregnant woman with the same choices as if the State had chosen not to operate any public hospitals at all."[13]

Given the indications in *Webster* that the Court was undergoing a crucial realignment on the issue of abortion, many anticipated that the *Planned Parenthood of Southeastern Pennsylvania v. Casey* (1992) decision would be a watershed for abortion rights. Indeed, *Casey* is an important decision, underlining the willingness of the Supreme Court to accept restrictions on abortion while upholding the basic principle of choice. Articulating an "undue burden" standard for reviewing laws that regulate abortion, the Court upheld regulations requiring informed consent, a twenty-four-hour wait after counseling before an abortion can be performed, and parental consent before a minor can have an abortion. But the centrist coalition of Justices O'Connor, Kennedy, and Souter, who authored the majority opinion, refused to overturn *Roe v. Wade,* arguing that "an entire generation has come of age free to assume *Roe*'s concept of liberty in defining the capacity of women to act in society, and to make reproductive decisions." The opinion accepts the essential similarity between deciding to have an abortion and deciding to use contraception, treating the right to control decisions that profoundly affect a person's life as a valid constitutional interest which, while open to regulation, still deserves protection.[14] But the Court's support for the central holding of *Roe* stems from *stare decisis* and concerns about the institutional legitimacy of the Court; that is, bowing to political pressure to reverse *Roe* in the absence of principled reasons to invalidate the earlier holding would send the wrong message about the Court's role. With respect to privacy, *Casey* was not a novel or clarifying decision; it covered the same doctrinal ground as *Roe* and its progeny, building on privacy without questioning the analogies (and false analogies) between *Griswold* and *Roe*.

In upholding laws in *Webster* and *Casey* that actively burden or interfere with a woman's decision to abort, the Court has taken a step beyond upholding the refusal to fund Medicaid abortions. But the justification continues to be similar to that in the abortion funding cases: so long as a law does not "unduly burden" a woman's decision, it is permissible under the right to privacy. By the mid-1990s the right to privacy barred only the most overt and absolute interferences with reproductive choice.

Parental Notification and Consent

The Supreme Court's decisions dealing with parental consent and notification requirements for minors began in 1976 with *Danforth v. Planned Parenthood of Central Missouri* 425 U.S. 52 (1976), striking down requirements of spousal or parental consent which amounted to allowing a third party to veto a woman's decision to abort her pregnancy.[15] The Court followed this in 1979 with *Bellotti v. Baird II* 443 U.S. 662, which held that a Massachusetts law requiring parental consent for minors to request abortions was unconstitutional because the judicial bypass mechanism provided in the statute did not automatically permit exceptions to the consent requirement for mature minors or for minors whose best interest would be served by not seeking parental consent for an abortion.

Although the *Bellotti* decision came down on the side of pregnant minors, the Court was sympathetic to arguments for respecting family integrity and the value of parents' consulting with their minor daughters, and accepted the argument that parental consent could be valid if it provided for a sufficient judicial bypass alternative. Justice Powell's majority opinion in *Bellotti* makes a strong case for familial privacy, focusing both on minors' immaturity and need for counsel, and on the family's traditional and respected role as inculcator of values. Powell cites children's peculiar vulnerability and their need for concern, sympathy, and parental attention, the fact that "minors often lack the experience, perspective, and judgment to recognize and avoid choices that could be detrimental to them," and the common provision for "parental consent or involvement in important decisions by minors." Furthermore, because parents have a special obligation to provide their children with an education that will prepare them for adulthood and citizenship, the state is justified in deferring to, even encouraging, parents' control over their children.[16] Thus, the decision gave considerable weight to the claims and values of familial privacy, and set the groundwork for later decisions favoring parental consultation over the minor's right to decide to abort her pregnancy without telling her parents.

In its 1981 decision in *H.L. v. Matheson* 450 U.S. 398, the Supreme Court (Chief Justice Burger writing) took this reasoning a step further in upholding a Utah statute requiring that parents be notified before a minor has an abortion. Faced with a fifteen-year-old unmarried pregnant plaintiff who refused to answer questions about the problems that might arise if she told her parents about the pregnancy, or whether she was mature enough to decide on an abortion without consulting her parents, the Court treated the challenge to the Utah law only as it applied to the class of immature, unemancipated minors, and found it constitutional.

Since the Utah law mandated only parental notification, not consent, it was not viewed as raising the possibility of a parental veto of a minor daughter's decision to abort her pregnancy as were the laws challenged in *Danforth* and *Bellotti*. Also, because the plaintiff in *Matheson* was presumed to be immature, arguments about the need for parental guidance, emotional support, and counsel carried greater weight here than in *Bellotti*. Given these factual differences, concerns about protecting parents' decisions over raising their children, parental responsibility for caring for and nurturing their children, protecting adolescents, and the state interest in providing parents an opportunity to supply medical information to a physician easily overrode the concern that some minors might be inhibited from seeking an abortion because of the notice requirement.[17]

The movement from *Danforth* to *Bellotti* to *Matheson,* with each decision placing progressively greater weight on the state's interest in fostering consultation between parents and their minor daughters and less on the privacy interests in the autonomy of young pregnant women, culminated in the Supreme Court's decisions in *Ohio v. Akron Center for Reproductive Health* 497 U.S. 502 (1990) and *Hodgson v. Minnesota* 497 U.S. 417 (1990), which were handed down together in June 1990. I focus here on the *Hodgson* decision since the Court's response to Minnesota's two-parent notification requirement is more interesting than the narrowly focused technical issues involved in Ohio's bypass procedure.

The Minnesota statute upheld in *Hodgson v. Minnesota* required that both parents be notified, and the forty-eight hours elapse between parental notification and the abortion procedure. The two-parent notification requirement could be waived only if an immediate abortion were necessary to prevent the woman's death, if both parents had consented in writing, or if the woman declared that she was a victim of parental abuse or neglect, in which case notice of her declaration had to be given to the proper authorities, who could pursue an investigation of the alleged abuse or neglect while the abortion was pending.

Hodgson reveals deep cleavages among the justices about how much respect to accord the pregnant minor's interests in autonomy and how much to accord her parents' interests in knowing of their daughter's pregnancy and consulting with her or influencing her decision, as well as a central disagreement about the *kind* of familial privacy to be protected. Five of the justices argued that the requirement that *both* parents be notified was premised on an ideal of family life, with both biological parents living at home and involved in their children's upbringing, which is simply not true in a large percentage of cases.[18] The other four justices strongly supported the two-parent notification requirement, defending the right of both parents to be informed of an involved in their daughter's decision, whether or not they live with her, support her, or are good parents.[19]

The debate over the constitutionality of requiring that both parents be notified is important for analyzing the Supreme Court's evolving understanding of and respect for familial privacy. Although the Massachusetts law at issue in *Bellotti v. Baird* required both parents' consent for a minor to have an abortion, the Court barely touched on the problems of "nonstandard" or dysfunctional families in prescribing the kind of judicial bypass procedure that would make the two-parent consent requirement constitutional.[20] But in *Hodgson* four justices thought that the requirement that *both* parents be informed of their daughter's abortion should be consitutional *even in the absence of a judicial bypass procedure* that would allow the pregnant minor to have an abortion without telling one or both of her parents. This goes far beyond the recognition of claims of family privacy in *Bellotti* or *Matheson,* and marks the first explicit defense of the rights of noncustodial parents to be involved in a daughter's decision about abortion. Justice Kennedy wrote for the four dissenters (himself, Rehnquist, Scalia, and White):

All must acknowledge that it was reasonable for the legislature to conclude that in most cases notice to both parents will work to the minor's benefit. . . . This is true not only in what the Court calls the "ideal family setting," where both parents and the minor live under one roof, but also where the minor no longer lives with both parents. The Court does not deny that many absent parents maintain significant ties with their children, and seek to participate in their lives, to guide, to teach, and to care for them. It is beyond dispute that these attachments, in cases not involving mistreatment or abuse, are essential to the minor's well-being, and that parental notice is supportive of this kind of family tie. . . . As a general matter . . . it "remains cardinal with us that the custody, care and nurture of the child reside first in the parents, whose primary function and freedom include preparation for obligations the state can neither supply nor hinder."[21]

Putting the result in *Hodgson*—to uphold Minnesota's two-parent consent requirement if a bypass mechanism were included—together with the dissenters' strong endorsement of parents' rights to be informed about and involved in their minor daughters' decisions about abortion suggests that as of 1990, the Court was moving toward increasing respect of the rights of parents.

Although family privacy has a long history of respect from the courts, laws that require minor girls to notify their parents before seeking an abortion force us to weigh parents' and children's privacy interests against each other. Robert Keiter suggests that laws should be written to encourage rather than compel parental involvement in the child's decision making. On the one hand, Keiter thinks that children have "an interest in receiving guidance, assistance, and support when confronted with important personal matters. Parental assistance in these situations is certainly the norm, and it is consistent with the traditionally exercised and constitutionally recognized role of the parent. . . . Without parental support and guidance, the child may lack adequate insight and strength to confront responsibly and to resolve satisfactorily a personal matter as important as whether or not to bear a child." On the other hand, he believes that such parental involvement is likely to be beneficial only in stable and harmonious families, and that laws requiring parental notification or consent will not work in families characterized by discord and distrust. In the very situations where children would be least likely to tell their parents of their pregnancies, laws such as Minnesota's could force a less-than-supportive, even hostile response in the absence of bypass procedures to protect the privacy interests of pregnant minors.[22]

Given the diversity of family arrangements, sensitivity to both sides of the privacy conflict involved in parental notification and consent laws is crucial. Moves by conservatives on the Court to give greater weight to parents' interests in control over child rearing suggest a return to the roots of the right-to-privacy jurisprudence in decisions about parental control over children's upbringing and education and a disquieting depreciation of the privacy-as-autonomy interest of pregnant minors in deciding whether to abort a pregnancy.

Fetal Abuse

Women's privacy faces new challenges as fetuses are increasingly recognized as having distinct rights that need to be protected against detrimental maternal behavior. Pregnant women who refuse to consent to treatment deemed necessary to preserve or protect their fetus's life or health are often viewed as irrational, incompetent, or selfish. Judges are more likely to order medical treatment for poor pregnant women and women of color than they are for wealthier women who have private physicians. Cynthia Daniels reports that in one study, seventeen out of twenty-one pregnant women forced to undergo medical treatment were Black, Hispanic, or Asian, and five of them were not native speakers of English. Furthermore, almost all documented cases of women being forced to undergo casarean sections "involve women whose religious beliefs conflicted with the dominant culture."[23]

In the leading federal circuit court of appeals opinion in this area, *In re A.C.* 573 A.2d 1234 (1990), the majority upheld the right of a terminally ill woman not to have a cesarean section performed without her consent. Angela Carder became pregnant while her cancer was in remission. When her illness worsened about twenty-six weeks into the pregnancy, she was asked if she would consent to a cesarean section; she replied that she would do so after twenty-eight weeks, when the fetus's chances of survival would be much better. Carder lapsed into a coma, and an emergency cesarean section was performed without her consent. Both Carder and the baby died shortly afterward. Although the court of appeals upheld Carder's right under these circumstances to withhold consent, many suggest that *In re A.C.* is not a solid victory for the bodily integrity and autonomy of pregnant women. Carder was an unusually sympathetic figure whose ability to comprehend the medical arguments and whose self-sacrifice on behalf of her fetus distinguished her from many women who refuse medical treatment aimed at saving the fetus, making her a prototypical "good" mother rather than a selfish or incompetent one.[24] In addition, despite the ruling in Carder's favor, the majority accepted the notion that a fetus has protectable interests which must be balanced against the mother's; the decision in favor of Carder was based on her competence to decide about her medical treatment, not on the relative weight of maternal and fetal rights.

In the more usual situation, doctors or hospital administrators obtain court orders at rushed hearings allowing them to proceed with emergency treatment over the objections of the pregnant woman. "Bolstered by the ideology of the pregnant woman's duty to care, and motivated . . . by the fear of lawsuits in cases where they did not act to 'save' fetal life," they

become "much more inclined to compromise the patient's right to autonomy in the interests of fetal health," writes Daniels. In such a situation the
woman's objections to interference with her body are often discounted,
especially if she is viewed as deviating from the ideal of the nurturing, self-
sacrificing mother, as nonwhite, foreign-born, and poor women frequently
are.[25]

The tendency to see women who are willing to sacrifice their fetus's
health or life as monstrous and unnatural is even more marked in recent
prosecutions of pregnant drug abusers.[26] Class and race biases pervade this
policy area as well. Poor and nonwhite women are more likely than middle-class white women to be prosecuted or forced to undergo drug testing.
Dorothy Roberts and Lisa Bower both argue that the pregnant drug
abuser is rhetorically constructed as a poor black woman. One of the reasons why drug abuse during pregnancy is associated with nonwhite, particularly African American, women is the tendency of whites to view women
of color as "bad" mothers; consider the many stereotypes of black women
as crackheads, jezebels, welfare queens, and negligent mothers.[27] Another
is that, especially for poor and nonwhite women, drug use often coincides
with other factors that can harm fetal health, such as battering, poor nutrition, poverty, and lack of prenatal care. Also, poor and nonwhite women
are more often dependent on public assistance such as Medicaid, AFDC,
and public hospitals and do not have private physicians and health insurance to help shield them from postpartum drug testing and prosecution.

Why has the tendency to prosecute drug-abusing mothers for harm to
their fetuses and babies become so marked in recent years? Some point to
media coverage which has produced a sense of crisis. Others say the public
tends to focus on the behavior of pregnant women while ignoring larger
factors such as poverty, poor nutrition, and lack of prenatal care or the
possible damage done by fathers who abuse drugs, smoke, drink, are exposed to hazardous substances in the workplace, or batter their wives or
partners.[28] Once the issue is framed in terms of *women's* bahavior and *wom-
en's* fault, other contributing causes of harm are ignored or discounted.
Still another explanation is the tendency to view the fetus as a "baby person" with rights of its own. Many have commented on the persuasive
power of representations that show fetuses with clearly babylike features,
who appear to be free-floating, unconnected to an umbilical cord or their
mother's uterus. Such depictions lead people to think of the fetus as if it
were already a person, with interests deserving of protection.[29] The medical profession has responded to advances in technology that permit visual-
ization and earlier and more effective testing for fetal defects and prenatal

medical and surgical interventions by considering the care of their "second patient" to be equal in importance to the care of the pregnant woman, even when the interests of the fetus and the mother are potentially at odds. Part of the power of the fetal abuse issue stems from the expectation that women are especially self-sacrificing and nurturing when it comes to protecting and caring for their children. Women who refuse to act this way are viewed as monstrous "anti-mothers," selfish and withholding.[30] Thus they are especially likely to elicit rage for failing to curb their own appetites and addictions, thereby harming their babies.

Given the way forced medical treatment and fetal abuse have come to be defined as issues, and the apparent willingness of cultural institutions and state prosecutors to accept the stereotype of the negligent, abusive mother, notions of privacy and choice developed in the context of contraception and abortion appear especially inadequate to express or protect women's interests when they conflict with "fetal rights." Notions of autonomy, the right to control physical invasions of one's body or to determine what one consumes or puts into one's body, lack moral power when weighed against the ideology of maternal care and duty. As in the parental consent and notification decisions, the concept of woman's privacy as autonomy is undercut in the courts and in public discourse by notions of familial attachment.

Mary Shanley suggests another reason why autonomy is not a good basis for expressing the interest in controlling one's body while carrying a pregnancy to term. A pregnant woman's decisions and behaviors are not purely self-regarding, for they directly affect the fetus growing inside her. Shanley suggests that we think about fetal personhood as presupposing attachment and community between mother and fetus, and proposes that we adopt legal approaches that foster relationships of dependence and interdependence rather than assuming mother and fetus to be isolated, right-asserting individuals. In her view we can better appreciate the moral complexity of a relationship of connection, nurturance, and dependence if privacy and autonomy belong to the mother-fetus dyad, envisioned as a symbiotic unit or community for which the woman is the agent, than if we view the woman as acting alone in her privacy. The supposed privacy of the isolated individual not only distorts the maternal-fetal relationship but also invites us to see the autonomy interests of the fetus pitted against the mother's.[31]

As with other reproductive issues, the concept of privacy as individual autonomy also makes it hard to attend to the public context in which women become pregnant and carry their pregnancies. According to Daniels, it is tempting to counter the coerciveness of forced medical treatment and fetal abuse prosecutions by arguing that pregnant women should be treated the same as men, and asserting the liberal right to be "let alone." But the right to be let alone does not help us recognize the special demands and constraints that pregnancy places on women or the social and institutional context in which women become pregnant, a context where women are often economically dependent on men, where being pregnant is viewed as incompatible with being a responsible worker, where there are few supports for having and raising children, and where women are presumed to be primary parents. As in the abortion funding cases, asserting a right to privacy leaves women with no way to make positive claims for policies that recognize and assist them with the social burdens of pregnancy. The right to privacy is autonomy is simply the right to be let alone. In Daniels's words: "Until a new public agenda . . . addresses the . . . unique circumstances [surrounding pregnancy], the retreat into privacy for women will amount to a new form of disempowerment. Real reproductive choice rests upon recognition of reproduction as a social and collective responsibility, not simply a private and individual one."[32]

As I have suggested, the ability to exercise one's right to privacy in the contexts of forced medical treatment and fetal abuse prosecutions depends on a degree of economic privilege. Although in theory everyone has a right to privacy, in practice middle-class women have resources with which to protect and assert their privacy which poor women do not. Women who can afford to pay for abortions readily receive them; women who cannot, do not, since most states and the federal government ban funding for abortion under Medicaid. Women with private physicians and health insurance are often able to avoid being tested for drugs when hospitalized to give birth, whereas women dependent on Medicaid or public hospitals are not. Daniels underscores the cruelty of a right to privacy that provides no entitlement to the financial means for its exercise:

Just as poverty, for Marx, revealed the "political swindle" of the abstract liberal right to free contract, so pregnancy now reveals the swindle of free reproductive choice. A woman who has the formal right to choice, but no access to economic resources, health care, paid parental leave, or quality day care, does not have the free choice to bear and raise children with dignity. A woman who has the choice to continue her pregnancy, but who may in the process lose her right to control her own medical treatment or to make decisions about where to work and what to eat and drink, does not have access to real choice. Her right to pregnancy is burdened or qualified by her loss of civil liberties.[33]

Even for middle-class women, privacy does not provide an adequate rubric for protecting choice. In an essay analyzing the pressures women face in adjusting to ever-rising standards of prenatal care and intervention, Patricia Richard argues that even for affluent women, "choice" is a flawed way of thinking about or protecting reproductive freedom. Since most parents want what is best for their children, Richards fears that the majority of women will submit to dietary and exercise regimes, medical treatments, testing, monitoring, and even surgery if they think it will ensure healthy offspring. Most people's "perceptions of choice," she says, "are shaped by what they learn they should want. . . . The experience of choice is very real for those who want what society wants them to want."[34] It appears that in a society with a strong ideology of maternal self-sacrifice, choice or privacy is inadequate as a legal tool for protecting reproductive freedom, for middle-class women who "voluntarily" agree to treatments, surveillance, and medical interventions that invade their bodies and infringe their autonomy as well as for women forced to undergo medical treatment or face prosecution for drug use.

Bowers v. Hardwick *and Consensual Sodomy*

In its 1986 decision in *Bowers v. Hardwick* 478 U.S. 186, the Supreme Court considered a challenge to Georgia's sodomy law on the grounds that it unconstitutionally interfered with the privacy rights of consenting adult homosexuals. Justice White, speaking for a five-person majority, rejected what he characterized as a claim to "a fundamental right to engage in homosexual sodomy" on the basis of judicial deference to legislative judgment about the unacceptability and immorality of homosexual activity, the unwillingness to expand privacy protections given inadequate textual basis in the Constitution for doing so, and differences between homosexuals' interests in seeking constitutional protection for intimate sexual relationships and those at stake in cases relating to familial privacy and reproductive autonomy. White wrote:

[We think it evident that none of the rights announced in those cases [*Pierce v. Society of Sisters* (1925) and *Meyer v. Nebraska* (1923), dealing with child rearing and education; *Prince v. Massachusetts* (1944), dealing with family relations; *Skinner v. Oklahoma* (1942), dealing with procreation; *Loving v. Virginia* (1967) and *Griswold v. Connecticut,* dealing with marriage; *Eisenstadt v. Baird* (1972) on contraception; and *Roe v. Wade* (1973) on abortion] bears any resemblance to the claimed constitutional right of homosexuals to engage in acts of sodomy that is asserted in this case. No connection between family, marriage, or procreation on the one hand and homosexual activity on the other has been demonstrated.[35]

White's opinion sharply echoes the Court's move toward greater rec-ognition of notions of privacy that give weight to parental control and maternal obligation. Homosexual intimacy may be even more challenging to the prevailing familial predispositions reflected in the privacy jurispru-dence than the autonomy claims of pregnant teenagers or women. Justice White apparently thought so when he characterized as "facetious" Michael Hardwick's claim that homosexual intimacy is deeply rooted in this na-tion's history.[36] The majority's refusal to extend constitutional privacy pro-tections to consensual homosexual behavior abruptly curtailed the devel-opment of a broader notion of privacy as individual autonomy in favor of legislative judgments aimed at fostering conventional, socially condoned (i.e., heterosexual, marital, and familial) forms of intimacy.[37]

In contrast, Justice Blackmun's dissenting opinion in *Bowers* cast the issue in terms of the central importance of intimate relationships to the development of human identity and personality. He asks us not to close "our eyes to the basic reasons why certain rights associated with the family have been accorded shelter," but to recognize that we protect family pri-vacy because it forms a central part of an individual's life. Blackmun argues for a robust conception of privacy that would protect the intimacies of human association because of what they contribute to an individual's sense of self, rather than protecting only the privacy of marriage, heterosexual sex, and socially condoned families, which some see as rooted in our na-tion's traditions:

"The concept of privacy embodies the 'moral fact that a person belongs to himself and not others nor to society as a whole.' " . . . We protect the decision whether to have a child because parenthood alters so dramatically an individual's self-determi-nation, not because of demographic considerations or the Bible's command to be fruitful and multiply. . . . And we protect the family because it contributes so powerfully to the happiness of individuals, not because of the preference for stereo-typical households. . . .

Only the most willful blindness could obscure the fact that sexual intimacy is "a sensitive, key relationship of human existence, central to family life, community welfare, and the development of human personality." . . . The fact that individuals define themselves in a significant way through their intimate sexual relationships with others suggests, in a Nation as diverse as ours, that there may be many "right" ways of conducting those relationships, and that much of the richness of a relation-ship will come from the freedom an individual has to *choose* the form and nature of these intensely personal bonds.[38]

White's and Blackmun's opinions in the *Bowers* decision give contrast-ing readings to the meaning of privacy, and invite a discussion of how best to understand the role of privacy in contemporary American constitutional law. Is privacy an essentially conservative idea or value, used in the service of powerful interests to reinforce traditionally condoned relationships and forms of intimacy, which we have long recognized as "private" and deserving of protection? Or is privacy a liberatory value, crucial to allowing people the freedom to develop manifold relationships, forms of intimacy, and notions of happiness? The first reading is closer to the analysis of the right-to-privacy decisions offered in this chapter, but the second is closer to the integral role privacy plays in human life, as I argued in Chapters 1–3. Which is correct?

The Right to Privacy: Protection, Privilege, and Privation

Throughout this chapter I have pursued a feminist reading of the constitutional right-to-privacy decisions of the last thirty years, pointing to the ways privacy has been interpreted to serve social goals of protecting marriages and parental interests while minimizing or excluding the privacy interests of pregnant teenagers and women and of gays, lesbians, and bisexuals. Although since the centrist decision in *Planned Parenthood v. Casey* (1992) the right to privacy which guarantees a woman's right to seek an abortion seems firmly established, the right is a limited tool, open to erosion and slippage. Regulations that burden a woman's decision to abort her pregnancy are permissible so long as government-imposed interference does not effectively bar choice. Interferences imposed by lack of financial resources, health insurance, or availability of clinics may make it difficult for women to obtain abortions, but they are not the result of government action and hence do not offend the constitutional right to privacy. Although the bare minimum of a right to choose abortion without any claim on entitlement to funding or access has been affirmed, the privacy argument will guarantee *only* such a minimal right, offering merely the illusion of choice to those without the resources to make it possible.

The fetal abuse cases also suggest that those with privileges are better able to protect and enjoy their privacy than those without. Babies born to women who rely on Medicaid or public hospitals are more likely to be tested for drugs than those of middle-class women; residents of public housing or recipients of AFDC benefits are more likely to have the privacy of their homes invaded by case workers or police officers than are homeowners; people who live in cramped spaces enjoy less privacy than people who live in dwellings where each sleeps in her or his own bedroom, and homeless people have next to no privacy. Having property thus makes it easier to assert and enjoy privacy. Privacy as a value and a right is a perquisite of the privileged; it verges on an empty promise for those who are poor. As Cynthia Halpern has put it, "Privacy protects property . . . and . . . property also provides privacy. . . . [W]ho pays for what in this society determines a great deal about the amount of privacy and protection from outside intervention that the individual is afforded."[39]

Not only is privacy a privilege enjoyed by those with means. As we have seen, it can also deprive an issue of public significance. When we treat decisions related to pregnancy as private, we set women up to see becoming pregnant as something they must cope with by themselves, a decision in which they have no proper claim on society or the state for support. Furthermore, defending reproductive choice in terms of privacy makes it harder to see that sexual intercourse, pregnancy, and child rearing are played out against a background of gendered social roles that shape men's and women's notions of pleasure, volition, and responsibility. Among the issues that become invisible to us when we think in terms of a right to privacy are the circumstances in which women become pregnant; the structuring of the job market around full-time workers with few domestic responsibilities; and notions of maternal self-sacrifice. The public debate about "suboptimal" fetuses and newborns is skewed toward mothers' behaviors, ignoring a variety of other factors, such as the behavior of fathers; society's failure to provide universal health and prenatal care; the omnipresence of poverty; toxic substances in the environment; and the reasons why women and men use addictive drugs.

Understanding an issue as a personal dilemma or a matter of one's privacy rights rather than as a systemic problem which can be addressed through collective action is disempowering to the individual coping with the dilemma, and depoliticizing and dangerous to the polity that closes off important problems from consideration by declaring them "private." Refusing to engage forms of power and injustice becomes easier when we treat issues as merely private. Thus "the social" grows at the expense of political engagement.

Many criticize privacy protections for gays, lesbians, and bisexuals on similar grounds. Protecting privacy hardly begins to address the potent political and cultural problems posed by homophobia. One often hears, "They're free to do what they want in private, I just don't think they should flaunt their lifestyle in public." Like the "Don't ask, don't tell" policy in the military, extending privacy protections to lesbian and gay sex would be like placing a welcome mat in the closet. Acceptance, and self-acceptance, of diverse forms of intimacy and familial relationships requires the uncovering and confronting of prejudices and forms of social power, the acknowledgment and appreciation of differences in public as well as private, not the pretense of assimilation and passing that privacy promotes. Protecting privacy would not help us recognize that the " ' "freedom to have impact on others—to make the 'statement' implicit in a public identity—is central to any adequate conception of the self" ' " or help to allay " 'pervasive discrimination against gays' in public society; it would not itself contribute, nor would it directly empower its beneficiaries to contribute, to 'heightening public awareness of homosexuality and thus broadening public acceptance of gay lifestyles.' " Defending privacy only burdens homosexuality with the "stigma of quarantine."[40]

Besides being a rhetorically debilitating political strategy, privacy is conceptually flawed: what is private in parents' decisions about their children's education or the use of contraceptives by married couples is mistakenly taken to explain what is private and valuable about decisions involving bodily autonomy. Furthermore, many fear that there is no conceptual core to the notion of privacy that makes it a workable tool for delineating, valuing, and protecting various aspects of human life. Have the courts articulated intellectually defensible criteria or reasons for valuing and protecting privacy? Do we have procedures or guidelines for weighing the value of privacy against competing values, such as protecting unborn life, enforcing community morality, or ensuring freedom of speech?[41]

On the depreciatory reading, privacy is a conservative value which has been used to reinforce heterosexual and marital intimacy and parental control over pregnant teenagers and to protect and reinforce the interests of those with power in our society: men who benefit from greater access to women's bodies under *Roe*;[42] police and judges who traditionally adopt a hands-off attitude to the battering of women in the home; middle-class white women who have the means to assert privacy interests in contexts ranging from sterilization to contraception to abortion to drug testing of their infants. Arguing that the public-private distinction is manipulated to prevent certain issues and forms of power from being contested, Cynthia Halpern makes explicit the connection between legally protected privacy rights, the depoliticizing character of privacy protections, and social and political power: "The public-private distinction is not a thing; it is not a found object. It is a political practice, one that does political work and has been used as a political instrument for and against particular constructions of power since the beginning. . . . It is . . . a tool of power and a stratagem of politics. It is a moveable barrier that is a way of enclosing, or opening up to political control, certain subjects and issues."[43] The image of privacy as a movable barrier is a potent one, and suggests the irony if not the futility of efforts to gain recognition of privacy claims and protections by groups that have long struggled to have their choices protected from hostile and moralistic majorities.

Given these powerful arguments that the right to privacy is a conceptually and politically flawed tool, what position should judges, advocates, and legal commentators take toward the right of privacy asserted by women seeking reproductive choice and gays, lesbians, and bisexuals seeking sexual choice? Should we abandon privacy and look for more useful legal doctrines, such as equality? Should we shut our eyes to the problems and fight for constitutional and legal privacy protections tooth and nail, arguing against any restrictions or regulations that limit a woman's or gay person's privacy? Should we continue to make critical, intelligent arguments for privacy in the hope of eventually gaining legal and political recognition of privacy as a central and empowering value in our political life?

For pragmatic and strategic reasons I would not at this point propose an alternate legal or constitutional basis for protecting reproductive and sexual freedom. Ruth Gavison has defended the Court's initial reliance on the right to privacy, arguing that expanding the right enunciated in *Griswold* was a more defensible approach than announcing a new departure in equal protection analysis or simply defending abortion in terms of liberty.[44] Her prudential reasons for favoring privacy still hold. Defending privacy has political resonance for conservatives as well as liberals, dovetailing with a conservative agenda that favors less government involvement in providing services and in regulation. Had abortion rights been defended in terms of equality, the decision probably would not have weathered attacks on judicial overreaching and on moral grounds as well as it has with privacy.[45]

Continuing to rely on privacy as the basis for protecting reproductive and sexual choice does not mean, however, that we should uncritically endorse the privacy doctrine. I do not accept the position that privacy rights are so beleaguered that criticizing the doctrine the Court has developed is dangerous. Like Rhonda Copelon, I think that "the way we claim our rights is the foundation for their future realization."[46] Not talking about the problems privacy poses for the abortion funding cases, or the progressive assimilation of family values to privacy doctrine, or the connection between privacy and forms of social privilege, or the political character of the contexts in which choices are made, will not in the long run serve the development of constitutional protections for personal autonomy in matters related to sex and reproduction. What is needed are thoughtful and concrete proposals for making privacy a stronger and more inclusive tool for protecting choice.

For example, many argue that protecting privacy should be accompanied by a strong commitment to equality, so that privacy becomes something more than a privilege of those with means. Dorothy Roberts argues that privacy should be expanded beyond a negative proscription against government control to an affirmative duty "to protect the individual's personhood from degradation and to facilitate the processes of choice and self-determination." She is echoed by Copelon, who argues that privacy is not just a negative liberty, but should be viewed as "integral to charting one's own destiny," to autonomy and choosing who one will be. Peggy Cooper Davis argues that privacy should be central to preserving diversity in various types of families and approaches to raising children.[47] Davis's proposal that privacy be used to protect a variety of forms of intimacy and family life, taken together with Copelon's argument that privacy is integral to choosing who one will be, points toward how we might reconstruct privacy as a way of guaranteeing full citizenship to all.

Justice Blackmun's dissenting opinion in *Bowers v. Hardwick* might be a starting point for a more empowering way to read the struggle for privacy rights. Blackmun cast the issue posed by Michael Hardwick's constitutional challenge to Georgia's sodomy law as asking whether there is a fundamental right for individuals to make decisions that cut to the core of their identity, and whether there are certain places, such as the home, where the individual's privacy interests are especially strong. In Blackmun's view the right to privacy protects both the decision-making and the spatial aspects of privacy; and it does not protect only those relationships and choices that are sanctified by tradition or that the majority regards as uncontroversial and worthy of reinforcement. As Morris Kaplan puts it, for Blackmun the reasons for protecting privacy "have less to do with some calculus of social benefits to be derived from family institutions than 'because they form so central a part of an individual's life.' "[48] Blackmun's argument for respecting privacy parallels the argument I have made, building on Arendt and anthropological philosophers such as Post and Schoeman, for the importance of a protected space where central, constitutive aspects of human life and personality can develop and flourish in private.

Morris Kaplan and Frank Michelman offer political-philosophical justifications for thinking that constitutional protection for privacy "has a legitimate and important place in constitutional adjudication" and in a civic-republican approach to thinking about citizenship and inclusiveness.[49] Their arguments help clarify the affinity between my general arguments for valuing privacy and arguments favoring generous interpretations of protections for privacy in American constitutional law.

Like Blackmun, Kaplan sees respect for privacy as a way of affirming "the centrality of uncoerced individual decision-making in important areas of human activity. In Kantian terms, morality requires recognition of the autonomy of the person. Such recognition implies the right to participate in the ethical life of a society in which each is free to join with others in creating the institutions necessary for pursuing a good life."[50] Recognizing the autonomy of the person means respecting the individual's ability to define her identity independently through intimate sexual relationships with others, her decisions to form a family, have children, and so on. But respect for privacy is not just about respecting a life led in isolation, walled off in one's home. Although Kaplan respects the "domain of intimacy through which mutual personal decisions are not only insulated against interference from government or society but also given a place in the world," he does not see the domestic or intimate sphere as separate from a life built around associations and memberships in various communities. Privacy is protected in order to allow us to decide about issues central to our identity, especially our intimate associations, but also in order to allow us "the positive capacity to create intimate spaces and the social support of personal choices that enable individuals to establish and develop their relationships."[51]

Kaplan's discussion of the associational character of privacy interests, like Ferdinand Schoeman's notion of privacy as a value that allows people to negotiate a variety of social involvements and private spheres rather than one that shields the individual from such interactions, underlines the multiple settings and identities that help define a person. He writes: "In modern societies the individual is situated in a plurality of institutional settings. Thus, one may be a lesbian, a mother, a Jew, a daughter of working class parents, a university teacher, and a psychoanalyst. Such diversity of social roles may subject the individual to conflicting ethical demands which go to the very heart of her personal identity. The major point here is that recognition of the moral personality as socially situated in a plurality of communities leads back to acknowledgement of the centrality of individual choice in the shaping of a life."[52] Privacy is important, therefore, because it helps us develop multifaceted identities, and to create and join communities where we can develop and display different parts of ourselves. On this reading, protecting a person's privacy is central to both her status as a moral agent and her ability to negotiate multiple institutional and social settings. To put this more concretely: the privacy interests of the lesbian mother psychoanalyst extend beyond what she does in her bedroom, to her ability to choose and move freely in various social and institutional networks, and perhaps especially to have friends with whom, and settings in which, she can be open. For Kaplan, the concept of privacy has been in important ways about facilitating associational freedoms from its very inception in *Griswold,* and he argues that this is still how we should understand the role privacy plays in our public life, especially for those seeking the right to express unconventional notions of sexual intimacy.

Michelman offers a rereading of constitutionalism inspired by the political theory of civic republicans which would justify striking down Georgia's sodomy law. He makes a powerful argument about the political significance of privacy based on the centrality of the right to privacy to notions of citizenship, equality, and membership. Like Kaplan, Michelman argues that the roots of respect for privacy are deeper and more generous than the notion of protecting socially condoned forms of intimacy and familial relationships. His argument for the political significance of privacy "involves . . . a definitive decoupling of rights of 'privacy' and 'intimate association' from a certain 'traditional' cult of the family. The argument re-collects the authorities and recasts the tradition along the axes of self-formation and diversity rather than those of dominant social expectation and conformity."[53]

Michelman argues that Georgia's purpose in passing a law criminalizing sodomy—"to brand and punish as criminal the engagement by homosexual partners, but not heterosexual partners, in certain forms of sexual intimacy"—"is deeply suspect under the modern republican commitment to social plurality." This is so, Michelman believes, because attraction to partners of the same sex is not just a passing fancy; instead, "homosexuality has come to signify not just a certain sort of inclination that 'anyone' might feel, but a more personally constitutive and distinctive way, or ways, of being. Homosexuality has come to be experienced, claimed, socially reflected and—if ambiguously—confirmed as an aspect of identity demanding respect." When a law punishes citizens for aspects of their identity that are deeply, inextricably related to who they are, "it seems very likely that [its] effects . . . on persons for whom homosexuality is an aspect of identity [include] denial or impairment of their citizenship, in the broad sense . . . of admission to full and effective participation in the various arenas of public life. It has this effect, in the first place, as a public expression endorsing and reinforcing majoritarian denigration and suppression of homosexual identity." Under a political theory that values equality and social plurality, and maintains that "the renovation of political communities, by inclusion of those who have been excluded, enhances everyone's political freedom," such denigration and exclusion from full citizenship is clearly suspect.[54]

In addition to guaranteeing full citizenship to members of sexual minorities, Michelman believes, privacy is a key political right. It is not incidental to him that a law such as Georgia's "also . . . denies citizenship by violating privacy." For Michelman, privacy is more than simply a curb on state power. It functions as a political right, like property rights, which provides an essential underpinning for the independence and authenticity of the citizen's contribution to the collective determinations of public life.[55]

Michelman's political-theoretical approach to justifying an active judicial reworking of the right to privacy in order to protect the decisions of lesbians, gays, and bisexuals to choose sexually and emotionally satisfying relationships suggests a liberatory understanding of the role privacy plays in preserving intimate life associations and decisions. Of course, privacy is not always liberating in this way; that is why Michelman—and Kaplan and Blackmun—spend so much time distinguishing the conservative approach to privacy as protection for socially ratified "familial attachments" taken by the majority in *Bowers v. Hardwick* from the approach of rooting privacy interests in the core interests involved in the ability to shape one's self or identity free from legally enforced criminal sanctions. But the Blackmun approach to recasting the right to privacy, as developed by Kaplan's and Michelman's theoretically astute defenses of privacy as a political value with the potential to protect personality from social and official coercion, suggests a reading that is consonant with my own deepest inclinations.

So which is correct, the feminist reading of privacy or the reconstructive reading based on privacy's role in defending personality, identity, and full membership in the polity? I think both are. Both the deconstructive feminist approach and the reconstructive gay liberationist approach are important ways of looking at privacy, and capture conflicting but real aspects of what privacy means. We need both kinds of vision: we need to be critical of privacy's shortcomings but also visionary about the uses to which privacy can be put, about the kind of politics we want and the kind of civic privacy value our aspirations recommend.

We also need to remember that outside the courts, discussions of sexual and reproductive choice are not constrained to frame issues in terms of the value or right of privacy, nor should they be. As we come to see when we think about the contexts in which women make reproductive decisions, or when we recognize the inadequacy of recommending the closet as a means for combating homophobia, conceptual languages richer than the language of privacy are crucial for identifying the shared, systemic, public character of the various forms of social power that constrain sexual and reproductive freedom.

Five

The Democratic
Potential of Mothering

I RETURN NOW TO THE PROBLEM, INTRODUCED IN
Chapter 3, of translating issues rooted in intimate life into
perspectives and claims that are politically negotiable. My
discussion wrestles with two related difficulties: the dangers posed to
democratic citizenship by introducing into politics problems and perspectives pertaining to mothering, and those posed by *failing* to do so.

Work in feminist democratic theory has spawned a variety of arguments. Some embrace the notion of participatory politics while rejecting
the exclusion of household life from politics.[1] Others, meanwhile, maintain
that politics is about matters of general and shared concern, and hence
must transcend the perspectives of narrow group interest or care for the
lives of particular loved ones.[2] Here I focus on the debate between those
who argue that women, particularly mothers, have a distinctive moral perspective which can transform public life, and those who argue that feminist
citizens must make explicitly political matters their first concern.[3] Each
side of the debate—the "maternal thinkers" and the "civic feminists"—has
something important to contribute to developing a democratic theory that
encompasses the household. Maternal thinking is right to emphasize the
activity of nurturing as a source of political values and judgment, and civic
feminism rightly insists on the need to transform the private interest, attachment, or insight of the individual mother into claims that are politically negotiable. Yet neither side listens carefully or sympathetically to the
other, so that each misses what is valuable in the other's argument, to the
detriment of our thinking about feminist notions of democratic citizenship.

I review the debate over mothering and citizenship, first addressing the
argument that women as mothers develop a style of thinking about ethical

112

problems and responsibility for nurture which is politically valuable. Then I examine the argument that maternal thinking leads neither to democratic nor to feminist consciousness. I go on to argue that there are two ways mothering can draw women toward citizenship: by giving rise to political activism and participation which transform interest into a broader concern with the processes of participation, and by turning the experiences of the nurturer into a source of the collective values we wish to pursue as a polity.

Maternal Thinking

A number of writers have argued that women have a distinctive mode of thought or set of emotional predilections which they develop as mothers, and that these are particularly worthy or valuable and should inform our political life.[4] What is this mode of thought, sometimes referred to as "maternal thinking"? What attributes, virtues, and distinctive values do mothers learn? Sara Ruddick calls maternal thinking a "discipline" that leads mothers "to ask certain questions rather than others," and to establish "criteria for the truth, adequacy, and relevance of proposed answers. . . . Like any discipline, [a mother's] has *characteristic* errors, temptations, and goals. . . . To describe the capacities, judgments, metaphysical attitudes, and values of maternal thought does not presume maternal achievement. It is to describe a *conception* of achievement, the end to which maternal efforts are directed, conceptions and ends that are different from dominant public ones." In Ruddick's view maternal thought is not just a different set of values or commitments but a different way of thinking altogether: "Out of maternal practices distinctive ways of conceptualizing, ordering, and valuing arise. We *think* differently about what it *means* and what it takes to be 'wonderful,' to be a person, to be real." This way of thinking gives priority to preserving vulnerable life, and honors a moral "style" that makes central the values of humility, resilient good humor, and attentiveness to others.[5]

There is much to be said for the idea that there is a distinctively maternal or feminine approach to thinking about care and relationships, or to assessing matters of moral obligation and fairness. Not only does this notion capture and dignify the experience of many women in a society structured along gender lines, but also, as many have argued, it has the power to transform our public values. Ruddick suggests that politically organized maternal thinkers might be a force for pacifism. Jean Elshtain argues that maternal thinkers who make responsibility to children and families their central commitments could radically reform public values, perhaps even create an "ethical polity" devoted to a politics of compassion and citizen involvement. And Dorothy Dinnerstein argues that women's nurturing, conserving attitude toward life and nature can begin to counteract the destructive impulses of male fascination with technology and domination, which have heretofore directed public life.[6] The notion of a public life committed to "maternal" values such as peace, preserving the world, living in harmony with nature, and nurturing healthy and well-educated children is surely an appealing one.

Under present gendered social arrangements, mothering is a fundamental, constitutive activity for women in a number of senses: because of the ways mother-raised girls and boys resolve issues of attachment and separation;[7] because of the nurture women learn to provide their own children as primary parents; and because of the problems that domestic responsibilities pose for mothers (but not most fathers) who work outside the home. But though the intimate-life experience of being responsible for the care of helpless little human beings probably leads most nurturers to develop capacities for self-restraint, patience, empathy, and responsiveness to others, I am skeptical of arguments that treat women's "monopoly" over child rearing as a given and assert that a specifically *maternal* consciousness could work fundamental changes in our political life.[8] Such arguments are troubling on several grounds: (1) they wrongly assume the distinctively feminine nature of certain values, qualities, or ways of thinking; (2) they overlook differences among women; (3) they uncritically accept the social arrangements that give women in our society responsibility for mothering (thus "allowing" them to become maternal thinkers); and (4) they do not adequately show how maternal values or perspectives can be transformed into political ones, or explain how mothering might teach women to become good citizens. Let us address these points in more detail.

First, Ruddick's and Elshtain's versions of maternal thinking do not question why only women can become, or need become, maternal thinkers. Nor do they help us explore other possible styles of caring for children (e.g., "paternal thinking"),[9] or whether "maternal thinking" is shorthand for the mode of thought that *anyone* responsible for taking care of little ones can, and normally does, learn. That is, this approach to maternal thinking subsumes nurturance to a culturally specific practice of mothering, and wrongly ascribes it only to females.

Assuming the distinctive and ineluctable quality of "maternal" or "feminine" thought is troubling. At least some of the time, women (mothers and nonmothers alike) do not think and feel like nurturers, such as when they move in "male" realms of discourse and activity, but often even in the realm of mothering. There is something odd about the claim that women and men think differently. As the philosopher Jean Grimshaw puts it:

> I wish to resist . . . a view that sees women's moral reasoning, insofar as it may differ from that of men, as context-bound or situational, if these things are understood as sharply opposed to principles or general reasons for action. . . . I suspect that it is sometimes the case, not that women do not act on principles, but that the principles on which they act are not recognised (especially by men) as valid or important ones. . . . I think there are real dangers that a representation of women's moral reasoning based on such a sharp opposition will merely become a shadow of the belief that women perceive and act intuitively, situationally, pragmatically, 'from the heart', and that their processes of *reasoning,* if they exist at all, are nebulous or unfathomable.[10]

In addition to the danger that identifying "female" modes of reasoning will make it easier to dismiss or discount them as not "reasoning" at all, it can also make nurturant values or moral perspectives seem more innate and special than they really are. There are many relationships that are based on nurturance and dependency besides the mother-child one: teacher-student, mentor-protégé, sibling relations, marriage, sexual partnerships, friendship. Surely the point should be that care, nurture, and preservation of relationships are simply part of adulthood or ethical maturity, and ought not to be associated with or defended as part of a specifically *maternal* or feminine kind of thought and practice.

Second, maternal thinking often sounds monolithic, as though the experience of mothering always teaches or evokes the same responses. Furthermore, Elshtain's and Ruddick's descriptions seem to be premised on the experience of white middle-class married women. But, as many critics of essentialism remind us, such generalizations are misleading.[11] Women who are struggling to make a living, single mothers, reluctant mothers, young mothers, mothers of different races or cultures all may have very different notions of what it means to keep a child before the mind's eye.

The third difficulty with work that posits a "woman's voice" is that it often fails to consider that maternal thinking is a mode of thought women have learned in response to oppressive social arrangements.[12] That is, the virtues that theorists such as Elshtain and Ruddick praise women for are virtues they have developed because they have *had* to be responsible for nurture and care in a society that assigns women such work, and that values men's and women's work very differently. Of course, there is much to praise in maternal practice and thinking, much we might wish were more broadly diffused in our society and our public values. But surely mothers can be better nurturers when they are not oppressed, when there is no amalgam of bitterness or regret mixed with the affection they feel toward their children. We make a mistake in valuing maternal thinking without attending to the oppressive social relations that give rise to it, particularly the illusion that only women are responsible for child rearing and that nurturance is only a female virtue or task.

Nor is it likely to be of much use simply to encourage greater respect for "women's" nurturing work and the "unique" ethical perspective to which it gives rise in a society that rewards skilled productive work outside the home but not the humble, repetitive tasks of cleaning, cooking, and caring for children. How can we expect maternal thinking to infuse our public life if we can do no more than urge mothers to act politically as a group on the basis of their "maternal" values and perspectives? Few women, and fewer mothers, are in positions of public power, and few men take responsibility for caring for young children. Under present social conditions, the paths to public power rarely include primary parenting. Changing the world so that men are commonly responsible for raising children and women are commonly responsible for public decision making is the only way we are likely to introduce values of care, maintaining relationships, and preservation into political life.[13]

Finally, advocates of maternal thought say little about how to transform maternal values into political ones, nor do they show mothers how to become active, involved citizens. Ruddick and Elshtain suggest that the "attentive love" a mother feels toward her child can be transformed into a politically significant attitude of concern for *all* children. But they are not very specific in describing how this transformation is to occur, treating it more as a matter of course than a problematic move from particular to general, "mine" to "ours."[14] We might well wonder if the love mothers feel toward their own children *can* be translated into a more diffuse or generalized political sentiment of love or concern for *all* children. As Mary Dietz puts it, if "intimacy, love, and attentiveness are precious things . . . because they are exclusive and so cannot be experienced just anywhere or by just anyone with just any other," they cannot "be made the basis of political action and discourse."[15]

If maternal thinking is supposed to transform our political life, we might well ask what kinds of lessons women, children, and men learn about citizenship from mothering. For example, Dietz argues that mothering is the wrong relationship on which to model citizenship because the relationship between mother and child is nothing like the relationship among citizens: "The special and distinctive aspects of mothering emerge out of a decidedly unequal relationship, even if benign or loving, in which one person is responsible for a given period of time for the care and preservation of another. This is an intimate, exclusive, and particular activity," quite unlike democratic citizenship, which "is collective, inclusive, and generalized" and in which "individuals aim at being equal." Dietz thinks that if women treated other citizens the way they treat their children, the maternal voice in politics would be one that chastens or corrects, not one that treats fellow citizens as equals with whom one deliberates and compromises.[16]

In sum, theorists of maternal thought emphasize nurture as an activity that has moral and political significance and offers an implicit critique of existing public values. But these theorists tend to be uncritical of existing gender arrangements, making a virtue out of female responsibility for child rearing while paying scant attention to men's possible role as nurturers or primary parents. They overlook issues of public power and status, and assume rather than explain the transformation of maternal thought into a political perspective. In so doing, they appear to advocate introducing the attentive love of the mother into the world of citizens and strangers, where it does not belong.

Civic Feminism

Let us turn to the other side of the debate about mothering and democratic citizenship and examine "civic feminist" arguments for protecting political life from the inappropriate attitudes of intimate life.

Mary Dietz is the theorist who has most forthrightly argued the civic feminist position. She roots her discussion of citizenship "with a feminist face" in the Aristotelian notion of politics as the activity in which "human beings can collectively and inclusively relate to one another not as strong over weak, fast over slow, master over apprentice, or mother over child, but as equals who render judgments on matters of shared importance, deliberate over issues of common concern, and act in concert with one another."[17] Dietz powerfully evokes this image of politics as the pursuit of freedom through collective self-determination to show why "maternal consciousness" cannot be a basis for democratic citizenship. Yet one is left wondering just what her citizens are left to talk about, what sorts of issues or concerns are acceptable or appropriate for the collective, inclusive relationship among equals deliberating over issues of common concern.

Even though Dietz's intent is to reject the appropriateness for democratic politics of an untransformed "maternal consciousness," her argument seems at times to slide into a more far-reaching rejection of the notion that maternal interests or perspectives can ever have democratic or feminist potential. For example, she characterizes political activity by mothers as a temporary, periodic attraction to politics based on the interests they have in protecting (their) children. She finds it of little use for cultivating genuine democratic politics, rooted in "commitment to democratic values, participatory citizenship, and egalitarianism" and "the practice . . . of engaging with other citizens in determining and pursuing individual and common interests in relation to the public good."[18]

Although Dietz's examples of Mothers Against Drunk Driving and Mothers of Love Canal may be instances of narrow interest group activity with little promise of generating long-term commitment to democratic politics, they do not take in all the possible ways mothering might be relevant to citizenship or might raise issues important to a democratic polity. Dietz does not consider whether there may be other, better ways to connect the experiences or problems of mothering to politics, but suggests rather that such experiences are always narrow and unpolitical. Thus, she claims that a feminist consciousness rooted in the political situation that mothers have in common with "other women, some of whom are mothers, some of whom are not," is the only basis feminists have for pursuing explicitly political values such as freedom, equality, and community power: "If we are to locate a dimension of women's experience that is unique to us as women, we would do well to look to our history, our organizational styles, and our distinctive modes of political discourse—but not to our role as (potential) mothers. The latter collapses our identity into a single dimension, however nurturing and loving that may be in some possible world."[19]

This is a troubling position. In urging women to find a feminist consciousness based on what all women have in common, and to look to their history, organizational styles, and modes of political discourse, but not to their role as (potential) mothers, Dietz overlooks how often women's organizational styles and their role as mothers have been connected. Women's distinctive approach to political organizing in many cases has had, and continues to have, much to do with their role as mothers. Think, for example, of the social reform movements of the nineteenth and twentieth centuries (urban renewal, temperance, compulsory education, social work), the

movements for making contraception and abortion legal and widely available, and the pro-life movement. Furthermore, one could take her to be
saying that feminists' most promising route to democratic citizenship is to
discover a feminist consciousness based on the experience of women who
are able to lead lives that are most like men's. Although the experience
women have *qua* women (rather than *qua* mothers) may in truth be a
better basis for political participation than the experiences of mothers,
surely this is not what Dietz means.[20] Defending the primacy of political
concerns against the inappropriately intimate perspective of maternal
thinking and the narrow claims of "mothers' interest groups" without trying to find credible, serious ways to connect such perspectives and interests
to civic values leads Dietz to a conclusion that undermines her own vision
of democratic politics.

Because of the way her concern shifts from maternal thinking to mater-
nality per se, her images of feminism and citizenship end up seeming formal and exclusive. She appears to suggest that public or civic notions of
freedom, justice, and community power have nothing to do with one's
private experience in the home or family, and that women's history and
experience of political organizing have nothing to do with their anatomy
or their socially determined responsibility for taking care of children. Like
Hannah Arendt, Dietz wants to bar the private, intimate life of body,
home, and family from politics rather than determine how to bring intimate-life problems into politics in a spirit conducive to democratic citizenship.

Thus, the debate about mothering and citizenship is promising but
incomplete, with the maternal thinkers and the civic feminists failing to
engage each other's arguments or to learn from each other's criticisms. The
maternal thinkers insist that we question the inclusiveness of our political
values and processes, and they present the values of the caring mother as
an antidote to the prevailing goals and values of politics. Dietz, by contrast, argues that maternal thinking simply posits the political importance
of mothers' affection for their children, failing utterly to transform this
intimate attitude into shared civic values of freedom, equality, and community power. Both are right. Supporters of maternal thinking do not
adequately address the problem of transforming private values into public
ones, instead treating as incidental a problem that lies at the very heart of
the argument that the experiences of intimate life have something to teach
us about citizenship. And Dietz seems more interested in consigning the
intimate-realm experiences of the mother to political irrelevance than in

helping mothers articulate their insights and needs in politically appropriate ways.

Translating Intimate-Life Experiences into Political Perspectives

We can use the approaches of both civic feminism and maternal thinking to work on the problem of transforming intimate-life insights into political claims and perspectives. First, let us focus on maternal interest as we explore the challenge of transforming the mother into a citizen. Then we can consider some ways to think about the political significance of maternal thought.

I have referred to arguments grounded in civic feminist concerns about introducing private-life matters into politics in the right spirit. We start here with Hannah Arendt's worries about allowing private matters of the body and the household to enter public life. As we saw in Chapter 3, the problem is not, as Arendt believed, that private concerns inevitably contaminate public discourse and lead to a dilution of distinctively political life; rather, the problem is that those who are stuck in the routine dailiness of household life, or absorbed in the needs of filling empty stomachs, may forget (or may never know) how to act like citizens, and will approach public life in the wrong spirit. This "wrong spirit" can take many forms: one may feel that nothing one does can make a difference, or that the only thing that matters is earning a paycheck and supporting a life of consumption, or that caring for one's own close circle of loved ones is not only an all-consuming task but a morally sufficient end for a human life. So the problem for democratic politics is not how to bar private matters from politics, but how to introduce those matters and the people who care about them to public life in a spirit that is conducive to democratic citizenship.

A variety of "mothers' issues" have been widely recognized as public or political issues, such as the ability to choose whether and when to become a mother, the responsibility women owe to their prospective children, the availability of health care for children and pregnant women, shared responsibility for child rearing, the capacity and willingness of the workplace to accommodate the needs of working parents, the "glass ceiling," and the availability and cost of good day care.[21] The brute fact that many more women, and many more mothers, work than was the case fifteen or twenty years ago accounts for the emergence of "mothers' issues" within the workplace and on the national agenda. Most women work out of economic necessity; they must support themselves or their families or contribute a needed second income.[22]

Although a lot more women are working, there is still a persistent wage gap, with women's earnings averaging only about 70 percent of men's. Because of the rising divorce rate, many more women are supporting a family on these relatively low wages, which means that they often live in conditions of extreme economic hardship.

Although the financial situation of working couples is not as desperate as that of single mothers, research indicates that women take most of the responsibility for domestic work and caring for children.[23] Women's responsibility for this "second shift" is enormously taxing for them, their children, and their relationship with their partner, toward whom they often feel resentment (consider the frenetic pace of such a woman's ordinary day, and how little time she has left over to relax, read, take classes, make friends, exercise, or participate in politics).

Increasingly working mothers are coming to understand these difficulties not as a result of personal inadequacy but in political terms.[24] Instead of blaming themselves or seeing their "private" problems as beyond the scope of effective public action and therefore irremediable, mothers are making connections between private circumstances and notions of justice, as well as to institutional factors that can be changed. The standard assumption that workers have no significant domestic responsibilities puts mothers at a serious disadvantage in the workplace whenever they take time off or interrupt their career to have babies, miss work because of sick children or breakdowns in child care arrangements, or fail to put in the extra hours necessary to demonstrate their dedication to the job. Increasingly, working parents are responding to these pressures by asking employers to recognize and accommodate their needs.[25] Companies have been asked to institute maternity and parental leave, to permit flexible scheduling and job sharing, and to allow for—and treat as a normal part of men's and women's working life—a "parental phase" in which parents of small children would work part-time until their children were in school.[26] The lack of social support for children and families, such as state-supported paid parental leave and day care centers, has also come under attack. Further organized efforts to pressure employers and the government for policies that will accommodate the needs of working parents are sure to be made.

Fine, a civic feminist might respond; working mothers are mobilizing into an effective interest group. But what promise does that hold for transforming interest into a broader concern with participation in the political process, for transforming "groupies" into citizens?[27]

In the process of bringing new needs and demands to the workplace, parents must learn how to talk to bosses, co-workers, and fellow union members in ways that appeal to established language, standards, and values about notions of fairness which are relatively novel. At the same time, they must come to recognize the justice of others' claims as well.[28] Take, for example, the claim that employee disability leaves and benefits should cover pregnant workers who take time off when their children are born. Such a claim might be framed in terms of the desirability of conveying the message that having children is a normal thing to do, which ought to be covered as a predictable period of disability so that employees will not feel that they are being either stigmatized or indulged for becoming parents.

But a collective bargaining unit or fringe benefits committee will have other claims to consider as well. Such a group may be very concerned with issues of affordability as the cost of health and disability insurance continues to climb. They might attempt to draw distinctions between illnesses or disabilities that can be prevented or planned (such as pregnancy) and those that unexpectedly incapacitate workers (such as heart attacks or accidents).[29] They might argue about the desirability of helping older employees with severe or debilitating diseases rather than younger workers, who usually can decide when they want to have children, and can predict and budget for the expenses involved. They may point out that pregnancy is not an illness but a condition that poses little risk to most women's health, and one that is usually welcomed and looked forward to with anticipation.

So the would-be mother approaches her bargaining unit with interests in hand, makes her arguments about why in the name of justice and ideals of sexual equality pregnant employees should receive paid disability leave, and then finds herself confronted with very different arguments about fairness, ones that give weight to issues such as cost and the ability to plan and pay for pregnancy as opposed to other, more permanently disabling conditions. She may feel outnumbered or outranked by older (male) colleagues who are less sympathetic to her problems than to problems more likely to affect them. But she may also learn something about the standards to which members of this community appeal. If cost and efficiency are important considerations, then she may find ways to explain why it is practical for the company to welcome and retain competent female workers through interruptions and periods of low productivity. At the same time, she may press for recognition of the principle of equality for women in the workplace as her way of broadening the community's standards beyond the notion of economic rationality to a more inclusive and generous model of fair play.

The point of the example is that participation in this kind of collective decision making (whether it is about disability benefits or "parental phases") has the potential to help the worker learn how to think like a citizen, to care for political processes and democratic decision making. Of course, this can happen only if her opinion really *does* matter, if she is able to influence policies and decisions that have an important impact on her life. For many working parents, the possibility of getting one's company or one's colleagues to recognize and accommodate their needs gives them a push toward participation with the potential for broader engagement in civic democracy. "Mothers' issues" also have this kind of democratic potential in the sense that many parents are founders of or participants in local grass-roots organizations: cooperative day care centers, playgroups, baby-sitting cooperatives, alternative schools, and the like. Such community-oriented groups, though they clearly do not all address large issues of common concern, have the potential to teach parents some of the skills and satisfactions of political participation.

So far I have been working with the idea that the intimate-realm concerns and perspectives of mothers could be "properly clothed" to go out in public through the activity of political participation and appeals to justice. Now I want to turn from the problem of transforming maternal *interest* into political demands to the problem of translating maternal *thought* into a political perspective and source of knowledge.

The problem of translating maternal thought into a political perspective is at present inextricable from feminist concerns with making a characteristically female moral voice more credible and effective in public life. But the ability to nurture does not belong exclusively to women or mothers, however much our present social and cultural arrangements would have us believe that nurturance is a maternal or feminine quality. We make a mistake and perpetuate stereotypical thinking when we equate the outlook of the nurturer with a specifically *maternal* view; after all, many mothers are not very nurturing, and many fathers are. Rather than treat maternal thinking as a laudable or appropriate aspiration for women, perhaps we should think of it more as a guide to the qualities that women often or characteristically develop and are praised for, but that men tend to develop only in an attenuated or narrowly channeled way (for example, in the notion that a father's "proper" role with his children is to be the disciplinarian, or the idea that men have to look gruff or detached when they express affection toward their children).

Rather than think in terms of translating maternal thinking as it now exists into a political perspective, value, or movement, I propose that we treat men's responsibility for nurturing babies and children, men's capacity to think of specific others, to preserve relationships, and to provide attentive love, as matters for public discussion and goals of political activism.[30] There are two reasons for taking this approach, even though it undermines women's claim to a distinctive moral perspective and contribution to public life. First, treating the responsibility for nurture as a public issue gives us a way to think about, and see connections between, the marginalization of women and "women's work," the injustice and inequality of our gender arrangements, and the existence of a category of human beings who are not held responsible for our earliest and most intense feelings of helplessness, rage, and frustration (as well as for feelings of satisfaction and love).[31] If men shared the responsibility for caring for our helpless young, they too would be the focus of these feelings, and they would begin to develop more fully the capacity to nurture, to care for society's helpless or needy children, and to think about the needs of *particular* children. Relieved of sole responsibility for nurturing, women might then feel able to take on more of the direction of collective life.

Second, if men were responsible for raising children, public institutions (including employers and the government) would have to recognize that the activities of nurturing are both valuable and time-consuming. The refusal to compartmentalize nurturing work by sex would mean that there would no longer be a category of workers who are presumptively free from domestic obligations, and against whom women (at least those who are mothers) measure up as marginal, replaceable, less committed. Employers could no longer ignore the impact of domestic obligations on their employees but would have to accommodate workers' needs for career interruptions, flexible scheduling, and time off to care for sick children or aging parents. Public institutions would be forced to recognize the public value of nurturing as an activity that competes for the time and attention of working people, as well as one that can at its best produce bright, able children who in time will themselves become productive workers and discerning citizens. Political and policy dialogue would be transformed by employees' demands for changes in the workplace to accommodate their domestic responsibilities and by the demands of a broad cross-section of citizens that government provide social services to help families. In turn, men and women who nurture would bring the values of the caring parent into their deliberations about a variety of issues that concern the governance of the workplace, the community, and the nation.

Is it possible to treat shared responsibility for parenting as a matter for public discussion and political activism without unduly intruding into intimate life? I think so, but it is useful to repeat Cynthia Halpern's distinction between appropriate and inappropriate ways to politicize domestic life: "The division of labor in the household is political, but the point is not to institute cadres of diaper-changing and dishwashing police, but to empower women to insist on their own equal importance and value in the allocation of daily tasks and the making of family decisions."[32] Sharing responsibility for parenting would make a radical change from dominant, culturally accepted gender roles. At this point I attempt only to articulate the value of such an approach for children and adults, for transforming practices that make mothers the culpable parents, and for invigorating political participation.

Initial attempts to articulate maternal thought as a source of political regeneration were unconvincing. The theorists assumed that all mothers learn attitudes of concern for the needs of their children—along with humor, patience, and the skills for preserving the constantly frayed web of human life—and that this concern straightforwardly leads mothers into broader concerns with protecting vulnerable children and resources that maintain life and families. They ignored issues of power and the difficulty of legitimizing and valuing nurturing work that is unpaid and disrespected. Given the inadequacy of simply calling for a broad-based political movement predicated on the values of the maternal thinker, how might "maternal" modes of moral reasoning and attentive love be translated into political values or perspectives?

Many feminists criticize central concepts in Western political thought because they generalize from male experience without attending to the experience of women's lives. Feminists have shown how the practices of intimate, domestic life affect how women experience and understand political notions such as consent, obligation, and justice.[33] As we saw in Chapter 1, Western political theory has been attacked for defining intimate life as private and placing it beyond collective attention, criticism, and remedy. Such work shows how overlooking women's private experience can lead the theorist to make mistakes, and points to the importance of the values of intimate life to a more inclusive and accurate understanding of our shared public life. For example, who "we" are and what justice means to "us" cannot be extrapolated from singularly male experiences of autonomy or modes of moral reasoning, since in societies structured along gender lines, women are likely to develop *different* moral sensibilities and conceptions of the self in relation to others.[34]

This sort of criticism can be extended to democratic theory. Theorists of democratic citizenship have emphasized that politics is a realm where people think, talk, and act differently than they do anywhere else: "Man is the animal born to live in the polis," said Aristotle in *The Politics*. Hannah Arendt writes: "A life without speech and without action . . . is literally dead to the world; it has ceased to be a human life because it is no longer lived among men."[35] Sheldon Wolin writes: "The citizen has to decide what to do, not in a setting where each has the same interest as the other, but in one where there are differences that have to be taken into account and, ideally, incorporated into the decision. The citizen, unlike the groupie, has to acquire a perspective of commonality, to think integrally and comprehensively rather than exclusively."[36] Politics is a realm of action where citizens treat one another as equals, make collective decisions about issues of common concern, and strive for freedom. Such a vision of politics is broadly inclusive. Anyone can become a citizen; all that is required is that one come to politics ready to engage in dialogue, to respect others' arguments and claims, and to appeal to shared understandings in making one's own claims. Thus, feminist citizens must pursue explicitly *political* values such as equality, freedom, and community power rather than narrowly maternal concerns and interests.[37]

But where do our shared, public, political values come from? What is the mother-turned-citizen to draw upon? What informs her thinking about justice, equality, community, authority, freedom, power, or for that matter compassion, responsibility, and nurture? It is striking that democratic theorists often treat as unproblematic the content of "our" shared public values, our ability to make arguments and claims that are mutually comprehensible. Even more than this, because of the need to protect politics from inappropriate ways of thinking (expedience, utility, process thinking, preoccupation with one's own children), democratic theorists such as Arendt and Dietz have argued quite forcefully that the household, maternal thinking, and maternal practice have nothing to teach citizens.[38]

Emphasizing the separation and distinctiveness of politics and intimate life can make the democratic theorist seem insensitive to the needs and interests of parents, as well as to the perspectives and values women and men learn in the process of caring for small children. The ways we think in everyday, intimate life about what it means to make a moral decision, to be responsible, to be mature, to be a good parent inform what we mean by justice and fairness, what qualities we respect in our fellow citizens and leaders, maybe even what we expect of ourselves as citizens or participants in politics. Denying that intimate life has anything to teach us about what we take justice or authority to mean seems foolish. These intimate-life insights and perspectives should be not excluded but translated into collective action and purpose.

How this translation might occur is a question of great interest. Recognizing that "mothers" is not a homogeneous category but includes women who raise children in a variety of situations and with a variety of values and family arrangements is an important first step. Attending to the different standards and attitudes mothers develop as they learn to care for their children under circumstances of racism, poverty, immaturity, joblessness, violence, and the absence of others to share the burden of parenting will make the concept of maternal thinking more nuanced, not simply a reflection of the experience of certain middle-class white women as the representative or generic case. (Indeed, one could speak more broadly about an ethic of care and the activities of caring which are not solely the province of mothers or women, a move Joan Tronto makes in *Moral Boundaries,* where she discusses people who care, take care of, care for, give care, and are taken care of, and analyzes why such actions and those who perform them are held in low esteem).

When are the values and attitudes one learns by nurturing *politically* significant? It will not do to assume that such attitudes are *always* political: the moral aspirations of a nurturer do not necessarily imply political values or indeed *any* political involvement. Indeed, we all know mothers who are so busy raising their children that they simply "tune out" politics, finding the tasks of daily life and the responsibilities of caring for their own families all-absorbing.

One provisional answer might be that maternal thinking becomes political when it becomes an impetus for political action or demands for social change. When people take up an issue out of concern for their own children—be it unsafe neighborhoods, the number of children living in poverty in the United States, universal health care or prenatal care, improving schools, or increasing parent representation on school boards— the concern with preserving vulnerable life has become active and the ethical outlook of the nurturing mother has become political.

But the political landscape of the 1990s suggests otherwise. The midterm elections of 1994 pointed to yet another return to the "taxpayer revolt" mentality of the 1980s. Overwhelming support for denying the children of illegal aliens access to public schools and medical treatment was expressed in the vote on Proposition 187 in California. For many, the idea of nurturing *my* children means spending less of my income on taxes to support *other people's* children. Most Americans try to give their own children the best possible chance in life they can, often by moving to a school district where children perform well on standardized tests, teachers are well paid, and schools are safe and well equipped. Public debate on taxes and government spending, and in particular on health care reform, poverty, and welfare reform, is often mean-spirited, as people look out for the welfare of their own household economy while finding ways to avoid compassion or responsibility for the increasing number of children born into poverty.

We might discover a rather different way to think about how the values of a nurturing parent can be transformed into a political consciousness in the imagery of the nation-as-family. Earlier we heard Mary Dietz's objection to the idea that nurturers might learn to think about all children the same way they think about their own children; and certainly the phenomena of white flight, rabid demonstrations against integrating public schools, the taxpayer revolt, and the animus against welfare programs lend weight to Dietz's point. But consider the contrast between social policy in Europe (especially in Scandinavia, but also in France, Britain, and Germany) and the United States. European countries have well-developed welfare states, premised on the idea that people who are in need because they are out of work or have become pregnant or are raising small children have simply fallen on hard times and need temporary assistance to get back on their feet. It could happen to anyone, the people say; welfare recipients ought to be treated with generosity because such misfortunes might befall us or our children someday too.

In the United States the story we tell is not one about the essential likeness of all citizens and the need to take care of those who have fallen on hard times, but a story about "us" and "them." "They" aren't like "us"—hardworking, self-sacrificing, trying to live the American dream of pulling ourselves up by our bootstraps, getting an education, making a better life for our children than we had. "They" are a permanent underclass of poor people who exploit the welfare system, are lazy and improvident, take drugs, are responsible for the enormous increase in violence in our society. "They" don't have decent families, don't care about their children, and are mainly black or brown. We do not need to feel any essential likeness to or sympathy for their situation: it's their fault that they don't want to work hard and make something of themselves. Bad things don't happen to people who are industrious and try hard. That's why "we" aren't like "them."

If we were to take the attitude of a caring parent as a model for thinking about our fellow citizens, our approach to social policy would be more like the European one. When my children are having a hard time at school, I don't automatically assume that they're not working hard enough, or shrug my shoulders and resign myself to having children who don't perform well in school, or scold my kids for being ne'er-do-wells. My reaction is to urge them to spend more time on homework, but also to find out if the teachers are doing enough to explain the material they find confusing, to wonder if they are being picked on by the teacher or other children, to look at the books and see if the lesson is being clearly presented, even sometimes to phone the principal and find out if there is something the school might do to help my children learn better. If we could think about everyone's children as if they were our own, we would not simply blame them for not trying hard enough; we would try to find ways to help them flourish.

Now, of course nobody really thinks of all children the same way they think of their own. But obviously there is a difference between countries where people think of those who are poor or out of work as people like themselves who have simply fallen on hard times and our own country, where a large segment of the population sees poor people as essentially unlike themselves and define their interests (in having more disposable income, in sending their kids to good schools) as at odds with helping the poor. One way to transform the attitudes of the nurturing parent into a political perspective might be to think of families of different classes, races, and ethnicities the same way we think about our own families, to ask how well the system has served them and what they need in order to thrive. It would be an enormous step to move away from thinking in terms of "us" versus "them," away from thinking in terms of narrow self-interest—What will benefit me and my children?—to thinking about the collective good: What will benefit all of us and all of our children?

Another way to transform personal concern with preserving life and being attentive to others' needs into politically negotiable values or claims would be to connect them to the idea of justice.[39] Joan Tronto makes an extended argument for the importance of the ethic of care (which I take here to be an extension of the idea of maternal thinking) to democratic citizenship. She shows that care as a moral and political approach is marginalized: those who take responsibility for caring work are usually low-paid, low-status members of our society: women, people of color, the poor. Bodily functions are considered dirty, and the work of caring for them is likewise considered dirty and low in status. Not only is the work not respected, but also women's private caring duties have much to do with keeping them out of public life.[40] Furthermore, Tronto believes that care is devalued in our society because the bifurcations between morality and politics, public and private, deprive the moral sensibilities of care givers of public importance, making them seem appropriate and valuable only in personal, intimate relationships.

But, Tronto writes, the qualities of attentiveness, responsibility, competence, and responsiveness "need not be restricted to the immediate objects of our care, but can also inform our practices as citizens." If people become more adept at care giving, they will become not only "more caring and more moral people" but also "better citizens in a democracy."[41] Tronto's argument about the political significance of care is by way of justice: in her view, care is not distinct from justice, but requires us to think about justice differently. Taking care seriously pushes us in the direction of thinking of people not as autonomous individuals with abstract rights and responsibilities, but as mutually engaged and interdependent, all of us caring and receiving care at different points in our lives. Tronto insists that "care needs to be connected to a theory of justice and to be relentlessly democratic in its disposition. . . . What would make care democratic is . . . its focus on needs, and on the balance between care-givers and care-receivers." Attending to needs and how well they are met gives us a way to evaluate policies and the consequences of capitalist developments. In her view the fact "that health care is not available for all, and that children are disproportionately represented among the poor, are evidence of profound failures of caring."[42] Care also gives us a way to evaluate the political process, and to judge groups "in terms of the extent to which they are permitted to be care demanders and required to be care providers" so that we can expose "the ways in which the powerful have access to too many resources [and] at the same time . . . provide . . . the powerful with a vision of what they stand to gain in a well-ordered and well-cared-for society."[43]

Tronto understands that ultimately, if one wants to challenge the legitimacy of the existing social order, one must find a way to show people that their being deprived and excluded is wrong. Her attempt to do this by arguing that justice must be concerned with caring and nurturing, and that people must be understood as always involved in relations of care and being cared for, is another model for translating maternal thinking into politically negotiable, and potentially transformative, claims.

The responsibility for nurturing, and especially for raising children, may provide an avenue to political involvement and active citizenship for caregiving women and men. I have proposed several ways in which issues and moral attitudes that grow out of nurturing might be translated into political issues, claims, and perspectives. Interest—whether in making the workplace more responsive to the needs of those with significant domestic responsibilities, or in seeking benefits that will help parents and families—can draw mothers into political involvement, where they may find other reasons to concern themselves with political life. Increasing men's involvement in nurturing would make it easier to politicize "mothers' issues." Thinking about the least advantaged of our society's children as if they were our own could be a way to dispel the "us"–"them" cleavages that pit middle class against poor, white against black, in political debates related to public welfare policies.

This process of translating private to public is crucial because of the need to find political ways of understanding arrangements that otherwise go unquestioned, but produce injustices and inequalities. It is also crucial to transforming attitudes and outlooks that make sense in the context of loving relationships with particular others into perspectives that make sense as ways of thinking about relationships with strangers and fellow citizens, and as ways of turning "maternal woman" into a citizen.

Six

"The Personal Is Political":
The Closet, Identity Politics, and Outing

I N A COUNTRY WITH A LONG TRADITION OF
groups that have been discriminated against and degraded
by the majority—blacks, women, ethnic groups, Native
Americans—transforming the characteristics that have been vilified into
sources of self-esteem and pride, the movement of gays, lesbians, and bisexuals out of the closet is nothing new. Nor is the translation into political
issues of practices once regarded as merely private or social. Think, for
example, of the transition from *Plessy v. Ferguson* (1896), in which the U.S.
Supreme Court held that equality between the races could not be enforced
in "social" settings such as railroad cars, recreational facilities, and schools,
to *Brown v. Board of Education* (1954), which held that intentional racial
segregation in public schools irreparably harmed black children.

In this chapter I explore several issues related to gay identity: the
closet, coming out, gay "ethnic" politics, identity politics, and "outing."
Whereas the focus in Chapter 5 was on possible ways of appropriately
"dressing" maternal thinking to go out in public, here the focus is on inappropriate ways of politicizing private life.

On the Closet and Coming Out

Being gay is different from other stigmatizing conditions such as race,
gender, or age, which are usually immediately apparent in a person.[1] Not
only is gayness often not visible, but also it is made even less apparent by
the working assumption in this society that everyone is heterosexual. In

many or most social situations in mainstream society one is presumed to be straight, and because of this presumption, being "in the closet" is built into the condition of being gay.[2] Add to this the social stigma and disapproval, the danger of being physically attacked, and the legal disadvantage attached to being gay in a heterosexist society, and it is understandable why gay men, lesbians, and bisexuals choose to pass in many situations, even those who most of the time are open about their sexual identity. As Eve Sedgwick puts it:

The deadly elasticity of heterosexist presumption means that, like Wendy in *Peter Pan*, people find new walls springing up around them even as they drowse: every encounter with a new classful of students, to say nothing of a new boss, social worker, loan officer, landlord, doctor, erects new closets. . . . Even an out gay person deals daily with interlocutors about whom she doesn't know whether they know or not; it is equally difficult to guess for any given interlocutor whether, if they did know, the knowledge would seem very important. Nor . . . is it unaccountable that someone who wanted a job, custody or visiting rights, insurance, protection from violence, from "therapy," from distorting stereotype, from insulting scrutiny, from simple insult . . . could deliberately choose to remain in or to reenter the closet in some or all segments of their life. . . . For gay people [the closet] is still the fundamental feature of social life; . . . there can be few gay people, however courageous and forthright by habit, however fortunate in the support of their immediate communities, in whose lives the closet is not still a shaping presence.[3]

"Coming out of the closet" refers to making public information that had previously been kept secret about one's choice of sexual partners or one's affiliation as gay. Sedgwick's image of new closets springing up makes it clear that coming out is a recurrent, never-finished process since all of us are constantly meeting new people, encountering new social and work situations, and thus having to confront over and over again how much of ourselves we wish to reveal.[4]

Coming out is also a recurrent and ongoing process in the sense of being, at least for many, a perpetual struggle, first consciously to recognize and admit to oneself one's same-sex attractions, then to "come out" to a small circle of gay friends and intimates, then straight ones, and gradually to become more comfortable with one's identity as gay until one is "out" even in more difficult contexts, such as in the workplace or with one's parents and other relatives.[5] Depending on what kind of support network exists, how homophobic or accepting is the community where one lives, whether one is married, bisexual, has children, and the like, this can be a slow and difficult struggle. Peter Davies reflects on the ambivalence coming out can cause:

It is usually assumed that the process of disclosure is ever onward and outward: the tendency will be to tell more and more people—and to an extent this is inevitable: you cannot un-tell someone that you are gay. . . . This diffusion process is further assumed to be correlated with the process of individuation: the progressive retreat from living a lie. But it remains an undeniable feature of the society and culture in which we live that disclosure can, in many circumstances, have damaging, indeed disastrous effects: the loss of job, friends, house, family, etc. Thus, for some, indeed many individuals the costs of full disclosure quite heavily outweigh the benefits. Some individuals will, therefore, seek to maintain a partial disclosure over a period of time.[6]

The use of the phrase "coming out" to refer to situations other than being lesbian or gay can help us understand what the term implies. For example, we hear that Magic Johnson "came out" as HIV positive. One can "come out" as an incest survivor or a recovering substance abuser. We even read that "coming out" is a process "relevant for all individuals struggling to define their uniqueness vis-á-vis a society which molds them."[7] In the examples of "coming out" as, say, HIV positive or an incest survivor, the phrase means making public information about oneself that would otherwise not be obvious or likely to be known by casual acquaintances or strangers. Nor is it just any information about oneself that had been hidden, but information that is likely to be viewed as central to one's personality or identity, and as shameful or discreditable, at least by some.[8]

Even more interesting for our thinking about what "coming out" means are examples involving characteristics that are obvious or known. Sedgwick writes: "I recently heard someone on National Public Radio refer to the sixties as the decade when Black people came out of the closet. For that matter, I recently gave an MLA talk purporting to explain how it's possible to come out of the closet as a fat woman."[9] Now, what can it mean to "come out" as black or as fat? After all, these are usually characteristics that are immediately apparent, not ones that are hidden or secret. In this context I think "coming out" means that one takes ownership of the characteristic in question as an important, defining quality about oneself. Being black or being fat is not an inconsequential characteristic that ought to make no difference in how one is treated, as is commonly asserted in naive antiracist discourse; being black or being fat is *central* to who one is. "Black pride" or "fat pride" or "gay pride" is a way of acknowledging and resisting the structures of meaning and power in our society which have made skin color, body shape, and sexual identity important, determining, and sometimes negative qualities.[10]

"Coming out" may also make formal and speakable a piece of information or an aspect of a relationship which has been known or suspected but not acknowledged. Sedgwick frames her ruminations in *Epistemology of the Closet* with such an example:

I think of a man and a woman I know, best friends, who for years canvassed freely the emotional complications of each other's erotic lives—the man's eroticism happening to focus exclusively on men. But it was only after one particular conversational moment, fully a decade into this relationship, that it seemed to either of these friends that permission had been given to the woman to refer to the man, in their conversation together, as *a gay man*. Discussing it much later, both agreed they had felt at the time that this one moment had constituted a clear-cut act of coming out, even in the context of years and years beforehand of exchange predicated on the man's *being* gay.[11]

Sedgwick's examples suggest that coming out is a matter of declaring that the information, even if already visible, known, or suspected, is in fact central to who one is, a focus of one's political commitments, and something that can be acknowledged and talked about.

Coming out is viewed by many as the central political act of the gay liberation movement.[12] It is seen as a way of rejecting the negative valuation of gayness which permeates society at large. Instead of buying into the message that gays are weird, perverse, unnatural, despised, doing something that should be shunned and hidden away, the individual coming out of the closet asserts her identity as lesbian as a defining part of who she is and something she is proud of. Coming out is a way for gays and lesbians to assert their self-respect.[13]

Coming out is important as a collective or public endeavor as well. The argument is often made that if all queer people were to come out, so many straight people who thought that they didn't know anyone who was gay would find they had sons, daughters, sisters, brothers, parents, friends, colleagues, clients, teachers, acquaintances, and so on who were gay that homophobia would become a dead letter. Thus, all are urged to come out in order to do their part in breaking down stereotypes by giving gay America a human face.[14]

Coming out is also viewed as a way of forming and becoming part of a supportive and safe community of "out" lesbians and gay men. For Mark Blasius, by coming out one simultaneously constitutes oneself as a member and constitutes the community to which one belongs. Coming out creates a lesbian and gay ethical and political community, or "ethos." "Coming out is a preeminently *political* experience," says Blasius, one that should be understood as a lifelong process of publicly asserting that one is lesbian or gay, and seeking and producing individual and collective empowerment in the face of "heterosexist domination and homophobic subjection."[15]

So coming out is political in a number of ways: as an act of self-affirmation, as a way of standing up to heterosexism and homophobia, of forcing one's friends, family, and colleagues to confront their homophobia, and of joining and sustaining a community of openly gay people. Coming out is not an easy thing to do; it can be dangerous, and it is almost always risky. For many it is tempting to pass as straight, with most people anyway, for much or all of their lives. Coming out challenges social power and calls into question dominant norms and expectations about sexuality, masculinity, and femininity. Those who come out as gay, lesbian, or bisexual are usually stigmatized and harassed, and often lose the easy acceptance of their peers and the advantages of social practices and laws that reward heterosexual unions and families. They know full well that by coming out, they will become social outcasts, or pariahs in Hannah Arendt's term, and it is this willingness to forgo the comfort of living a lie by passing in order to challenge powerful social norms and institutions that makes coming out an important political act of resistance.[16]

Coming out is facilitated by the existence of an active gay or lesbian community, a supportive environment in which to meet other gay people, work on issues related to sexual identity, and take the risky step of declaring oneself gay in a homophobic society. In turn, the willingness of individuals to come out, to openly declare themselves gay or lesbian and live their lives as such, is what sustains these communities. The community provides a sense of belonging and safety to those who must deal with constant hostility and harassment from straight society.[17] The fundamental basis for community building is the common experience of being gay or lesbian: it is what gives the community a collective sense, as Blasius puts it, of "who we are." Without question, the creation of gay and lesbian communities has been a significant achievement, empowering to many who would otherwise have remained frightened and closeted, or silently suffered harassment and discrimination.

But what visions of politics and what appreciations of privacy are afforded by the politics of community building? Do gay activists need to be careful about *how* they make the personal political? Or about what aspects of the personal they choose to make political? Let us explore the core concern of this chapter, the transition from private to public, personal to political, involved in different approaches to a politics of gay liberation.

Differing Interpretations of "The Personal Is Political"

My study of words related to "public," "private," and "politics" in Chapter 2 underlined the variety and nuance in meanings within this word "family." Confusion or disagreement about the meaning of "politics" is evident in recent work on gay and lesbian community building. Let us now consider several different senses of "political" by looking at various interpretations of the phrase "The personal is political." We shall find that it encompasses the proposition that gays and lesbians develop an "ethnic" identity to become effective competitors in interest groups politics; the notion of "identity politics" as a strategy for community building to protect against the oppressive power of the majority as well as divergent practices or beliefs *within* the community; the hardball politics of "outing"; and a civic notion of politics as deliberation among citizens who are equals but not necessarily friends or compatriots, who come to public life with different perspectives, needs, and interests, and who must appeal to one another's standards and power to arrive at actions and policies.

Gay "Ethnic" Politics

A plausible and frequently used notion of politics is that of interest group competition. Working from this model, Steven Epstein proposes that gays and lesbians develop an "ethnic" consciousness similar to that of racial and ethnic minority groups in the United States. He believes that gay and lesbian identities have emerged which function much like ethnic identities, giving the gay community a sense of geographic location, pride, and, in some urban communities, local political power:

> By the late 1970s . . . the "ethnic" self-understanding truly seemed to correspond to the reality of the burgeoning gay male communities, which had become, at least in New York and San Francisco, wholly contained cities-within-cities. . . . While lesbian communities were neither as visible nor as territorially based, they, too, provided a variety of cultural supports and institutions, fostering a sense of minority-group identity that was furthered by separatist tendencies. Little wonder, then, that lesbians and gay men began to be seen as, and to think of themselves as, almost a distinct type of being, on an ontological par with "Irish-Americans" or "Japanese-Americans."[18]

Epstein sees many advantages to thinking of one's membership in the gay or lesbian community as a kind of ethnic identity. It permits gay people to organize effectively in a society where interest group competition and civil rights struggles have a long history. And it allows gays and lesbians, like racial and ethnic groups, to tap into traditional American values such as equality, fairness, and freedom from persecution. In addition, the emergence of gay neighborhoods has made gay people a force in urban political decision making; and the gay liberation movement, like the earlier movement for racial equality, has created a positive identity for lesbians and gay men and redefined "legitimate sexual and affectional possibilities."[19]

These are important claims. Thinking of themselves as a minority group struggling to redefine the meaning of sexual identity and working for fairness and equality, as blacks and other minority groups in the United States have done, is clearly a powerful and empowering model of politics for gay activists. But the pluralist model of politics also raises problems for transcending the perspective of narrow self-interest which moves people to coalesce as a group in the first place, as Epstein acknowledges: "There are a number of questions that can be raised, from a progressive standpoint, about the political manifestations of 'ethnicity.' It would be unfortunate to reduce the politics of gay liberation to nothing more than the self-interested actions of an interest group, in competition with other such groups for various resources; such a model would imply that gays have no interests in common with other oppressed groups, and would almost entirely abandon any notion of a broader role for the gay movement in radical politics."[20] Thinking about politics in terms of "what's in it for me" is a natural, even typical approach to political involvement in the United States, but not one that seems to hold much promise for sustaining a lasting commitment to political participation. After I get what I want, why should I stick around to debate and decide *your* issues?

As we saw in Chapter 5, participating in political life may help transform a narrowly self-interested utility-maximizer into a citizen. Hanna Pitkin describes the transformative potential of participation:

The . . . outlook [expediency] characterizes us when we come to politics with our private interest firmly in hand, seeking by any means necessary to get as much as we can out of the system. It is a common condition, for the private is immediately visible in our daily lives and face-to-face relationships. But actual participation in political action, deliberation, and conflict may make us aware of our more remote and indirect connections with others, the long-range and large-scale significance of what we want and are doing. Drawn into public life by personal need, fear, ambition or interest, we are there forced to acknowledge the power of others and appeal to their standards, even as we try to get them to acknowledge our power and standards. We are forced to find or create a common language of purposes and aspirations, not merely to clothe our private outlook in public disguise, but to become aware ourselves of its public meaning. We are forced, as Joseph Tussman has put it, to transform "I want" into "I am entitled to," a claim that becomes negotiable by public standards.[21]

Perhaps an interest-based politics of "ethnic" identity holds promise for bringing gays and lesbians into politics in pursuit of their interests, where they may then find themselves transformed into citizens with a stake in larger debates about justice and the standards that should be used to judge different claims. Or perhaps in some cities relatively well off gay men will lobby for their interests on the model of interest group pluralism, without any lasting commitment to political life.

Identity Politics

Some historians of the gay liberation movement use the phrase "The personal is political" to talk about building a communal political consciousness out of shared personal experiences. Thus, Jeffrey Escoffier writes:

In the early stages of creating a collective subjectivity, politically mobilized homosexuals . . . adopted norms and codes of conduct that served as "recipes for an appropriate attitude regarding the self." These norms, often articulated in opposition to homophobia, provided a platform for politics and social criticism. But they also addressed the personal distress and thematized the experience of humiliation that homosexuals had suffered. Thus the personal became the political. . . . The mobilization of homosexuals as collective subjects emphasized our *shared* experiences of oppression. It therefore was a militant affirmation of all that is the same among us.[22]

The "militant affirmation of all that is the same among us" has been a motif for various identity-based political movements. Here I explore identity politics among lesbian feminists, drawing on Shane Phelan's work. It should be noted that lesbian feminists are simply an example of a broader phenomenon. Similar pressures exist in many identity-based political movements, not only among lesbian feminists, and not in the same way now as ten years ago even among lesbians.

From the point of view of lesbian feminist community building, making a primary commitment to women is fundamentally a political act. Lesbians are the vanguard of the women's movement because they choose women for lovers rather than consorting with the male "enemy."[23] Phelan describes this position: "The personal is political, and in fact the most personal is the most political; if we engage in activism outside the home, even outside the bedroom, and then go to bed with a man, we will lose what we have fought for. The bedrock of women's oppression is heterosexuality. . . . By sleeping with women, lesbians express their commitment to a world that values women, and, conversely, heterosexual women reveal themselves as torn, half-hearted victims not entirely to be trusted. One's body and its desires become a more reliable guide to one's loyalties than words or public deeds."[24]

The argument that heterosexual women are traitors to the feminist cause because of their sexual involvement with men, and the assertion of a special political virtue that comes from being lesbian, raise important questions: How minutely should citizens be able to inquire into one another's private lives? Are there areas of life that should be shielded from public knowledge? What kinds of private actions or commitments have political relevance, and what kinds do not?

In general, I believe that we should shield intimate life from public knowledge, and we should not treat one another's intimate lives as matters of public or political significance unless there is special reason to do so—for example, because a person's private life sheds light on his or her character as a public leader, or because there is reason to think that someone is being hurt or exploited. There are three problems that arise when intimate life is open to public scrutiny: the problem of majorities coercing "deviant" minorities; the incompatibility of politics and exclusivity; and the problem of reducing people to their sexual identity.

As to the first problem, in her book *Identity Politics* Shane Phelan shows how lesbian feminists have made intimate and sexual attachments and commitments a basis for excluding lesbian sadomasochists (and others) from the lesbian community. Given lesbian feminism's premise that one's intimate and sexual commitments are a guide to one's political convictions, and the general encouragement of openness about one's choice of sexual partner and sexual practices, it is not surprising that lesbian sadomasochists were self-reflective and open about declaring and explaining their sexual practices. This openness generated a major debate within the lesbian community around the question, "Is lesbian sadomasochism consistent with feminism?" Rather than arguing for tolerance and respect for diversity, "mainstream" lesbian feminists created a hierarchy of sexual behavior, with long-term monogamous relationships at the top, a belief that "real women don't want weird sex," and an aversion to fantasy, power differentials, and role playing.[25] This new orthodoxy was used to argue that sadomasochism was not feminist.

This debate within the lesbian community is instructive. Making the personal political became a way of defining the lesbian feminist community

and excluding certain groups—bisexuals, heterosexuals, S/M lesbians—
with profoundly coercive and conformist results:

> Within an embattled atmosphere, these women simply cannot afford to appreciate
> diversity or any politics that assumes it. Appeals for the recognition of differences
> among women—whether they be differences of class, race, sexual preference, or
> any other—are translated in this context into threats against a movement, elements
> that would splinter and destroy the true, the central, the most important unity. . . .
> [T]he inability . . . to account for irreducible multiplicity among women, leads
> only to political isolation and individual conformism. The threat of community
> expulsion and withdrawal of validation serves to keep lesbians in place just as surely
> as does the charge of pathology.[26]

Ironically, the "tyranny of transparency," a phrase used to describe the
pressure for self-revelation and openness about intimate life in conjunction
with threats of excommunication if one's commitments or practices fail to
meet the community's standards, parallels the exclusion and medicalization
of homosexuality by heterosexual society. The danger of making intimate-
life commitments and attachments the basis for political acceptance is that
a person may be relegated to one of the "deviant" groups and become the
target of exclusion, hostility, or persecution at the hands of the majority.
Since none of us can be certain that our intimate lives would pass muster
according to the standards of mainstream society, the lesbian community,
or other conceivable future political communities, it is better not to submit
our intimate lives to such searching scrutiny.[27]

In terms of the second problem—the incompatibility of politics and
exclusivity—the argument that one's intimate-life affiliations are an indica-
tion of one's political commitments is troubling because pressures to conform to particular practices or choices of sexual partner flatten out the
diversity that distinguishes political life. At its best, citizenship is an inclusive relationship that draws together members of a society in deciding the
largest, most important issues they face as a collectivity. Given this broadly
inclusive relationship, it is incumbent on us as citizens to recognize that
there are some questions we should not ask.

What one thinks about the private choices and practices of people one
chooses for *friends* is one matter. If I would not feel comfortable with
homophobes, fundamentalists, bigots, or other people with whom I do
not agree or whose lifestyle I do not like, I would not choose those people
to be my friends. But *citizens* relate to one another in a less personal, more
distant way, as members of a broader political community that deliberates
about and acts on matters of common concern. Politics takes place among

citizens, some of whom we like and agree with, some of whom we do not, not among intimates or fellow believers. Plurality—the existence of a multiplicity of views and ideas, priorities and commitments—is part of what makes political life possible. Insisting that one's intimate sexual or emotional commitment to a same-sex partner is a *political* commitment exerts tremendous pressure on people to conform to the mores of the community, and undermines the diversity that is the distinctive quality of political life.

Third, the argument that being a lesbian is a political act not only flattens out the divisions and differences that mark political life but also tends to flatten the *individual's* identity into one dimension, treating her choice of sexual partner as her *defining* political trait. This is problematic not only in the senses I have just explored of exposing the individual to normalizing pressures on her intimate expression and failing to respect the diversity of political life, but also in the sense that it does not do justice to what a person is.

Of course, gay people are likely to think that issues related to sexuality are important. Thus, one may favor laws and ordinances that prevent discrimination on the basis of sexual orientation, or that prohibit denying health insurance benefits to people with AIDS, or that make sexual orientation irrelevant in child custody proceedings. One may vote for or against a particular candidate because of his or her position on gay rights. In a sense this is true for all of us: we are all led to politics by our tangible stake in the decisions the polity makes.

But the slogan, and much gay and lesbian political discourse, makes it sound as if one's sexual choices are determinative of one's political position, indeed, as if one's sexual identity *were* one's identity as a citizen and as a person. That clearly is not true: people have many different identities and affiliations, including their sexual ones. A woman can be lesbian, a marathoner, a mother, an author of controversial articles in scientific journals, and a staunch Republican. As Jeffrey Escoffier puts it: "Everyone's identity exists at the nexus of a web of opposing, contradictory, or merely different group affiliations and personal commitments."[28]

Jeb Rubenfeld makes an even more telling criticism, arguing that it is not just that sexual identity competes and interacts with other identities and commitments, but that it may simply not be central to one's self-definition: "In the very concept of a homosexual identity there is something potentially disserving—if not disrespectful—to the cause advocated. . . . Those who engage in homosexual sex may or may not perceive themselves as bearing a 'homosexual identity.' Their homosexual relations may be a pleasure they take or an intimacy they value without constituting . . . something definitive of their character."[29] "The personal is political" when applied to gay issues supposes that choice of sexual partner is constitutive of the person and her politics, which is not always the case.

In sum, making one's intimate and sexual affiliations a litmus test for one's political commitments is invasive, for making whom we love and what we do in bed matters for public inquiry and political membership constrains our openness in intimate matters that need to be uninhibited, hidden from public view and protected from censure. Furthermore, there are many ways for a woman to show her "commitment to a world that values women" besides sleeping with other women. Surely one's public words and deeds are a better guide to one's politics than one's body and its desires. Making intimate-life affiliations a basis for community membership invites (indeed, requires) conformity and exclusivity, and hence endangers the diversity that is a hallmark of political life. Finally, sexual identity is one aspect, and not always the most important one, of a person's whole self.

According to Shane Phelan's description of highly polarized and moralistic issues which may not be typical of more ordinary disputes and disagreements, identity politics at its most embattled, as in the debates within the lesbian feminist community over the anti-pornography movement and S/M, seems to be about maintaining a clear definition of the community and protecting its boundaries from practices and factions that step outside accepted notions of feminism and lesbianism. "Politics" in this sense has to do with infighting—us versus them, friends versus enemies, insiders versus outsiders—as one would use the adjective *political* to describe an especially acrimonious dispute or decision within an organization.

Insofar as identity politics has to do with defining and maintaining a politically pure community, there is little resemblance between this notion of politics and a broader, more inclusive notion of politics as citizen participation. In fact, when the personal is "political" in the sense of defining a tightly closed community, it is almost the opposite of "political" in the sense of involvement in collective decision making by citizens of diverse backgrounds and interests who negotiate their differences and treat one another as equals.[30]

Policing the Community: The "Outing" Controversy

Central to the argument for outing—the practice of making public the sexual orientation of a lesbian or gay man without her or his consent—is a revaluation of the closet. For the homophile groups of the 1950s and

1960s, and for many mainstream gay rights activists now, protecting the privacy rights of gays, and respecting the decision to keep one's homosexuality private, were and are essential strategies. The split mirrors the one we saw in my discussion of *Bowers v. Hardwick* in Chapter 4, in which some commentators oppose fighting for constitutional protections for the privacy to choose one's intimate sexual associations, while others think that recognition of such a right would be an important victory in the movement toward equal rights and respect for gays. Advocates of outing such as Michelangelo Signorile, Gabriel Rotello, and Richard Mohr turn the value of the closet upside down, arguing that the closet, reinforced by mainstream heterosexual society, is a source of pain and oppression, and should be dismantled rather than protected. Signorile writes: "Within the gay community, outing helped reshape the definition of the closet. Previously, the closet was seen by many as a place people had a 'right' to be—a safe, comfortable place where everyone had to stay. . . . But outing focused attention on the closet and what a horrible, pitiful place the closet is. Outing demands that everyone come out, and defines the closeted—especially those with power—as cowards who are stalling progress at a critical time. With outing, the tables have turned completely: It is now an embarrassment to be *in* the closet."[31] The outers' view is that the closet is shameful and deforming because it reinforces heterosexist norms and insists on self-contempt, hiding, and secrecy for gay men and women.[32] The point of gay liberation is to reject the hegemony of heterosexual values and to assert homosexuality as an identity equal to that of heterosexuality. For these writers and activists, coming out of the closet and outing famous and powerful closeted gays and lesbians are actions essential to affirming a positive identity as gay by refusing to hide any longer or to be complicit in anyone else's decision to hide.[33]

Advocates of outing often draw parallels between gays, lesbians, and bisexuals and other stigmatized groups who refuse any longer to engage or assist in the hypocrisy of passing. Gabriel Rotello writes: "We live in an anti-Semitic and a racist society. There are very real penalties for being Jewish or Black. Yet it's inconceivable that Jews or Blacks would insist that their most successful members have an inherent right to actively lie, decry their own kind and pass for Gentile or white. It's even more inconceivable that those minorities would demand that the press has a moral obligation to respect and reprint such lies. Yet that is exactly what gays opposed to outing are arguing."[34] Similarly, Signorile argues that our society is in the process of accepting homosexuality as ordinary newsworthy information, rather than something so taboo that it cannot be mentioned, in much the same way that drug abuse, alcoholism, extramarital affairs, and cancer—all of which were considered off-limits thirty or forty years ago—are now openly discussed.[35]

Advocates of outing are also making broader conceptual arguments about the nature and scope of privacy. Signorile asks: "Is being gay or lesbian a 'private' issue in this country . . . when so many millions of younger, more liberated Americans see their homosexuality as no different from such 'public' issues as race, gender, and ethnicity? If, as we've been saying all along, being gay is not about sex acts or about what we do in our bedrooms but is a much larger matter regarding identity and culture and community, then how can the mere fact of being gay be private? How can being gay be private when being *straight* isn't? Sex is private. But by outing we do not discuss anyone's sex life. We only say they're gay."[36] Thus, even though what one does in the bedroom is private, a person's sexual preference is not private information, any more than one's marital status. Drawing on the extensive literature articulating and defending privacy rights with regard to abortion and gay sex, Richard Mohr argues that the right to privacy does not obligate third parties to respect the secrecy of information about one's choice of sexual partners. Indeed, he believes that requiring other gay people to keep the secret of one's identity as gay is degrading and reduces them "to the level of abjection dictated for gays by the dominant culture." Mohr distinguishes between privacy and secrecy, arguing that privacy is not at stake in protecting information about one's sexual orientation, only the secrecy of this information. And, he says, we do not recognize any "right to secrecy."[37]

Some who defend outing argue that the gay community must be able to defend itself from closeted homosexuals who voice or pursue homophobic ideas or policies, or who are in a position of institutional or public importance where they could resist such ideas and policies but do not.[38] Others argue that outing is a way to deal with the "free rider" problem, by forcing those closeted gays and lesbians to come out who have benefited from the struggles and risks undertaken by those who are already out.[39] Many advocates of outing argue that it can provide positive role models for young gays and an effective way to further the gay liberation movement by increasing its visibility and pushing gays and lesbians in positions of power to pursue pro-gay policies and goals.[40]

The best arguments for outing—those which suggest that the closet is an institution premised on fear and self-hatred; which portray gay sexual orientation as a matter of identity, culture, and community rather than private acts performed in the bedroom; and which draw analogies between passing as straight and passing as Gentile or white—appeal to the individu-al's courage and dignity. Other arguments have a more pragmatic or tacti-cal cast: outing is justified because it can provide role models for young gays; because, even though it may cause some pain, it can accomplish change far more quickly and effectively than gentler reformist strategies; and because it can goad or intimidate closeted gays and lesbians in posi-tions of power into opposing homophobic policies. As with "identity poli-tics," here the personal is political in the sense of expressing a concern with forging a community and policing its boundaries. It is also political in a tough-minded, ends-justify-the-means sense: outers are playing hardball politics, using in-your-face tactics to further the goals of the community and the movement.

Like lesbian community building, outing raises important questions about privacy and politics: What counts as private? Is privacy ever some-thing that should be respected and protected? Have the claims of closeted lesbians and gays to privacy become politically reactionary or counterpro-ductive? Are the notions of politics behind outing consistent with plurality and democratic notions of citizen participation?

To answer these questions, it may be useful to think back to the discus-sion in Chapter 2 of the etymology and ordinary use of the words *public* and *private*. Recall that *private* comes from the Latin word *privare*, mean-ing to bereave, deprive, dispossess; the past principle *privatus* means with-drawn from public life, deprived of office, peculiar to oneself. Yet most of the time in contemporary American English, *private* has a protective, ex-clusive feel: for example, we often describe as "private" places or events one cannot visit or attend without an invitation, information or personal decisions that are nobody else's business, or property that is owned and managed in the interest of the owner.

Keeping in mind the privative and protective strands, both of which inform what we mean when we say that something is "private," helps us understand the concept of privacy itself. Even though we most commonly use "private" to talk about controlling access (to certain places, to informa-tion about outselves), our privacy is not always empowering or protective. Keeping something private—our preference for same-sex partners, for ex-ample—may keep others from finding out about something we do not want them to know. But it may also make it more difficult for us to claim that the ability to choose sexual partners freely is a matter of legitimate public and political concern. Privacy is protective, but it can also *deprive* issues of public significance. Outing plays on this tension. Activists argue that homosexuality is much more widespread, especially among the respected and powerful, than most people realize, and that forcing closeted gays to come out will force the public to take gay rights issues seriously. But in the drive to gain public recognition for the gay community and gay rights issues, outing neglects the importance of the protective sense of privacy.

Recall the distinction in our language between *making* something public and *keeping* something private. The *keep* expressions suggest that we view the privateness of the information as something that must be protected or guarded from intrusion or scrutiny. We do not talk about *making* something private. Once the secret is out, it cannot be made private again (though it may be hushed up); we cannot recapture the safe, hidden quality our language suggests when we talk about *keeping* something private. Again, our language suggests important insights. Privacy is valuable and fragile; it must be preserved, guarded, and kept, and it cannot be restored once lost. It suggests that privacy is not always the enemy of authenticity but, by hiding the self, may protect and nurture what is most authentic.

Advocates of outing give too little respect to the interest in being able to control information about oneself. The closet is discernibly related to recognized privacy interests in protecting information about oneself, and in protecting what goes on in settings where one has a legitimate expectation of privacy, such as the home or the bedroom. Much of the point of privacy as control over information about oneself is to prevent discreditable or embarrassing facts about oneself from becoming known to others—whether having been an incest or rape victim, having been arrested for shoplifting as a teenager, or having had an abortion.[41] Such protection is essential to the spontaneity, intimacy, intellectual and emotional curiosity, and exploration which can only flourish outside the glare of public life, in the absence of unwanted intrusions.

Being in the closet is related to these privacy interests in controlling information about oneself and controlling access to places where one rightfully expects to be left alone. The closet is an instance of retaining control over such information: it is a matter of hiding a part of one's self—one's sexual identity—from other people because one is afraid of losing the respect of one's associates, being ridiculed, being hated, losing friends, or losing one's job. If anything, there is an even greater interest in protecting the privacy of one's identity as gay than there is for other kinds of personal information which are less coded as shameful or likely to give rise to discrimination.

Arguments that the sexual orientation of closeted gays is not private but secret, or that only the actual sexual acts one performs are private, trivialize the importance of respecting the intimacy of human sexuality and of controlling how one is perceived in the world, especially when the information in question is likely to be viewed as discreditable.[42] For example, Mohr argues that although "who one marries is a private matter, . . . it is virtually never a secret matter." Since such information is usually known and acknowledged, Mohr argues that a gay person who tries to be continuously closeted is "morally abnormal," like a married person who doesn't acknowledge the fact that he is married.[43]

The analogy here between being married and being gay is strained. First, one may wish to hide one's marital status more often than Mohr suggests. For example, a married man might want to keep that information quiet when he tries to pick up a woman at a bar, or a woman might not want to let a prospective employer know she is married for fear she will hurt her chances of being hired. Although it is usual for people to know if one is married, it is telling that the circumstances where it makes sense to talk about protecting the privacy of that information are ones where being married would be viewed with disfavor.

Second, there is a world of difference in this society telling someone that you're married and telling them that you're gay. Being married is socially condoned, and rarely results in discrimination or disadvantage, whereas being gay is socially condemned and almost always results in discrimination and disadvantage. Privacy does not mean much if it means that one cannot keep private information that is likely to lead to disapproval or discrimination. Characterizing the interest in keeping one's identity as homosexual quiet as "secrecy" rather than "privacy" strikes me as disingenuous, and worse, as premised on the very notion Mohr wishes to reject: that being gay is shameful and discreditable.

Mohr also argues that asserting a privacy right against outing means that the individual must view herself or himself "as properly, in the nature of things, disgusting for being gay."[44] In a homophobic society, protecting the privacy of one's sexual identity is based on a calculation about what one thinks *other* people will think, not on one's own acceptance of the negative valuation others give to the fact that one is gay. There is no necessary connection between recognizing that being known as gay will be viewed with disapprobation and may well result in concrete harms and losses, and believing and accepting anti-gay stereotypes oneself, in essence hating oneself for being gay.[45] Having said this, I think Mohr is right to argue that there is no right to privacy enforceable against a third party which can force that person to keep quiet about one's sexual preference. There is, however, a widespread norm of respecting the "closets" or privacy of other gay people, and this is what Mohr and Signorile and others are arguing against.[46]

Many critics of outing argue that it is coercive and likely to result in harm to the person who is outed.[47] Hunter Madsen points out that "when you take it upon yourself to force others out of the closet you may wreak havoc in unintended ways. . . . Your intentions may be good, but your timing atrocious. Your highhanded intervention might expose them to real hardships and discrimination that they should have had a chance to weigh for themselves—keeping in mind, after all, that coming out isn't *everything* in life."[48] For example, outing may result in closeted gays or lesbians becoming estranged from their children, friends, or family, or losing their jobs, custody battles, or insurance. It may make them targets of homophobic hostility or attack. The response Signorile and others make—that such consequences are the fault not of the outers but of homophobic institutions and practices—is disingenous and dangerous. As C. Carr puts it: "By the twisted logic he often applies in his *OutWeek* column, Signorile has insisted that he doesn't ruin careers; homophobia and straight people do that. In other words, 'I just push 'em in front of the truck. The *truck* hits 'em.' "[49]

In addition to posing ethical questions about using homophobia to coerce or punish powerful closeted gays, forcing closet cases out of the closet does not accomplish that same thing as coming out on their own would. Recall my earlier discussion of coming out as black or as a fat woman. "Coming out" about such obvious, visible characteristics, I suggested, means that one is consciously owning one's identity as black or fat, positioning oneself as a person shaped by and aware of structures of power and meaning that have made skin color and body size crucial characteristics in this society. Mark Blasius draws on this understanding of coming out when he distinguishes between the conscious decision to come out of the closet, and being outed as gay: "As a process of becoming, one does not come out passively or accidentally. Thus one can never really be 'outed' by another (except in the very narrow sense of exposing sexual behavior that had been kept secret). . . . A lesbian and gay community . . . cannot be *produced* through outing."[50] As with the examples of coming out as black or fat, even though it may be publicly known that one is gay, this is not the same thing as claiming one's gayness as an essential part of oneself.[51] By the same token, forcing gays out of the closet is no way to provide young gays with positive role models. As E. J. Graff puts it: "Who wants public role models who are whining, wailing, and pulling their underwear back up as they try to crawl back into the closet? . . . If we want to show our community as gay and proud, we need public figures who are gay and proud. . . . We need to coax, not kick, them from the closet. And we do just that by building a strong, vocal, and supportive gay and lesbian community."[52]

Arguments for outing, like arguments for lesbian feminism, posit a fundamental likeness that unites all gay and lesbian people into "the gay community," ignoring or discrediting the variety of gay experience. The experience of being gay in a large urban community with a sizable, visible gay community is different from being gay in a small town with virtually no "out" community. Being lesbian is different from being gay; being exclusively lesbian or gay is different from being bisexual; leading a gay life without children is different from leading a gay life with them. As with lesbian feminism, there is a danger here of flattening personal identity and politics into one dimension, that of sexual identity, instead of acknowledging and respecting the diverse ways of being gay and the different roles gayness can play in a person's life.[53]

Fran Lebowitz explains what she finds objectionable about this tendency to make the gay community seem more homogenous than it really is:

[Interviewer:] You've said that you don't believe there's such a thing as the gay community or the heterosexual community per se.

[Lebowitz:] I think it's a very simpleminded and stupid way to divide people. I don't think that the fact of someone's sexuality necessarily gives him things in common with other people of that sexuality other than sexuality. People are a little more various than that.[54]

Carr, too, cherishes the variety of the "gay community," and criticizes what she sees as the outers' authoritarian mindset: "The more who *do* come out, the better. But I don't want to be told how to be gay. . . . I find . . . most upsetting . . . the idea that there are authorities (mostly male) who know what's best for all of us, who are qualified to tell us how to present outselves to the world and how to express our sexuality."[55]

In my view coming out is a highly variable experience, with different risks and meanings in different people's lives. Asserting that coming out is the primary goal and strategy of the gay liberation movement, and outing those powerful lesbians and gay men who do not come out on their own, seem to fly in the face of the experience of coming out of the closet as Eve Sedgwick describes it, in which "every encounter with a new classful of students . . . a new boss, social worker, loan officer, landlord, doctor, erects new closets." Except (possibly) for the famous, coming out is not a one-time act but a circumstantial decision which must be made over and over again. Outing robs the individual of the ability to decide how to present herself in different situations where she is the one best able to appreciate the impact of her decision.

In short, the outing controversy reflects the tension in our language between the "privacy" that deprives problems of public, political recognition and the senses of "privacy" that are connected to our ability to control information about our intimate selves. Advocates of outing believe that making public the sexual identities of powerful closeted gays and lesbians is an effective way to push for political changes that will help gays and lesbians avoid discrimination and feel normal and accepted. They redefine the closet, attacking it as a metaphor for hiding and shame rather than seeing it in terms of claims of privacy which preserve the individual's control over his identity and protect him from social opprobrium. Although outing gets at the problem of gay issues' being deprived of public status, it fosters a notion of the political that resembles a cross between the idea of identity policies and that of politics as ruthlessness. Outing does not respect intimacy, and pays little regard to the individual's ability to control harmful information or to the importance of being able to decide on one's own when and to whom to come out. Outing can have punitive consequences, but, more essentially, erases and ignores differences among gay people.

In this section I have examined several interpretations of the phrase "The personal is political," premised on varying understandings of "political." One sense of the term is that in which gays are seen as an effective constituency in interest group politics, where political involvement is usually brief and aimed at achieving the group's goals. A broader and more lasting commitment to the political process may be possible if political participation helps make the interest-seeker aware of his or her connection with others and of the long-range and large-scale significance of the community's public actions.

In the identity politics interpretation of "The personal is political," whom one chooses for a sexual partner is a decisive statement about one's politics. Here the notion of "political" has to do with creating and protecting a community based on lesbian feminism. Such an identity politics is defensive and exclusive, however; it undermines pluralism and compresses identity and politics alike into the single dimension of sexuality. It thus poses problems for a democratic politics of citizen participation, in which people relate as equals and have widely varying opinions, viewpoints, and sexual practices.

Outing makes public information that closeted gays, lesbians, and bi-sexuals may wish to hide. Its aim is to bolster the visibility and clout of the gay community; but, like lesbian identity politics, it presumes a more homogeneous gay community than in fact exists, and exposes gay men and women as such, rather than respecting the many reasons they may have for choosing not to reveal their sexual orientation. Outing thus taps into the notion of political that we associate with hard-nosed, ruthless strategy.

Participatory democratic politics has been the implicit reference point for my discussion of different notions of politics in this chapter. I turn now to this notion of political life, and suggest how we might make injus-tices located in or associated with intimate life available to political recog-nition, discussion, and action while respecting the privacy of intimate life and the need for control over information about oneself.

The Political

When we wrestle with the problem of translating intimate-life issues related to sexuality into politically negotiable issues, it matters which no-tion of the political informs our thinking: there are crucial differences be-tween the political as the existence of power and oppression, as narrowly focused interest group competition, as sectarian battles, conformist pres-sure, or coercive tactics to build and preserve community, or as the process whereby citizens of diverse opinions and backgrounds deliberate and de-cide together as equals about questions of broad public concern. Of course, all of these things are recognizably "political"; all have something to do with political life as we know and practice it. Politics *is* about power; but it is also about who has it, how it is exercised, and to what ends. Politics *is* concerned with effective strategy, whether interest group mobili-zation or the outing of gays and lesbians in positions of power. Building communities based on a group's identity—as black or lesbian or gay or female—provides enclaves where members can effectively resist the racist or sexist or homophobic values and messages of the dominant society and nurture alternative, oppositional visions of themselves and of justice. But to treat the transition from personal to political in any one of these ways alone is to risk the full, genuine practice of politics for partial, limited aspects of it.

To judge the adequacy of different notions of the political, we need to recover an older, broader meaning of politics. The word derives from the ancient Greek *politikos* (from *polis,* meaning city, state), pertaining to citizens, civic, the civil.[56] Aristotle called politics "the most sovereign and inclusive" of all associations, and argued that participation in politics is what makes human life distinctively human. Politics is the common endeavor to create the public world through collective decision making by citizens who rule and are ruled in turn, and who relate to one another not as bureaucrat and client, technician/expert and passive consumer, lovers, intimates, or even friends, but as equals.[57] Politics aims to address and decide large, encompassing questions: What is a good life? What is justice? How can these goods be attained?

Politics as a process takes place among people who are fundamentally different. Plurality and diversity, challenge, competition, widely differing appeals to common standards, disagreement about the standards themselves, persuasion, negotiation, and compromise all characterize politics. Political debate and vision assume and require a variety of positions, angles of vision, perspectives.

Power and interest are also crucial aspects of political life. People are drawn to political life by what interests them, by their particular needs and concerns, and because it *matters,* because contending over resources and priorities, programs and policies, values and goals, can make a concrete difference to their lives. In the process of becoming citizens and participating in political life, they learn to recognize and appeal to others' power and standards, and to frame their issues and concerns in terms of claims that are negotiable by public standards.

What, then, does it mean to make "the personal," especially intimate-life affiliations and sexual commitments, "political" in this sense? What is needed is a way to recognize and articulate problems first experienced in private or in isolation from others—perhaps because they usually occur in the context of the home, the family, friendships, or sexual relationships—not as problems of personal biography (my problem because I am so unusual, neurotic, maladjusted), but as *systemic* problems that affect many or most people in the same situation, and are reinforced by social values and practices, as well as official sanctions, laws, and policies. When their problems are recognized and articulated in this way, people can begin to make claims about how they themselves ought to be treated, what they are entitled to, and what justice requires—claims that are negotiable as political claims.[58] To do so does not mean that they will always *win* their political battles, that others will always accept their claims; it means only that they have begun to deal as citizens with their intimate-life problems and grievances. They have begun to make arguments that appeal to common standards, to argue about the standards themselves, and to make a commitment to engage in political discourse about a whole range of important issues, not just their own.

On this understanding of the political, even though most decisions and practices related to consenting adult sexuality are private in the sense of being nobody else's business, and usually take place hidden from view, social patterns of homophobia and heterosexism raise issues of injustice that are properly political. The harassment, hatred, humiliation, and discrimination suffered because of one's homosexuality should be viewed as political rather than personal experiences because such experiences are rooted in a social structure that makes homosexuality a salient fact about a person, and not in personal biographies of pathology or maladjustment. Social structure can be transformed only through political action to make it more just. Seeing the personal as political in this way changes the questions one asks from "Why do I have to be gay? What did I do wrong?" to "Why does society have to be homophobic? How can oppressive norms, practices, institutions, and laws that produce heterosexism and homophobia be changed?"

Making intimate-life matters political in the civic, participatory sense of politics means that we as citizens must approach the life we live in common as citizens differently than do gays in pursuit of their narrow self-interest, or lesbians affirming their membership is a closed, protective community, or gays who "out" other gays against their will. Rather than treating opponents with contempt as the victims of brainwashing or false consciousness, we have to respect them and treat them as equals who are capable of making up their minds and are worth arguing with.[59] In this vein, Phelan says that we need to embrace "the liberal *sentiment,* that which appreciates, even enjoys, the ambiguity and contestation of public life. The bearer of such a sentiment need not abstract from the particulars of my existence to respect me; neither must she agree that my understanding of a good life is the true, the best, the purest. What she need do is believe that I mean what I say; that is, she must agree to treat me as a being competent to speak of my own desires and motives directly, even if she suspects that I am not."[60] Citizens treat opponents as worthy and stay to argue, rather than stalking off in disdain to commune with the like-minded. Although community building and identity politics may be necessary stages on the way to developing the confidence needed to make one's claims to one's fellow citizens at large, communities based on exclusivity or on ignoring and erasing the diversity of their members are not schools of democratic citizenship. Politics is characterized not by unanimity and harmony but by diversity, conflict, and contention. Perhaps there is no necessary reason for community building to give rise to exclusivity, fractures, defensiveness; but working in coalitions may hold out more promise for effective political action that respects differences.[61]

Here is an example of the kind of claim that furthers the politics of democratic participation:

When the leader of the New York Gay Men's Chorus proclaims: "We show the straight community that we're just as normal as they are," this would seem on the face of it to be a rather conservative proposition, reminiscent of the accommodationist politics of the 1950s homophile movements. And yet in fact the comparison is inappropriate. When the members of homophile organizations stressed their "normality," they meant: We're the same as you, so please stop excluding us. But the sense of the above quote is quite different; it is saying: We're different from you, and that doesn't make us any less human.[62]

For gays, contesting standards of what is "normal" and making demands on the broader straight community to recognize their humanity are important steps toward a genuinely political dialogue. So is the Gay Men's Chorus's strategy of asserting their difference and asking for recognition and respect, rather than emphasizing their sameness with straights and struggling for assimilation. By downplaying or papering over differences, assimilation replicates many of the pitfalls of communities that exclude "deviants" or that pressure members to conform or reveal themselves—to act like parvenus, in Arendt's language. Ignoring or silencing differences—whether between gays and straights, whites and blacks, poor and rich, or *among* gays and lesbians—does not make them go away; it simply drives them underground, and reproduces invisibility, silence, and oppression. Many have begun to reconsider the kind of exclusionary identity politics criticized here, in particular rejecting the idea of a community based on familiar, safe, protected boundaries and identities with no recognition of the exclusions, oppressions, and silences these cause.[63]

Finally, there is the problem of respecting privacy. Throughout this book I have struggled to keep alive the tension between privacy as privative and privacy as protective. On the one hand, there is no question that sometimes the division drawn in liberal political thought between public and private is false and politically disempowering. Power is exercised unjustly in many non-state, non-governmental venues, such as the informal social relations between men and women, heterosexuals and homosexuals, rich and poor, white and black (and, especially in other countries, along religious and ethnic lines: Christian and Muslim, Protestant and Catholic, Jewish and Palestinian, Serb and Croat). Informal social relations often have widespread impact, affecting the chances for different groups to gain education, prosperity, acceptance, and dignity. Although protecting private life from public scrutiny and government regulation may, as John Stuart Mill claimed, foster intellectual debate, idiosyncrasy, and religious toleration, it also shields the exercise of private power from political analysis and action, and masks how privacy is connected to economic, gender, race, and heterosexual privilege.

On the other hand, there are important reasons to respect the privateness of sexual impression and intimate relationships. There is much value in protecting certain spaces or aspects of human life, such as sexual expression, intimacy, and religious or moral conviction, from public scrutiny and intrusion. Earlier I said that translating problems rooted in intimate, private life was a way to keep them from being deprived of public significance and thus to escape the "privative" sense of privacy. But that process of translation needs to remain attentive to the sense of privacy as protection, the sense of *keeping* things private that will be injured or destroyed if they are made public. A polity that did not value and respect privacy—the notion that certain parts of one's life, certain activities, decisions, and places are off-limits to others, not open to public scrutiny, not politically relevant—would be a frightening one, with little room or tolerance for differences in sexual practices, notions of the erotic, religious and ethical beliefs, and much else. I think it is possible, indeed crucial, to address what is problematic in our shared public life about social structures of power and patterns of homophobia and heterosexism, which are unjust and properly political, while respecting the individual's privacy when it comes to what goes on behind the bedroom door, one's choice of a sexual partner, or what fantasies one entertains. That is why it is particular practices rooted in "private" life—sexism, racism, homophobia, and economic inequality—that must be attacked, and not the value of privacy per se.

Conclusion

Privacy and Democratic Citizenship

MY ANALYSIS HAS BEEN INTENDED TO UNSETtle rigidities and complacencies in our thought about public and private. I have attempted to sensitize readers to the conflicting dimensions of privacy, arguing for greater tolerance for ambiguity and complexity. I urge advocates and analysts to make genuinely political claims about justice and equal citizenship but also to respect the privateness that protects the ways of life out of which these issues emerge. The approach I argue for is especially significant in light of crucial and contentious political issues that have begun to emerge from their home in intimate life.

There are three central dangers in current approaches to thinking about public and private which we need to beware of as we attempt to make theoretical and practical connections between private and public realms of experience. One is the danger that respecting privacy can reify various forms of power and privilege, making it seem that social arrangements are not open to question or change. The second is the danger of a "politics of authenticity." The third, which Arendt warned against, is of the progressive "socialization" of political life.

The danger contemporary feminist theory most persistently warns of is that respecting privacy can reinforce and make invisible forms of social power and privilege and lead to political quietism. We are led to accept that what goes on in private cannot be a matter for political recognition or action. Overlooking connections between the institutions and arrangements of private life and the public institutions and laws that support them leads people who suffer in their private roles to blame their problems on their own inadequacies rather than on larger, systemic power structures. In this form, respect for privacy keeps people from recognizing and challenging historically developed forms of power, and makes those who suffer in the isolation of the home or the closet feel powerless.

By the politics of authenticity, I mean the practice in some oppositional political groups of using aspects of their members' intimate lives—for example, their choice of sexual partner—to gauge their political acceptability, or as information that can be made public to further the objectives of the movement, such as attacking homophobia. But these practices marginalize, exclude, or make invisible group members who do not fit the group's image, and define group politics in terms of a single characteristic. This process not only undermines the spontaneity and trust of intimate life but also causes the diversity of people's personal and political commitments to fade into insignificance. Such a politics does not respect privacy's role in protecting and making possible a variety of human interactions, including relations premised on trust and intimacy. Moreover, many people view it as a kind of "moral authoritarianism."[1] Certainly it seems poor grounds for building an inclusive civic notion of political activism, whereby citizens of a diverse polity interact with fellow citizens, mostly strangers, some of whom they like and agree with, some of whom they do not.

Hannah Arendt's book *The Human Condition* warns us of the third danger, the looming presence of "the social" in modern life. Here I read the social as a way to talk about matters that become public in such a way that we cannot engage them politically, either because of the way we understand ourselves or because of the way we understand the issues. For example, ordinary citizens often think it wise to leave issues of great technological complexity to the experts who understand them best.[2] Or issues involving private-life matters—family policy, for example—are introduced in such a way that those most directly affected feel that they are merely clients, there for the state to serve or protect but not consulted or involved in figuring out what ought to be done.[3] Or perhaps we come to politics only occasionally, our own issues and interests foremost in our minds. For many Americans, cynicism and disillusionment are the predominant feelings about national public life, and our ordinary experience of "the political" is apt to refer to instrumental senses of politics, to power plays and inappropriately politicized decision-making processes, to positions and labels rather than to commitment to the standards we judge by as participants in our common life as citizens.

A symptom of the "socialization" of politics—that is to say, the loss of a distinctively political sphere as citizens become dispirited, passive clients of giant welfare states—is the theoretical move Bonnie Honig makes in her reading of Arendt's "agonal" politics. Honig suggests that we ought no longer to privilege institutional sites of politics but rather should see as political acts of resistance which occur in a number of possible sites. Her view seems unduly pessimistic about the possibilities for politics as an association among citizens and jettisons much, if not all, of the older, richer notion of political life which I defend.

Many people have called, as I do here, for citizens once again to discover participation in public life as an intrinsic satisfaction and a form of collective self-determination rather than merely a means to defend personal interests. Finding ways to address problems that really matter to people's lives—especially the recurrent problems of daily life, such as sexism, homophobia, and racism—may be one way to rekindle this older civic notion of politics.

I feel conflicted about the value of privacy. Over and over, I find, I have set up "on the one hand"/"on the other hand" strategies for explaining what is important about privacy. I find convincing both the criticism that "the private" obscures questions of power and the argument that privacy protects central and defining aspects of human life. This construction of oppositions and tensions is no accident; it is essential to the character of privacy as an idea and a practice in our society. In some contexts privacy serves us well, whether as a legal strategy we use with varying degrees of effectiveness to safeguard choice, a value that helps us interact appropriately in a variety of private and public settings at various levels of social distance and intimacy, or a central political value that allows us to choose our defining relationships and form our own identities. But privacy also obscures differences in social and political power, makes us feel that we are stuck in unalterable social arrangements, and leads us to believe that our problems are individual rather than connected to larger structures of power. Privacy works both ways simultaneously, and we need to nurture our ability to see the tensions so that we do not falsely characterize privacy as merely one thing or the other.

Just as I resist one-sided ways of thinking about privacy, I also endeavor to keep alive tensions and complexities in our concept and practice of politics, so that we do not refer to it in its instrumental or power-derived or ideological senses without also keeping in mind the notion of politics as the collective engagement of citizens in determining how they shall live. If the goal is to foster active involvement in the life of the polity, something more than the mere assertion that private-life relationships are founded on power is needed to render them political. It is crucial to transform private-life problems into issues that everyone can recognize as raising politically negotiable questions because to do so makes them actionable, and it changes private sufferers into citizens with a stake in the standards by which the community judges different claims. Political engagement depends on our discovering how our private lives are connected to politics; the task is to learn to translate private need into political claim.

Notes

Chapter One. Why the Personal Is Not Always Political

[1]Jean Bethke Elshtain, *Public Man, Private Woman* (Princeton, N.J.: Princeton University Press, 1981); and Wendy Brown, *Manhood and Politics* (Totowa, N.J.: Rowman & Littlefield, 1988) are leading examples.

[2]See three works by Jean Bethke Elshtain: *Public Man, Private Woman;* "Moral Woman and Immoral Man: A Consideration of the Public-Private Split and Its Political Ramifications," *Politics and Society* 4 (1974): 453–73; and "Antigone's Daughters: Reflections on Female Identity and the State," in *Families, Politics, and Public Policy,* ed. Irene Diamond (New York: Longman, 1983), pp. 300–311.

[3]See Sara Ruddick, "Maternal Thinking" and "Preservative Love and Military Destructiveness," both in *Mothering: Essays in Feminist Theory,* ed. Joyce Trebilcot (Totowa, N.J.: Rowman & Allanheld, 1983); pp. 213–62; Carol Gilligan, *In a Different Voice* (Cambridge: Harvard University Press, 1982).

[4]Brown, *Manhood and Politics,* pp. 205–6; see also pp. 189, 190–91.

[5]For examples of Brown's criticism of notions of politics that ignore the "private" life of bodies and necessity, see *Manhood and Politics,* pp. 44–45, 63.

[6]Carole Pateman, *The Sexual Contract* (Stanford: Stanford University Press, 1988).

[7]Pateman writes: "The combination of public equality and private inequality, as the story of the sexual contract shows, is not a contradiction of modern patriarchy. Juridical equality and social inequality—public/private, civil/natural, men/women—form a coherent social structure." Ibid., p. 229.

[8]Ibid., p. 17. Frances Olsen echoes the argument that the public-private distinction reinforces male power and privilege when she points out that were it "not for our habits of thinking about public and private, it would perhaps seem peculiar that what a victim of rape might have done that titillated the defendant is considered legally relevant while what a slain wife-beating husband did to terrorize his wife before she killed him is often not considered legally relevant." Frances Olsen, "Constitutional Law: Feminist Critiques of the Public/Private Distinction," *Constitutional Commentary* 10 (1993): 327.

[9]Carole Pateman, "Feminist Critiques of the Public/Private Dichotomy," in *Public and Private in Social Life,* ed. S. I. Benn and G. F. Gaus (London: Croom Helm, 1983), pp. 295, 297. Recent feminist scholarship fleshes out these arguments. For example, developments in criminal law such as the recognition of a cause of action for marital rape and increasing acceptance of the "battered woman" defense (as in the celebrated Bobbitt trial) mirror growing public awareness that relationships in the intimate realm can be oppressive. To take another example, women's primary responsibility for child rearing has been linked to the ghettoization of women in low-pay, low-status jobs that are more tolerant of work interruptions, "mommy tracks," high stress rates owing to the responsibility for a double work shift, and low numbers of women elected to public office. See generally Susan Moller Okin, *Justice,*

Gender, and the Family (New York: Basic Books, 1989); and Arlie Hochschild, *The Second Shift: Inside the Two-Job Marriage* (New York: Viking, 1989). The patriarchal impact of laws and policies affecting marriage, divorce, rape, abortion, child care, and the allocation of welfare benefits has also been well documented (see Pateman, "Feminist Critiques," p. 295). Other writers have developed Pateman's point about how public laws and policies shape domestic life. See, for example, Ann Showstack Sassoon, "Women's New Social Role: Contradictions of the Welfare State," in *Women and the State: The Shifting Boundaries of Public and Private,* ed. Ann Showstack Sassoon (London: Hutchinson, 1987). See also the essays collected in Linda Gordon, ed., *Women, the State, and Welfare* (Madison: University of Wisconsin Press, 1990).

[10]Susan Moller Okin, "Women, Equality, and Citizenship," *Queen's Quarterly* 90.1 (1992): 69; see also pp. 63–64, and Okin, *Justice, Gender, and the Family,* chap. 6.

[11]Okin, *Justice, Gender, and the Family,* pp. 103, 104, 155–56; Susan Moller Okin, "Justice and Gender," *Philosophy & Public Affairs* 16 (Winter 1987); "Gender Inequality and Cultural Preferences," *Political Theory* 22.1 (February 1994); "Women, Equality, and Citizenship." Cf. Carole Pateman, "Feminist Critiques," p. 299, and Mary G. Dietz, "Hannah Arendt and Feminist Politics," in *Feminist Interpretations and Political Theory,* ed. Mary Lyndon Shanley and Carole Pateman (University Park: Pennsylvania State University Press, 1991), p. 242.

[12]Okin, *Justice, Gender, and the Family,* pp. 99, 100.

[13]Although Okin relies on Nancy Chodorow's explanation of object relations theory (see Nancy Chodorow, *The Reproduction of Mothering* [Berkeley: University of California Press, 1978]), what follows here is my own gloss on Dorothy Dinnerstein's argument in *The Mermaid and the Minotaur* (New York: Harper Colophon, 1976), not Okin's. Okin suggests the psychological dimension of our child rearing practices and its impact on adult moral development, but she does not adequately explain Dinnerstein's and Chodorow's basic insight.

[14]This of course parallels Carol Gilligan's argument in *In a Different Voice.*

[15]Okin, *Justice, Gender, and the Family,* p. 107.

[16]Catharine MacKinnon, *Toward a Feminist Theory of the State* (Cambridge: Harvard University Press, 1989), p. 191.

[17]Catharine MacKinnon, "Feminism, Marxism, Method, and the State," in *Feminist Theory: A Critique of Ideology,* ed. Nannerl O. Keohane, Michelle Rosaldo, and Barbara Gelpi (Chicago: University of Chicago Press, 1981), p. 1. See also ibid., p. 19; idem, *Toward a Feminist Theory of the State,* p. 3; and much of MacKinnon's writing on pornography.

[18]MacKinnon argues that intimate relations is the location of women's oppression in *Toward a Feminist Theory of the State,* p. 191: "privacy doctrine is most at home at home, the place women experience the most force, in the family, and . . . centers on sex. . . . For women the measure of the intimacy has been the measure of the oppression." Also see "Feminism, Marxism," p. 21: "women's distinctive experience as women occurs within that sphere that has been socially lived as the personal—private, emotional, interiorized, particular, individuated, intimate—so that what it is to *know* the *politics* of woman's situation is to know women's personal lives."

[19]For examples of these lines of thought, see Catharine MacKinnon, *Feminism Unmodified* (Cambridge: Harvard University Press, 1987), and *Toward a Feminist Theory of the State.*

[20]Catharine MacKinnon, "Abortion: On Public and Private," in *Toward a Feminist Theory of the State,* pp. 187, 192. See also Wendy Brown, "Reproductive Freedom and the Right

to Privacy," in Diamond, *Families, Politics, and Public Policy,* pp. 322–38; and Ruth Bader Ginsburg, "Some Thoughts on Autonomy and Equality in Relation to *Roe v. Wade,*" North Carolina Law Review 63 (1985): 375–86, for similar arguments about the inadequacy of the right of privacy for addressing the issues raised by the abortion funding cases.

[21]MacKinnon, *Toward a Feminist Theory of the State,* p. 190.

[22]MacKinnon writes that "abortion policy has never been explicitly approached in the context of how women get pregnant; that is, as a consequence of intercourse under conditions of gender inequality; that is, as an issue of forced sex." Ibid., pp. 185–86.

[23]Ibid., pp. 188, 189, 190.

[24]Ibid., pp. 190, 191; emphasis added.

[25]MacKinnon, "Feminism, Marxism," pp. 21–27, 29.

[26]Ibid., pp. 27, 24, 19.

[27]Angela P. Harris, "Race and Essentialism in Feminist Legal Theory," in *Feminist Legal Theory,* ed. Katharine T. Bartlett and Rosanne Kennedy (Boulder: Westview Press, 1991), pp. 235–62.

[28]See Iris Marion Young, *Justice and the Politics of Difference* (Princeton: Princeton University Press, 1990).

[29]Ibid., pp. 116, 97.

[30]"Feelings, desires, and commitments do not cease to exist and motivate just because they have been excluded from the definition of moral reason. . . . The plurality of subjects is not in fact eliminated, but only expelled from the moral realm; the concrete interests, needs, and desires of persons and the feelings that differentiate them from one another become merely private, subjective. In modern political theory this dichotomy appears as that between a public authority that represents the general interest, on the one hand, and private individuals with their own private desires, unshareable and incommunicable." Ibid., p. 103.

[31]She *does* think, however, that impartiality and privacy play such a role: "An idea functions ideologically when belief in it helps reproduce relations of domination or oppression by justifying them or by obscuring possible more emancipatory social relations." Ibid., p. 112.

[32]Ibid., p. 119; emphasis added. See also p. 121: "Justice cannot stand opposed to personal need, feeling, and desire, but names the institutional conditions that enable people to meet their needs and express their desires. Needs can be expressed in their particularity in a heterogeneous public."

[33]Ibid., pp. 120–21.

[34]Ibid., p. 119. See also p. 118: "This manner of formulating the concepts of public and private, which is inspired by feminist confrontations with traditional political theory, does not deny their distinction. It does deny, however, a social division between public and private spheres, each with different kinds of institutions, activities, and human attributes."

[35]Ibid., p. 119.

[36]Ibid., p. 47.

[37]All of these examples touch on the not-very-distant past: the right of married couples to use contraception was not recognized in the United States until 1965, and some anti-miscegenation statutes were not struck down until 1967 (*Loving v. Virginia*). Most of the issues mentioned here—abortion rights, domestic violence, marital rape, sexual harassment, same-sex marriage, civil rights for gays and lesbians—are still hotly contested, at least in terms of what public policy is appropriate, and in many cases in terms of whether the issues presented should even be matters for political consideration.

[38]Pateman, "Feminist Critiques," p. 297.

[39]Okin, *Justice, Gender, and the Family*, p. 127. See also Young, *Justice and the Politics of Difference*, pp. 119–20.

[40]Pateman, "Feminist Critiques," p. 295; emphasis added.

[41]See Ian Shapiro, "Three Ways To Be a Democrat," *Political Theory* 22.1 (February 1994): 128; Mary G. Dietz, "Citizenship with a Feminist Face: The Problem with Maternal Thinking," *Political Theory* 13.1 (February 1985): 27–28; Young, *Justice and the Politics of Difference*, p. 121.

[42]See Ruth Gavison, "Feminism and the Public/Private Distinction," *Stanford Law Review* 45 (November 1992): 21, 36–37, 43–44, for arguments similar to mine.

[43]Responding to criticisms along these lines, Susan Okin has argued that her account of gender oppression holds up across different cultures. I find her suggestion that outsiders like herself may have a clearer idea than those immersed in oppressive relationships in poor countries patronizing and inattentive to the meaning structures of other cultures. See Susan Moller Okin, "Gender Inequality and Cultural Differences," *Political Theory* 22.1 (1994): 5–24.

[44]Harris, "Race and Essentialism in Feminist Legal Theory"; Shane Phelan, *Identity Politics* (Philadelphia: Temple University Press, 1989); Anita L. Allen, *Uneasy Access: Privacy for Women in a Free Society* (Totowa, N.J.: Rowman & Littlefield, 1988); Dorothy E. Roberts, "Punishing Drug Addicts Who Have Babies: Women of Color, Equality, and the Right of Privacy," *Harvard Law Review* 104.7 (1991): 1419–82; Peggy Cooper Davis, "Neglected Stories and the Lawfulness of *Roe v. Wade*," *Harvard Civil Rights–Civil Liberties Law Review* 28.2 (1993): 299–394.

[45]Several theorists implicitly adopted a broad "politics is whatever pertains to power and conflict" definition. For example, Ian Shapiro writes: "Politics are everywhere, however, because no realm of social life is immune from relations of conflict and power." Shapiro, "Three Ways to Be a Democrat," p. 130.

[46]Quoted in Pateman, "Feminist Critiques," p. 297.

[47]MacKinnon cites political scientists such as Harold Laswell and Robert Dahl, as well as Millett, in support of her definition of sex as politics. MacKinnon, *Toward a Feminist Theory of the State*, p. 161.

[48]Young, *Justice and the Politics of Difference*, pp. 118–19.

[49]Ibid., p. 107.

[50]Hanna Pitkin, "Justice: On Relating Private and Public," *Political Theory* 9.3 (1981): 347.

[51]Young, *Justice and the Politics of Difference*, p. 116.

[52]Ibid., p. 110.

[53]Hannah Arendt, *On Revolution* (New York: Viking Press, 1963).

[54]Gavison, "Feminism and the Public/Private Distinction," p. 43.

[55]Judith Jarvis Thomson, "The Right to Privacy," *Philosophy and Public Affairs* 4.4 (1974): 295–314.

[56]Edward Thomas Mulligan, "*Griswold* Revisited in Light of *Uplinger*: An Historical and Philosophical Exposition of Implied Autonomy Rights in the Constitution," *Review of Law and Social Change*, 13 (1984–85): 73, 75, writes: "It should be noted that the right addressed in the present context is not, as a literal reading of the phrase might suggest, the right to maintain secrecy with respect to one's affairs or personal behavior; rather, it is a right of independence in making certain kinds of important decisions. . . . *Roe vs. Wade* has everything to do with autonomy and little to do with privacy, a point Justice Rehnquist seized upon in

his *Roe* dissent. The act of abortion necessarily entails the loss of privacy. An abortion is performed by a third party in surroundings not at all conducive to a sense of personal security. Moreover, personal information must be released and medical records collected, contributing to a loss of privacy in the narrow, common law sense."

[57]Several theorists have suggested that the core value at stake in privacy cases is autonomy. See Louis Henkin, "Privacy and Autonomy," *Columbia Law Review* 74 (1974): 1410; Joel Feinberg, "Autonomy, Sovereignty, and Privacy: Moral Ideals in the Constitution?" *Notre Dame Law Review* 58 (1983): 445–92; David A. J. Richards, "Liberalism, Public Morality, and Constitutional Law: Prolegomenon to a Theory of the Constitutional Right of Privacy," *Law and Contemporary Problems* 51.1 (1988): 123–50; and Joseph Kupfer, "Privacy, Autonomy, and Self-Concept," *American Philosophical Quarterly* 24.1 (1987): 81–87.

[58]C. Keith Boone, "Privacy and Community," *Social Theory and Practice* 9.1 (1983): 8; Charles Fried, *An Anatomy of Values: Problems of Personal and Social Choice* (Cambridge: Harvard University Press, 1970); Jeffrey H. Reiman, "Privacy, Intimacy, and Personhood," *Philosophy & Public Affairs* 6.1 (1976): 26–44; James Rachels, "Why Privacy Is Important," in *Philosophical Dimensions of Privacy,* ed. Ferdinand Schoeman (Cambridge: Cambridge University Press, 1984); Robert S. Gerstein, "Intimacy and Privacy," *ethics* 89 (1978): 76–81. Several writers have argued that privacy can be especially helpful to reviled or oppressed groups, a point I touched on earlier. For instance, David Richards suggests that the privacy of homosexuals is in desperate need of protection—"certainly more than the contraceptive-using heterosexual majority." David A. J. Richards, "Constitutional Legitimacy and Constitutional Privacy," *New York University Law Review* 61 (1986): 853.

[59]Kupfer, "Privacy, Autonomy, and Self-Concept," pp. 82, 84. See also Robert C. Post, "The Social Foundations of Privacy: Community and Self in the Common Law Tort," *California Law Review* 77 (1989): 1008; Reiman, "Privacy, Intimacy, and Personhood," pp. 39–44; Ferdinand Schoeman, *Privacy and Social Freedom* (Cambridge: Cambridge University Press, 1992), p. 13. In the context of an article on the importance of privacy in the workplace, Richard Lippke does a nice job of explaining why respecting someone's privacy conveys to that person that he or she is worthy of being trusted and worthy of autonomy. Richard Lippke, "Work, Privacy, and Autonomy," *Public Affairs Quarterly* 3.2 (1989): 43.

[60]Richards, "Liberalism, Public Morality, and Constitutional Law," pp. 130–50.

[61]Ruth Gavison, "Too Early for a Requiem: Warren and Brandeis Were Right on Privacy vs. Free Speech," *South Carolina Law Review* 43.3 (1992): 461. The point is echoed by Richard Lippke: "The most autonomous person is one who evaluates his deepest convictions, or the most fundamental aspects of his life-plan. Privacy is essential to individuals having the concept that they can do this. It allows them to engage in this self-scrutiny without intrusion and distraction. When the most intimate aspects of their lives are up for scrutiny, individuals are vulnerable to ridicule or manipulation by others. It is vitally important for them to be able to remove themselves from observation and criticism by those they feel they cannot trust." Lippke, "Work, Privacy, and Autonomy," p. 43. Many argue that people need to be free from the scrutiny of strangers, not just to pursue self-reflection but to "rehearse" their thinking and behavior, have room to make mistakes or do wrong (Kupfer, "Privacy, Autonomy, and Self-Concept," pp. 83, 84), to be affectionate and sexually intimate, to fight and quarrel (Rachels, "Why Privacy Is Important," p. 296).

[62]Feinberg, "Autonomy, Sovereignty, and Privacy," pp. 453–54.

[63]See, for example, Allen, *Uneasy Access.*

[64]Feinberg, "Autonomy, Sovereignty, and Privacy," p. 483.

[65]Allen, *Uneasy Access,* p. 46.

[66]Henkin, "Privacy and Autonomy," p. 1426, suggests there is no such principle for deciding hard cases.

[67]Feinberg, "Autonomy, Sovereignty, and Privacy," p. 490.

[68]Boone, "Privacy and Community," p. 21.

[69]According to Rubenfeld, the originator of the idea of using "personhood" as a synonym for privacy was Paul Freund, but one of the most prominent commentators who defends privacy in terms of its connection to "personhood" is Laurence Tribe. See Laurence H. Tribe, *American Constitutional Law* (Mineola, N.Y.: Foundation Press, 1978). Jeb Rubenfeld, "The Right of Privacy," *Harvard Law Review* 102 (1989): 752.

[70]Rubenfeld, "The Right of Privacy," p. 770.

[71]Ibid., pp. 779–80, 782.

[72]Ibid., pp. 788, 799–800. For a critique of this argument, see Kendall Thomas, "Beyond the Privacy Principle," *Columbia Law Review* 92 (1992): 1431–1516.

[73]Rubenfeld, "Right to Privacy," p. 793.

[74]Ibid., pp. 804–5.

[75]Rubenfeld's political arguments for defending privacy have been echoed by Jean Cohen, who defends privacy against feminist attacks and argues that privacy rights are the best way to assert individual rights as limits to government power since the eclipse of property rights in the 1930s. She addresses arguments made by feminist legal commentators, focusing on Catharine MacKinnon, Frances Olsen, and Cass Sunstein. Jean Cohen, "Redescribing Privacy: Identity, Difference, and the Abortion Controversy," *Columbia Journal of Gender and Law* 3.1 (1992): 43–117, esp. 50–61.

[76]Schoeman, *Privacy and Social Freedom,* p. 156.

[77]Ibid., p. 66: "Autonomy uncompromised is sociopathic." See also pp. 98, 110, 116 (on the role of associations); p. 137 (on modulating social pressure); and generally chap. 8, "Privacy and Gossip," for good examples and explanations of how this modulation works.

[78]Ibid., p. 110.

[79]Ibid., pp. 154, 157.

[80]Ibid., pp. 174–75.

[81]John Hardwig, "Should Women Think in Terms of Rights?" *ethics* 94.3 (1984): 443; Schoeman, *Privacy and Social Freedom,* pp. 181, 191. See also Jeremy Waldron, "When Justice Replaces Affection: The Need for Rights," *Harvard Journal of Law and Public Policy* 11.3 (1988): 625–45.

[82]Rachels, "Why Privacy Is Important," p. 296.

[83]"What do you mean, 'our' way of life?" I anticipate readers asking. "Are you generalizing from your own limited white, middle-class, academic experience?" Robert Post, whose formulation I am drawing on here, addresses the issue this way: "It is something of a fiction to speak of a single, homogeneous community within a nation as large and diverse as the United States. There is every reason to expect that civility rules regarding privacy will differ 'among communities, between generations, and among ethnic, religious, or other social groups, as well as among individuals' " (quoting *Anderson v. Fisher Broadcasting Company* 712 P.2d 803, 809 [1986].) Having said this, Post goes on to explore the hegemonic function played by civility rules: "The common law tort purports to *speak for* a community. Yet this very ambition authoritatively to forge a community simultaneously requires the common law to displace the deviant communities. Under such conditions, community and hegemony necessarily entail each other." Post, "Social Foundations of Privacy," pp. 976, 978. To the

extent that I am talking about social practices that define a community, they *are* hegemonic. They are also experienced and observed differently in different communities. Insofar as privacy exists, it *is* something "we" recognize and value, an argument I spend some time making in the next few pages.

[84]Schoeman, *Privacy and Social Freedom*, pp. 82, 92.

[85]Post, "Social Foundations of Privacy," p. 1010. Ferdinand Schoeman's approach to thinking about privacy has much in common with Post's; Schoeman also believes that privacy is a culturally shared strategy that helps maintain a life in common, and that cultural values and traditions are not something we are entirely free to pick and choose but something that has authority for us. Schoeman, *Privacy and Social Fredom*, pp. 82, 92.

[86]Post, "Social Foundation of Privacy," pp. 971–72 (quoting from Erving Goffman, "The Territories of the Self").

[87]See Schoeman, *Privacy and Social Freedom*, pp. 138, 149, 162–63.

[88]Rachels, "Why Privacy Is Important," pp. 294, 295.

[89]Reiman, "Privacy, Intimacy, and Personhood," p. 39.

[90]Post, "Social Foundations of Privacy," p. 973.

[91]Patricia J. Williams, "On Being the Object of Property," in *Feminist Legal Theory*, ed. Katharine Bartlett and Rosanne Kennedy (Boulder: Westview Press, 1991), p. 169.

[92]Post, "Social Foundations of Privacy," p. 985 (quoting from Ferdinand Schoeman).

[93]Schoeman, *Privacy and Social Freedom*, p. 147.

[94]Ibid., pp. 142–43, 154–56.

[95]Post, "Social Foundations of Privacy," pp. 1007, 1009, 1010.

[96]The chief exception here is Anita Allen, who in *Uneasy Access* addresses the different ways women and men have access to, and need for, privacy.

[97]For example, Ruth Gavison responds to feminist arguments in defending the right to privacy, and so does Jean Cohen. As law professors, they usually choose as interlocutors other academics who publish in law reviews (e.g., Frances Olsen, Cass Sunstein, Catharine MacKinnon), or at any rate who address legal issues.

[98]See, for example, Cohen, "Redescribing Privacy," and Gavison, "Feminism and the Public/Private Distinction."

[99]See Dietz, "Citizenship with a Feminist Face," pp. 27–28.

[100]Susan Okin and Carole Pateman have suggested that privacy has all along benefited male heads of households more than it has their wives, children, or slaves. See Okin, "Women, Equality, and Citizenship," pp. 67–68; and Pateman, *Sexual Contract*.

[101]We have all engaged in "personal" conversations about public policies. For example, when my parents talk about why they favor national health care, they always relate the issue to the high cost of care for themselves as retirees, without making any broader connection to principles of justice or to the benefit of such a plan to large numbers of people who have no health insurance.

[102]An example may make this point clearer. A woman who is beaten by her husband, and understands her abuse as her personal misfortune, perhaps even as something she is responsible for, is not thinking politically about the power dynamics of her relationship. She must make connections between her personal experience and that of large numbers of women who are also beaten if she is to understand the problem as rooted in social forces larger than her own particular psyche or family, and to see it as unjust and soluble through collective action. Being able to make the link between the first perspective and the second is what I mean by translation. See Pitkin, "Justice," for a discussion of this kind of linkage.

[103]Here I use "lifestyle" as a shorthand for referring to issues located in the intimate sphere of family, sex, and control over making bodily decisions which share the character of being "private-and-public."

Chapter Two. Privation and Privilege

[1]For a fine discussion of entities and issues that combine public and private qualities, see Cynthia Halpern, "Property, Privacy, and Power," paper presented at the American Political Science Association annual meeting, New York, September 1–4, 1994.

[2]Some argue that the right-to-life position is stuck in a central hypocrisy because it denies abortions to women who unintentionally become pregnant, but then refuses to support parental leave or public assistance plans that would help these women deal with the burdens of raising small children. On another interpretation, however, both these positions are consistent with the ideology of "rugged individualism," whereby a woman should take responsibility for her actions and work hard to make something of herself and her children. (The responsibility *fathers* of unplanned children should bear is less clear.)

[3]For example, Mary Ann Glendon thinks that arguments for protecting the right to privacy have led us to think and talk as though the responsibility for pregnancy, abortion, and child rearing rests solely on the pregnant women, casting the debate about family policy in overly individualistic terms. She writes: "A Martian trying to infer our culture's attitude toward children from our abortion and social welfare laws might think we had deliberately decided to solve the problem of children in poverty by choosing to abort them rather than to support them with tax dollars." Mary Ann Glendon, *Abortion and Divorce in Western Law* (Cambridge: Harvard University Press, 1987), p. 55.

[4]For arguments to this effect, see the dissenting opinions of Justices Brennan, Marshall, and Blackburn in *Maher v. Roe* 432 U.S. 464 (1977); Wendy Brown, "Reproductive Freedom and the Right to Privacy: A Paradox for Feminists," in *Families, Politics, and Public Policy,* ed. Irene Diamond (New York: Longman, 1983); Catharine MacKinnon, *Toward a Feminist Theory of the State* (Cambridge: Harvard University Press, 1989), pp. 186–87, 192–93.

[5]As Hanna Pitkin has put it, "We can . . . back . . . off from the ontological question to the question of meaning, and from that to the question of use; and there we may find release from what is confusing us." Hanna Pitkin, *Wittgenstein and Justice* (Berkeley: University of California Press, 1972), p. 20.

[6]See Paul Ziff, *Semantic Analysis* (Ithaca: Cornell University Press, 1960), p. 54.

[7]J. L. Austin, "A Plea for Excuses," in *Philosophical Papers* (Oxford: Oxford University Press, 1961), p. 182.

[8]Pitkin, *Wittgenstein and Justice,* pp. 20–21.

[9]See, respectively, Hanna Pitkin, *The Concept of Representation* (Berkeley: University of California Press, 1967); Hanna Pitkin, "Are Freedom and Liberty Twins?" *Political Theory* 16.4 (November 1988): 523–52; Pitkin, *Wittgenstein and Justice,* chap. 8 ("Justice: Socrates and Thrasymachus"); David Laitin, *Politics, Language, and Thought: The Somali Experience* (Chicago: University of Chicago Press, 1977); and Jack Donnelly, *The Concept of Human Rights* (New York: St. Martin's Press, 1985).

[10]Pitkin expands on the point: "Grammar is what a child learns through experience and training, not explanation; it is what we all know but cannot say. Grammar includes all the patterns or regularities or rules in language, permitting new projections and yet controlling what projections will be acceptable." *Wittgenstein and Justice,* p. 80.

¹¹Ibid., p. 17. For an example of looking back and forth between verbal and worldly context, see J. L. Austin's story about the man who becomes angry with his donkey and goes out into his field to shoot it. He takes aim and fires, but just at the moment when the gun goes off, his neighbor's donkey steps in between him and his donkey and is shot instead. In such an instance, he argues, we should all be clear that "It was an accident" rather than "It was a mistake" is the right way to talk about killing the wrong donkey. "A Plea for Excuses," p. 185 n. 1.

¹²Pitkin, *Wittgenstein and Justice,* pp. 16–17.

¹³See Judith Jarvis Thomson, "A Defense of Abortion," *Philosophy and Public Affairs* 1.1 (1971): 48–49; and "The Right to Privacy," *Philosophy and Public Affairs* 4 (1975): 295.

¹⁴Pitkin, *Wittgenstein and Justice,* p. 95.

¹⁵Pitkin writes: "The meaning of a concept grows out of its use in actual human life. In conceptual speculation we want to think about that meaning entirely apart from its use, but it is only in use that an expression fully makes sense. . . . 'What is left out of an expression if it [is] used "outside its ordinary language game"? Not what the *words* mean (they mean what they always did, what a good dictionary says they mean), but what *we* mean in using them when and where we do. Their point, the point of *saying* them, is lost.' " Ibid., p. 98, quoting Stanley Cavell, "Claim to Rationality."

¹⁶Pitkin, *Wittgenstein and Justice,* p. 95; see also pp. 97, 98.

¹⁷For an early example of this criticism, see Herbert Marcuse, *One-Dimensional Man* (Boston: Beacon Press, 1964), p. 175. See also Michel Foucault, "The Discourse on Language," in *The Archaeology of Knowledge and The Discourse on Language* (New York: Pantheon, 1972), pp. 215–37; and Norman Fairclough, *Language and Power* (New York: Longman, 1990).

¹⁸Pitkin, *Wittgenstein and Justice,* p. 91; emphasis added; see also pp. 84–85, 89–90, 92–93.

¹⁹Ibid., pp. 85, 89, 90–91.

²⁰Etymologies and definitions are drawn from *The Compact Edition of the Oxford English Dictionary.* Unless otherwise noted, dates given are for first recorded usage.

²¹Aristotle's notion of man as a political animal is premised on the idea that human potential can be fully realized by living in a polis and participating actively in political life, by ruling and being ruled in turn. Evidently the ancient Latin word *privare* (*privatus*) retained some of this understanding of the centrality of politics to human life.

²²This is the sense of privacy Anita Allen treats as "paradigmatic," in *Uneasy Access: Privacy for Women in a Free Society* (Totowa, N.J.: Rowman & Littlefield, 1988).

²³This sense of *private* may evoke the idea of the person as essentially a separate, self-seeking individual, as in phrases such as "private profit," "satisfaction," "interest," "ambition," or "malice." I take this idea from the *OED*'s use of an example from Hobbes's *Leviathan* which cites "private interest" to illustrate the idea of limited impact.

²⁴Compare Hanna Pitkin's three axes of "publicness": access, impact, and governance. First, the dimension of access or attention sorts with the publicness of public opinion, public knowledge, or publicity, and has to do with what "is accessible to all, open to scrutiny by anyone, visible as a focus of attention," as in senses 1, 4, and sb 3 of *public.* This notion of publicness contrasts with what is reserved, closed, hidden, as in sense 2. Second, something may be public in its consequences and significance because it affects all or most of us, as in sense 1: "Here the opposite of public is not secluded or withdrawn, but personal, of limited impact, affecting only select individuals or groups," as in sense 5. Third is "the publicness of

government, public administration, and collective action," which sorts with senses 1, 2, 5, 6, sb 1, and sb 3, and contrasts with sense 1 of *private* (lacking in public office, rank, or distinction). Hanna Pitkin, "Justice: On Relating Private and Public," *Political Theory* 9.3 (August 1981): 329–30.

25Hanna Pitkin also makes this point in her pathbreaking essay on public and private; see ibid., p. 330.

26Austin uses an instructive example to help make this point: " 'Voluntarily' and 'involuntarily', then, are not opposed in the obvious sort of way that they are made to be in philosophy or jurisprudence. The 'opposite', or rather 'opposites', of 'voluntarily' might be 'under constraint' of some sort, duress or obligation or influence: the opposite of 'involuntarily' might be 'deliberately' or 'on purpose' or the like." "A Plea for Excuses," pp. 191–92.

27A variety of studies focus primarily on the protective character of privacy. They include Alan F. Westin, *Privacy and Freedom* (New York: Atheneum, 1967); David M. O'Brien, *Privacy, Law, and Public Policy* (New York: Praeger, 1979); Allen, *Uneasy Access;* and Julie C. Inness, *Privacy, Intimacy, and Isolation* (New York: Oxford University Press, 1992).

28Ziff, *Semantic Analysis,* p. 190.

29For examples of this argument, see Carole Pateman, *The Sexual Contract* (Stanford: Stanford University Press, 1988); Catharine MacKinnon, "Abortion: On Public and Private," in *Toward a Feminist Theory of the State* (Cambridge: Harvard University Press, 1989); and Halpern, "Property, Privacy and Power."

30See Samuel Kernell's book *Going Public: New Strategies of Presidential Leadership* (Washington, D.C.: CQ Press, 1986), which helped coin this new expression.

31This is a complicated issue in the media age, when opinion makers, shapers, and leaders have a large role in bringing matters to public attention and keeping them there. The matter is also complicated by the realities of representative government, as legislators or officials may find *their* interest ignited and sustained by the efforts of influential groups. Yet the regularities in our language suggest that action and volition are part of *making* something public, whereas the objective importance of a problem or issue is what *keeps* it public. Although lobbyists or protesters can make an issue public, it stays public because it commands the attention of most citizens.

32For arguments in favor of privatizing a variety of government services, see E. S. Savas, *Privatization: The Key to Better Government* (Chatham, N.J.: Chatham House, 1987).

33*Publicize* evokes the idea of public relations firms and "spin doctors"; *privatize,* a word that has gained currency since 1980, refers to devolving public services into the hands of the market or private contractors; *politicize* has a flavor of petty rivalries and undue influence.

34See *Bowers v. Hardwick* (1986), discussed in Chapter 4.

35For example, see Hannah Arendt, *The Human Condition* (Chicago: University of Chicago Press, 1958); Pitkin, "Justice"; Hanna Pitkin and Sara Shumer, "On Participation," *democracy* 2.4 (Fall 1982): 43; Sheldon Wolin, "What Revolutionary Action Means Today," *democracy* 2.4 (Fall 1982): 17–28.

Chapter Three. Arendt on Political Approaches to Intimate-Life Issues

1For a cultural critique that focuses on body images, see Susan Bordo, *Unbearable Weight* (Berkeley: University of California Press, 1993).

2A student once asked me if respecting the privacy of intimate life would not blind us to wrongs such as incest, spouse battering, rape, and other forms of psychological and sexual abuse. If we cherish intimacy, don't we put on blinders that put anything which takes place within an intimate relationship beyond the purview of critical public scrutiny? Don't we buy into a set of values that obscures the operations of power, both within relationships and families and from social and political institutions? I do not think so. I disagree with simplistic, overarching attacks on privacy, and at the same time insist on the need to make convincing arguments for the political significance of practices rooted in private life, which do often need to be treated as matters for political debate and activism.

[3]I draw on theorists who read Arendt's work on public and private through her own experiences as a Jew during the rise of anti-Semitism and the Holocaust, especially Dagmar Barnouw, *Visible Spaces: Hannah Arendt and the German-Jewish Experience* (Baltimore: Johns Hopkins University Press, 1990); Ron Feldman, introduction to Hannah Arendt, *The Jew as Pariah: Jewish Identity and Politics in the Modern Age* (New York: Grove Press, 1978); Jennifer Ring, "The Pariah as Hero: Hannah Arendt's Political Actor," *Political Theory* 19.3 (1991): 433–52; Seyla Benhabib, "Feminist Theory and Hannah Arendt's Concept of Public Space," *History of the Human Sciences* 6.2 (1993): 97–114; and Hanna Fenichel Pitkin, "Conformism, Housekeeping, and the Attack of the Blob: The Origins of Hannah Arendt's Concept of the Social"; Morris Kaplan, "Refiguring the Jewish Question: Arendt, Proust, and the Politics of Sexuality"; and Bonnie Honig, "Toward an Agonistic Feminism: Hannah Arendt and the Politics of Identity," all in *Feminist Interpretations of Hannah Arendt,* ed. Bonnie Honig (University Park: Pennsylvania State University Press, 1995); pp. 51–81, 105–33, 135–66 respectively.

[4]Hannah Arendt, *The Human Condition* (Chicago: University of Chicago Press, 1958), p. 37; see also pp. 28–49.

[5]Ibid., pp. 120, 29, 59.

[6]Ibid., pp. 24, 30–32, 26–27.

[7]"Without mastering the necessities of life in the household, neither life nor the 'good life' is possible, but politics is never for the sake of life. . . . No activity that served only the purpose of making a life, of sustaining only the life process, was permitted to enter the political realm." Ibid., p. 37.

[8]Ibid., pp. 28, 35, 72. Arendt laments not only the rise of society but also the emergence into public view of bodily necessities and those who attend to them; see, for example, pp. 72–73.

[9]Hannah Arendt, "The Crisis in Education," in *Between Past and Future* (New York: Viking Press, 1954), p. 188.

[10]For example, she writes: "The full development of the life of hearth and family into an inner and private space we owe to the extraordinary political sense of the Roman people who, unlike the Greeks, never sacrificed the private to the public, but on the contrary understood that these two realms could exist only in the form of coexistence." Arendt, *Human Condition,* p. 59.

[11]Ibid., pp. 119, 32. See also her reference to violent oppression in a slave society and exploitation in capitalist society, p. 88.

[12]Arendt, *On Revolution,* pp. 65, 88.

[13]Ibid., p. 68.

[14]Arendt, *Human Condition,* p. 2.

[15]Ibid., pp. 70–71, 120, 106, 107–8.

[16]Ibid., p. 38.

[17]Ibid., pp. 70, 71; see also pp. 62–63.

[18]Ibid., p. 51. Arendt describes the household as "the realm of birth and death which

must be hidden from the public realm because it harbors the things hidden from human eyes and impenetrable to human knowledge. It is hidden because man does not know where he comes from when he is born and where he goes when he dies." Ibid., pp. 62–63.

[19]Ibid., p. 71.

[20]Ibid., p. 133; see also pp. 134, 124, 5.

[21]Ibid., p. 134; see also pp. 3–5.

[22]Ibid., pp. 126–27; see also p. 46.

[23]Ring, "The Pariah as Hero," p. 439.

[24]Arendt also talks about the dangers of *Homo faber*'s attitude of instrumentalism, the mindset that permeates modern cost-benefit analysis and interest group politics. Because my focus here is on private versus public and ways to talk politically about "household" matters, I have chosen not to deal with *Homo faber*.

[25]I am indebted for this insight to Hanna Pitkin, "Justice: On Relating Private and Public," *Political Theory* 9.3 (1981): 346.

[26]Again I rely on Hanna Pitkin's analysis, ibid., pp. 342, 345. This reading may help mend the rift between the Hannah Arendt who reveres private life and laboring and reviles the injustice of forcing some to lead an exclusively private life, and the Arendt who attacks the merely private life of the household and laboring and idealizes the Greeks. But I am less concerned with whether this interpretation explains inconsistencies in Arendt's position than I am in seeing how many of Arendt's insights—about the sickness of consumer society, the need to labor repetitively at necessary chores, the importance of privacy as home to hidden aspects of human life, the need for a genuine political life—help us understand the world we live in.

[27]Arendt, *Human Condition,* pp. 51, 73; emphasis added. Arendt seems here, and throughout *The Human Condition,* to draw on one of the most common meanings of public and private: she thinks *spatially* about public and private *places* in the world, giving us an almost theatrical distinction between that which happens "onstage" and that which goes on "behind the scenes."

[28]Ibid., p. 57.

[29]Ibid., p. 52.

[30]See my discussion of anthropological philosophical approaches to privacy in Chapter 1.

[31]I am indebted here to Peter Steinberger for his perceptive comments on a paper I gave at the 1994 Western Political Science Association meetings, where he suggested thinking about public and private not as different spheres or spaces but as different "modes of being," variable ways of thinking and acting about the same matters.

[32]I discuss mainly the distinction between political and social approaches to issues rooted in private life. A fuller treatment of Arendt's thinking about public-private, political-social, and private-intimate distinctions would have to attend to her differentiation between private and intimate. She sees "the intimate" as developed in opposition to the rise of "the social," and views it as a way to protect personal life from social pressures. "Intimate" is not the same as "private"; they differ in part because the latter is related to physical location (private property, walls and laws that protect what goes on in private from public view), whereas the former refers to the manifold richness of our individual emotional lives under modernity. Intimacy provides a space for personal development and meaning that make up for the loss of meaningful public life.

[33]Hannah Arendt, *Rahel Varnhagen: The Life of a Jewish Woman* (New York: Harcourt,

Brace, Jovanovich, 1974); Arendt, *Jew as Pariah*; Hannah Arendt, *Eichmann in Jerusalem: A Report on the Banality of Evil* (New York: Penguin, 1963).

[34]Hannah Arendt, *The Origins of Totalitarianism* (New York: Harcourt, Brace, and World, 1951); Arendt, "The Moral of History" (1946), in *Jew as Pariah*, p. 107; Arendt, *Rahel Varnhagen*, p. 85.

[35]Arendt, *Rahel Varnhagen*, pp. 204–5, 208.

[36]Rahel's deathbed words, as reported by her husband, were: "The thing which all my life seemed to me the greatest shame, which was the misery and misfortune of my life—having been born a Jewess—this I should on no account now wish to have missed." Ibid., p. 3; see also p. 177.

[37]Arendt, "We Refugees" (1943), in *Jew as Pariah*, pp. 60–61; see also pp. 62–63.

[38]Arendt, "Moral of History," p. 110; Hannah Arendt, "Portrait of a Period" (1943), in *Jew as Pariah*, p. 115; Hannah Arendt, "Jew as Pariah: A Hidden Tradition" (1944), in *Jew as Pariah*, p. 77.

[39]Ring, "The Pariah as Hero," p. 441.

[40]Pitkin, "Conformism, Housekeeping, and the Attack of the Blob," pp. 60–63.

[41]Arendt does, however, recount several examples in *Eichmann in Jerusalem* of courageous people who stood up to the Nazi policy of exterminating the Jews: the Scholls, a brother and sister who were students at Munich University, who distributed leaflets calling Hitler a mass murderer (p. 104); Dutch students who went on strike when Jewish professors were dismissed from universities (p. 169); Danish and Swedish resistance to handing Jews over to the Germans (pp. 171–75); Anton Schmidt, a sergeant in the German army who helped members of the Jewish underground for some five months (p. 230). After listening to testimony about Sergeant Schmidt, Arendt wonders "how utterly different everything would be today in this courtroom, in Israel, in Germany, in all of Europe, and perhaps in all countries of the world, if only more such stories could have been told" (p. 231).

[42]Arendt, *Human Condition*, p. 58.

[43]David Greider argues strongly for ordinary citizens' taking the responsibility to judge matters such as economic policy, rather than deferring to experts, in his book describing the genesis of "supply side" economic policy, *The Education of David Stockman and Other Americans* (New York: Signet, 1986). For a similar argument to the one I make here about allowing political decisions to be treated as administrative ones, see Benhabib, "Hannah Arendt's Concept of Public Space," p. 110.

[44]There is an extensive literature about "passing" by gays, lesbians, and bisexuals, some of which is extremely critical of closeted homosexuals. See, for example, Richard Mohr, *Gay Ideas: Outing and Other Controversies* (Boston: Beacon Press, 1992), chap. 1. I explore this literature in detail in Chapter 6. For a theoretical argument comparing passing by gays, lesbians, and bisexuals to assimilation by Jews in the context of Arendt's distinction between parvenus and pariahs, see Kaplan, "Refiguring the Jewish Question."

[45]Both Kaplan and Honig point admiringly to Arendt's independence from social convention and wariness of membership in identity communities as part of her intellectual disposition, and Honig and Benhabib speak to the importance of protecting private life. See Kaplan, "Refiguring the Jewish Question, p. 108; Honig, "Toward an Agonistic Feminism," pp. 150, 145; and Benhabib, "Hannah Arendt's Concept of Public Space," pp. 106–7.

[46]Pitkin writes: "Drawn into public life by personal need, fear, ambition or interest, we are there forced to acknowledge the power of others and appeal to their standards, even as we try to get them to acknowledge our power and standards. We are forced to find or create

a common language of purposes and aspirations, not merely to clothe our private outlook in public disguise, but to become aware ourselves of its public meaning. . . . In the process, we learn to think about the standards themselves, about our stake in the existence of standards, of justice, of our community, even of our opponents and enemies in the community; so that afterwards we are changed. Economic man becomes a citizen" ("Justice," p. 347).

[47]Honig, "Toward an Agonistic Feminism," p. 143.

[48]Wendy Brown suggests this as an alternative to traditional notions of the political, which are often intertwined with "macho" values of daring and aggression. See Wendy Brown, *Manhood and Politics: A Feminist Reading in Political Theory* (Totowa, N.J.: Rowman & Littlefield, 1988), pp. 205–6. One example of a way to express respect for the sustained efforts of nurturing human life would be to give "nurturing parents" (parents who spend at least two years out of the work force while their children are babies) an automatic lifetime preference in seeking civil service jobs. (I model this imaginary policy on *Personnel Administrator of Massachusetts v. Feeney* [1979], in which a woman challenged a lifetime civil service preference for veterans on gender discrimination grounds.)

[49]Hanna Pitkin writes, "Our public life is an empty form—at best a meaningless diversion for a few, at worst a hateful, hypocritical mask for privilege—unless it actively engages the unplanned drift and the private social power that shape people's lives" ("Justice," p. 346).

[50]For arguments about the centrality of justice for moving from private sufferer to citizen, see Pitkin, "Justice," p. 348; Richard J. Bernstein, "Rethinking the Social and the Political," *Graduate Faculty Philosophy Journal* 11.1 (1986): 125; and Mary G. Dietz, "Feminist Receptions of Hannah Arendt," in Honig, *Feminist Interpretations of Hannah Arendt*, p. 40.

[51]Benhabib, "Hannah Arendt's Concept of Public Space," pp. 105, 110.

[52]Honig, "Toward an Agonistic Feminism," pp. 155, 147, 146.

[53]Arendt, *Human Condition*, p. 50.

[54]Paul Monette, *Becoming a Man: Half a Life Story* (New York: Harcourt, Brace, Jovanovich, 1992). See also Paul Monette, *Borrowed Time: An AIDS Memoir* (San Diego: Harcourt, Brace, Jovanovich, 1988); Rita Mae Brown, *Rubyfruit Jungle* (1973; rpt. New York: Quality Paperback Books, 1993); Adrienne Rich, *Of Woman Born* (New York: Norton, 1976); Maya Angelou, *I Know Why the Caged Bird Sings* (New York: Random House, 1969); Audre Lorde, *Zami* (Freedom, Calif.: Crossing Press, 1982).

[55]Kaplan, "Refiguring the Jewish Question."

[56]Benhabib, "Hannah Arendt's Concept of Public Space," p. 104.

[57]Benhabib carefully dissociates her notion of "home" from any particular kind of family or intimacy, and argues that "private property" in the sense of ownership is not central to Arendt's concept of a private space. Ibid., p. 107.

[58]For criticisms of identity politics, see Shane Phelan's discussion of lesbian community in *Identity Politics* (Philadelphia: Temple University Press, 1989); Bernice Johnson Reagon's critique of "the barred room" of identity politics in her speech "Coalition Politics: Turning the Century," in *Home Girls: A Black Feminist Anthology,* ed. Barbara Smith (New York: Kitchen Table/Women of Color Press, 1983); Honig, "Toward an Agonistic Feminism," pp. 148–50, 154–55; Kaplan, "Refiguring the Jewish Question," pp. 126, 129–31.

[59]Students frequently ask me, for example, about women changing their surname when they marry: "If I change my name, does that mean I'm not a feminist? If the decision to keep or change one's name is not a valid way to judge one's politics, how come so many seem to judge my feminist credentials lacking if I take my husband's name?" (The same is often asked about other superficial characteristics associated with being a feminist.) As I argue in the text,

I think it prudent to avoid the temptation to judge others on the basis of their intimate life affiliations or personal style, but to focus instead on the more crucial aspect of feminism, which is to empower women to question and struggle against injustices and inequalities.

[60]Cynthia Perwin Halpern, "Property, Privacy, and Power," paper presented at the American Political Science Association annual meeting, New York City, September 1–4, 1994, p. 43.

Chapter Four. Problems with the Right to Privacy

[1]Samuel Warren and Louis Brandeis are often credited with originating the idea of a right to privacy because of their influential *Harvard Law Review* piece in 1890, in which they argued that the individual has a right to an "inviolate personality" and cannot be subjected to unwanted publicity. See Samuel D. Warren and Louis D. Brandeis, "The Right to Privacy," *Harvard Law Review* 4 (1890): 193–220. According to the *Restatement of Torts,* actions may lie for intrusion into one's seclusion or solitude, especially if one gains access through deception; for public disclosure of embarrassing private facts; for publicity that places one in a false light; or for appropriation of one's likeness or name without permission for pecuniary advantage.

[2]One can see this preoccupation in a cursory glance at a constitutional law syllabus (covering, e.g., the turn-of-the-century fixation with protecting liberty of contract, separating intrastate production from interstate commerce, striking down regulatory uses of taxation) or list of law school courses, including contracts, real property, trusts and estates, and corporations. Jennifer Nedelsky has argued for the central role property rights played in curbing government power up until the 1930s in *Private Property and the Limits of American Constitutionalism* (Chicago: University of Chicago Press, 1990).

[3]This is Morris Kaplan's phrase. His analysis of the grounds of Justice Douglas's *Griswold* decision is quite fine. See Morris B. Kaplan, "Intimacy and Equality: The Question of Lesbian and Gay Marriage," *Philosophical Forum* 25.4 (1994): 333–60, 341.

[4]381 U.S. 479 at 486, 485.

[5]405 U.S. 438 at 453. The approach in *Eisenstadt* was reiterated in *Carey v. Population Services, International* 431 U.S. 678 (1977), where Justice Brennan again wrote the majority opinion. That decision states: "Read in light of its progeny [especially *Eisenstadt v. Baird* and *Roe v. Wade*], the teaching of *Griswold* is that the Constitution protects individual decisions in matters of childbearing from unjustified intrusion by the State." Quoted in Herma Kay, *Sex-Based Discrimination: Texts, Cases and Materials,* 2d ed. (Saint Paul, Minn.: West Publishing, 1981), p. 405.

[6]"The right of privacy . . . is broad enough to encompass a woman's decision whether or not to terminate her pregnancy. The detriment that the State would impose upon the pregnant woman by denying this choice altogether is apparent. Specific and direct harm medically diagnosable even in early pregnancy may be involved. Maternity, or additional offspring, may force upon the woman a distressful life and future. Psychological harm may be imminent. Mental and physical health may be taxed by child care. There is also the distress, by all concerned, associated with the unwanted child, and there is the problem of bringing a child into a family already unable, psychologically and otherwise, to care for it. In other cases, as in this one, the additional difficulties and continuing stigma of unwed motherhood may be involved. All these are factors the woman and her responsible physician necessarily will consider in consultation." 410 U.S. at 153.

[7]Joel Feinberg, "Autonomy, Sovereignty, and Privacy: Moral Ideals in the Constitu-

tion?," *Notre Dame Law Review* 58 (February 1983): 445–92; Jeb Rubenfeld, "The Right of Privacy," *Harvard Law Review* 102 (1989): 737–807; David A. J. Richards, "Constitutional Legitimacy and Constitutional Privacy," *New York University Law Review* 61 (1986): 800; and Kaplan, "Intimacy and Equality," make such arguments.

[8]See Kristin Luker, *Taking Chances* (Berkeley: University of California Press, 1975); Catharine MacKinnon, *Feminism Unmodified* (Cambridge: Harvard University Press, 1987); Rosalind Petchesky, *Abortion and Women's Choice* (New York: Longman, 1984); Sylvia Law, "Rethinking Sex and the Constitution," *University of Pennsylvania Law Review* 132.5 (June 1984): 955–1040. See also Mary Ann Glendon, *Abortion and Divorce in Western Law* (Cambridge: Harvard University Press, 1987), and *Rights Talk* (New York: Free Press, 1991), for arguments that U.S. abortion law is overly individualistic and pays too little attention to the need for communal support, including public policies supporting families and child rearing.

[9]410 U.S. at 159.

[10]Two of the leading cases in this area are *In re A. C.* (D.C. Court of Appeals [1990] 573 A.2d 1234), dealing with a cesarean section performed on a terminally ill woman without her consent, and *Johnson v. State of Florida* (Supreme Court of Florida [1992] 602 So.2d 1288), a prosecution for delivery of drugs to a minor through the umbilical cord in the seconds after birth. For excellent discussions of these cases and of the issues they present, see Cynthia Daniels, *At Women's Expense* (Cambridge: Harvard University Press, 1993). See also Janna C. Merrick and Robert H. Blank, eds., "The Politics of Pregnancy: Policy Dilemmas in the Maternal-Fetal Relationship," *Women and Politics* 13.3–4 (1993): 1–224 (entire issue devoted to this theme); Faye D. Ginsburg and Rayna Rapp, eds., *Conceiving the New World Order: The Global Politics of Reproduction* (Berkeley: University of California Press, 1995); and Patricia Boling, ed., *Expecting Trouble: Surrogacy, Fetal Abuse, and New Reproductive Technologies* (Boulder, Colo.: Westview Press, 1995).

[11]For critical discussions, see Wendy Brown, "Reproductive Freedom and the Right to Privacy: A Paradox for Feminists," in *Families, Politics, and Public Policy*, ed. Irene Diamond (New York: Longman, 1983), pp. 322–38; Petchesky, *Abortion and Woman's Choice*, pp. 295–302; Catharine MacKinnon, *Toward a Feminist Theory of the State* (Cambridge: Harvard University Press, 1989), pp. 192–93; dissenting opinions of Justice Marshall and of Justice Blackmun (joined by Justices Brennan and Marshall), *Beal v. Doe* 432 U.S. 438, 455–63.

[12]Interestingly, this is the same argument Catharine MacKinnon makes in *attacking* the right to privacy. See *Toward a Feminist Theory of the State*, chap. 10, and *Feminism Unmodified*, chap. 8.

[13]492 U.S. 490, 509.

[14]120 L. Ed. 2d 674, 704; see also 701, 699.

[15]425 U.S. 52, 74 (1976).

[16]443 U.S. 662 (1979) at 635, 637. References throughout are to *Bellotti v. Baird II*, the second version of this case to reach the Supreme Court.

[17]450 U.S. at 408–13.

[18]The Court cites statistics that only 50 percent of Minnesota minors live with both biological parents (497 U.S. at 437).

[19]" 'The fundamental liberty interest of natural parents in the care, custody, and management of their child does not evaporate simply because they have not been model parents.' " Justice Kennedy, concurring in the judgment in part, dissenting in part, 497 U.S. at 485 (quoting *Santowsky v. Kramer* 455 U.S. 745, 753 [1972]).

[20]443 U.S. at 648–49.

[21]Justice Kennedy concurring in the judgment in part, dissenting in part, 497 U.S. at 491–92, 483–84; see also 489. This reasoning contributes to "normalizing" the family by accepting the assumption that it is desirable for both parents to be involved in their daughter's abortion decision, regardless of the circumstances—divorce, abandonment, failure to pay child support, estrangement, serious illness of one of the parents, and so on—of the particular family.

[22]Robert B. Keiter, "Privacy, Children, and Their Parents: Reflections On and Beyond the Supreme Court's Approach," *Minnesota Law Review* 66 (1982): 511, 505, 506.

[23]Daniels, *At Women's Expense,* p. 48; see also pp. 42–46.

[24]Ibid., pp. 50–51.

[25]Ibid., p. 49; see also p. 52.

[26]Daniels writes, "Pregnant addicts represented not the lost, confused, or misguided mother, but the *anti-mother.*" Ibid., p. 106. She reports at least 167 documented prosecutions of women for using illicit drugs or alcohol during pregnancy between 1985 and 1992. Between 1989 and 1992 eighty-seven cases were brought against women in South Carolina alone, and another forty-three women were forced to undergo treatment or face criminal charges (pp. 103, 104). Iris Young develops this argument: "It is not just anyone who has harmed their baby, say by shooting it up with cocaine. It's the child's *mother.* The mother is supposed to be the one who sacrifices herself, who will do anything for her child, who will preserve and nurture it. That's what mothering *means.* The rage directed at pregnant addicts unconsciously recalls the feeling we all had as children of rage toward our mothers who were not always there for us, did not always respond to our needs and desires, and sometimes pursued their own purposes and desires. The mother who harms her child is not merely a criminal, she is a monster." Iris Young, "Punishment, Treatment, Empowerment: Three Approaches to Policy for Pregnant Addicts," in Boling, *Expecting Trouble,* p. 111.

[27]Lisa C. Bower connects such stereotypes to the notion of Africanism in "The Trope of the Dark Continent in the Fetal Harm Debates: 'Africanism' and the Right to Choice," in Boling, *Expecting Trouble,* pp. 145–46; see also Dorothy E. Roberts, "Punishing Drug Addicts Who Have Babies: Women of Color, Equality, and the Right of Privacy," *Harvard Law Review* 104.7 (1991): 1419–82; Daniels, *At Women's Expense,* pp. 52, 103.

[28]Jean Reith Schroedel and Paul Peretz, "A Gender Analysis of Policy Formation: The Case of Fetal Abuse," in Boling, *Expecting Trouble,* pp. 85–108.

[29]Celeste Michele Condit, *Decoding Abortion Rhetoric: Communicating Social Change* (Urbana: University of Illinois Press, 1990); Rosalind Pollack Petchesky, "Fetal Images: The Power of Visual Culture in the Politics of Reproduction," *Feminist Studies* 13.2 (Summer 1987): 263–92; Dierdre Condit, "Fetal Personhood: Political Identity under Construction," in Boling, *Expecting Trouble,* pp. 25–54; Daniels, *At Women's Expense,* pp. 37–41.

[30]See note 26. Daniels, *At Women's Expense,* pp. 106, 146; Young, "Punishment, Treatment, Empowerment."

[31]Mary Lyndon Shanley, " 'Surrogate Mothering' and Women's Freedom: A Critique of Contracts for Human Reproduction," in Boling, *Expecting Trouble,* pp. 167–68.

[32]Daniels, *At Women's Expense,* p. 55.

[33]Ibid., p. 134.

[34]Patricia Bayer Richard, "The Tailor Made Child: Implications for Women and the State," in Boling, *Expecting Trouble,* p. 18.

[35]478 U.S. 186, 190–91.

[36]478 U.S. 186, 194. See also the observation that many conservatives see homosexual

families as the last straw in terms of new threats to "family values," in Kaplan, "Intimacy and Equality," p. 336.

[37]See June Aline Eichbaum, "Towards an Autonomy-Based Theory of Constitutional Privacy: Beyond the Ideology of Familial Privacy," *Harvard Civil Rights–Civil Liberties Law Review,* 14 (1979): 361–84, for an early critique of "familial" privacy on the basis of its bias in favor of conventional relationships. The Court decided *Romer v. Evans* 94–1039 on May 20, 1996, striking down as unconstitutional Colorado's Amendment 2, which made gay rights ordinances aimed at guaranteeing civil rights for gays and lesbians illegal. This is the first gay rights case the Court has taken up since *Bowers v. Hardwick*. Although it has no bearing on the issue of privacy protections, it has been heralded by gay rights and civil liberties groups as a major contribution to constitutional protections for gays, lesbians, and bisexuals. *New York Times,* May 21, 1996, p. A1.

[38]Justice Blackmun dissenting in 478 U.S. 186, 204–5.

[39]Cynthia Perwin Halpern, "Property, Privacy and Power," paper presented at the American Political Science Association annual meeting, New York City, September 1–4, 1994, p. 23. See also Alida Brill's arresting description of homeless people washing themselves first thing in the morning in Grand Central Station, in *Nobody's Business: Paradoxes of Privacy* (Reading, Mass.: Addison-Wesley, 1990), pp. xv–xvi.

[40]Frank Michelman, "Law's Republic," *Yale Law Journal* 97.8 (July 1988): 1493–1537, 1534, quoting Note, "The Constitutional Status of Sexual Orientation: Homosexuality as a Suspect Classification," *Harvard Law Review* 91 (1985): 1290–91 (quoting Laurence Tribe, *American Constitutional Law* [Mineola, N.Y.: Foundation Press, 1978]: 888); see also Kendall Thomas, "Beyond the Privacy Principle," *Columbia Law Review* 92 (1992): 1431–1516; and Note, "The Constitutional Status of Sexual Orientation: Homosexuality as a Suspect Classification," *Harvard Law Review* 98 (1985): 1285–1309.

[41]See, for example, Louis Henkin, "Privacy and Autonomy," *Columbia Law Review* 74 (1974): 1410.

[42]See MacKinnon's analysis in *Feminism Unmodified,* p. 99.

[43]Halpern, "Property, Privacy and Power," p. 24.

[44]Ruth Gavison, "Feminism and the Public/Private Distinction," *Stanford Law Review* 45 (November 1992): 32.

[45]Cass Sunstein makes a similar argument for gradualism in declaring sexual orientation a "suspect class" for Fourteenth Amendment equal protection analysis. See Cass Sunstein, "Homosexuality and the Constitution," *Indiana Law Journal* 70.1 (1994): 1–28.

[46]Rhonda Copelon, "Losing the Negative Right of Privacy: Building Sexual and Reproductive Freedom," *New York University Review of Law and Social Change* 18.1 (1990): 50.

[47]Copelon, "Losing the Negative Right of Privacy," pp. 44–45; Roberts, "Punishing Drug Addicts Who Have Babies," pp. 1479, 1480; Peggy Cooper Davis, "Neglected Stories and the Lawfulness of *Roe v. Wade,*" *Harvard Civil Rights–Civil Liberties Law Review* 28.2 (1993): 393–94, 386, 389.

[48]Kaplan, "Intimacy and Equality," p. 349.

[49]Morris B. Kaplan, "Autonomy, Equality, Community: The Question of Lesbian and Gay Rights," *Praxis International* 11.2 (July 1991): 201; Michelman, "Law's Republic."

[50]Kaplan, "Autonomy, Equality, Community," p. 206.

[51]Kaplan, "Intimacy and Equality," p. 350.

[52]Kaplan, "Autonomy, Equality, Community," p. 211.

[53]Michelman, "Law's Republic," p. 1536.

[54]Ibid., pp. 1533, 1495.

[55]Ibid., pp. 1533, 1535. See also Jean L. Cohen, "Redescribing Privacy: Identity, Difference, and the Abortion Controversy," *Columbia Journal of Gender and Law* 3.1 (1992): 43–117, for an argument that privacy is a key political right.

Chapter Five. The Democratic Potential of Mothering

[1]See, for example, Carole Pateman, "Feminist Critiques of the Public/Private Dichotomy," in *The Disorder of Women: Democracy, Feminism, and Political Theory* (Stanford: Stanford University Press, 1989). Pateman addressed issues related to mothering more directly in her Jefferson Memorial Lectures, delivered at Berkeley in February 1985, especially her third lecture, "The Personal and the Political." See also Susan Okin, *Justice, Gender and the Family* (New York: Basic Books, 1989); Jean Bethke Elshtain, *Public Man, Private Woman* (Princeton: Princeton University Press, 1981); Hanna Pitkin, "Justice: On Relating Private and Public," *Political Theory* 9.3 (August 1981): 327–52.

[2]Hannah Arendt, *The Human Condition* (Chicago: University of Chicago Press, 1958); Sheldon Wolin, *Politics and Vision* (Boston: Little, Brown, 1960); Sheldon Wolin, "What Revolutionary Action Means Today," *democracy* 2.4 (Fall 1982): 17–28; Mary G. Dietz, "Citizenship with a Feminist Face: The Problem with Maternal Thinking," *Political Theory* 13.1 (February 1985): 19–37; Joan C. Tronto, "Beyond Gender Difference to a Theory of Care," *Signs* 12.4 (Summer 1987): 644–63. Of course Arendt and Wolin are not arguing for a *feminist* democratic theory, just a democratic one.

[3]For the first view, see Elshtain, *Public Man, Private Woman;* Sara Ruddick, "Maternal Thinking" and "Preservative Love and Military Destructiveness," both in *Mothering: Essays in Feminist Theory,* ed. Joyce Trebilcot (Totowa, N.J.: Rowman & Allanheld, 1983), pp. 213–62; Carol Gilligan, *In a Different Voice* (Cambridge: Harvard University Press, 1982). For the second view, see Arendt, *Human Condition;* Dietz, "Citizenship with a Feminist Face"; Tronto, "Beyond Gender Difference."

[4]See Elshtain, *Public Man, Private Woman;* Ruddick, "Maternal Thinking" and "Preservative Love and Military Destructiveness"; Gilligan, *In a Different Voice;* Dorothy Dinnerstein, *The Mermaid and the Minotaur: Sexual Arrangements and Human Malaise* (New York: Harper Colophon, 1976).

[5]Ruddick, "Maternal Thinking," pp. 214, 224. Carol Gilligan's work on women's moral development (see *In a Different Voice*), especially her focus on the concern with preserving relationships and establishing care as central moral values, echoes the argument for maternal thought and generalizes it from mothers to all women. According to Gilligan, in our society girls and women learn to reason differently about moral issues not simply because they are or may become mothers, but because of our gendered social structures whereby women care for children. This leads girls to develop different feelings about attachment and autonomy than boys, who must early in life, and more completely than girls, differentiate themselves from their mothers. Unlike Ruddick and Elshtain, however, Gilligan does not propose that we reconstruct public life around an ethic of care. Instead she suggests that adults should be able both to think in terms of rights and justice and to sustain care and preserve relationships. See also Dinnerstein, *Mermaid and Minotaur.*

[6]Ruddick, "Preservative Love"; Elshtain, *Public Man, Private Woman,* pp. 322–53 passim; Dinnerstein, *Mermaid and Minotaur,* pp. 215, 217–18, and chap. 9 in general.

[7]See Dinnerstein, *Mermaid and Minotaur;* Nancy Chodorow, *The Reproduction of Mothering* (Berkeley: University of California Press, 1978).

[8]Elshtain and Ruddick have little to say about the psychological ramifications, or the injustice, of women's sole responsibility for child rearing. They treat male involvement in parenting as a possibly desirable but certainly not essential change in current gender arrangements. Ruddick, "Maternal Thinking," pp. 225–26; Elshtain, *Public Man, Private Woman,* pp. 326–39. Others, in contrast, argue that "maternal thinking" must be learned by all humans, not just women or mothers, if we are to transform our public life according to more humane values and aspire to visions of human and political maturity. See Dinnerstein, *Mermaid and Minotaur;* Gilligan, *In a Different Voice.*

[9]A friend who is a single mother of three teenage boys tells me that she must both mother and *father* her children, and that is hard for her to do, since she does not know how to be a good "father." Nurturing clearly has its male and female variants.

[10]Jean Grimshaw, *Philosophy and Feminist Thinking* (Minneapolis: University of Minnesota Press, 1986), pp. 210–11.

[11]Joan Tronto makes this criticism of the "ethic of care" in *Moral Boundaries* (New York: Routledge, 1993).

[12]Catharine MacKinnon, *Feminism Unmodified* (Cambridge: Harvard University Press, 1987), pp. 38–39; and Tronto, "Beyond Gender Difference," p. 649, make this point.

[13]Dinnerstein, *Mermaid and Minotaur,* argues this repeatedly.

[14]Ruddick, "Maternal Thinking," p. 226; "Preservative Love and Military Destructiveness," pp. 238–39, 256–58; Elshtain, *Public Man, Private Woman,* pp. 326–49.

[15]Dietz, "Citizenship with a Feminist Face," p. 32. See also Mary G. Dietz, "Context Is All: Feminism and Theories of Citizenship," *Daedalus* 116.4 (Fall 1987): 1–24. Jean Grimshaw also makes this criticism in *Philosophy and Feminist Thinking,* pp. 202–3.

[16]Dietz, "Citizenship with a Feminist Face," pp. 30–31, 32. This characterization of mothering, first used by Jean Elshtain in "Antigone's Daughters: Reflections on Female Identity and the State," in *Families, Politics, and Public Policy,* ed. Irene Diamond (New York: Longman, 1983), pp. 300–311, strikes me as unfair and unnuanced. Mothers are likely to chasten and correct toddlers but to reason with teenagers or adult children. And some parents do not chasten even small children, but strive to create a "democratic family" in which children are told the consequences of their actions in order to avoid constant nagging and correcting.

[17]Dietz, "Citizenship with a Feminist Face," p. 28.

[18]Ibid., p. 33. Although Dietz acknowledges that women may come to politics because of their needs and interests as mothers, she argues that they will be unlikely to sustain their interest and participation in politics. Instead, they will probably "retreat to their homes after a periodic—and rare—victory," thus contributing nothing "to a democratic ethical polity," but only recapitulating "the worst features of political participants in the liberal-capitalist state" (p. 33).

[19]Ibid., p. 34.

[20]Of course, neither women nor mothers are formally excluded from political participation, either in contemporary American society or in theories of active participatory democracy. But the animosity of such theories to concerns and issues that are housed in the intimate life of the family or household makes it sound as though many problems that matter to women, and especially to mothers, are too parochial to be dealt with politically.

[21]In large part such issues are not inspired by a "maternal perspective" of concern with preserving children (as in Dietz's example of Mothers Against Drunk Driving) but rather seek recognition of and help with the problems of caring for children and combining parenting with paid work.

[22]In the United States in 1950, 23 percent of mothers with children under the age of six worked; in 1986, 54 percent did. Even more startling, over 50 percent of mothers of babies under one year old now work. See Arlie Hochschild, *The Second Shift: Inside the Two-Job Marriage* (New York: Viking, 1989), p. 2; John P. Fernandez, *Child Care and Corporate Productivity: Resolving Family/Work Conflicts* (Lexington, Mass.: Lexington Books, 1986), pp. 8–9.

[23]Hochschild, *The Second Shift*, pp. 1–9.

[24]Even though many of the problems I talk about also apply to men who are primary parents, the vast majority of primary parents are mothers. In addition, women earn lower wages on average than men; and it is mainly women who face the problems of the second shift, and who are assumed to be the primary parent in early infancy (see Dinnerstein, *Mermaid and Minotaur*). In referring exclusively to mothers, I do not mean to reinforce existing gender roles, or to ignore the problems faced by fathers who are primary nurturers. Primary caretaker fathers—a role women have every reason to want to encourage—receive even more criticism than working mothers. Under the prevailing corporate male ethic, men who take time off to care for their kids, or who refuse overtime or transfers for family reasons, are viewed in an even worse light than women who do so, since men are still presumed to be breadwinners and must be seen as "serious" about their jobs. See Felice N. Schwartz, "Management Women and the New Facts of Life," *Harvard Business Review* 67.1 (January–February 1989): 65–76.

[25]For a good discussion of this movement toward changing the "male definition of work," see Anne Showstack Sassoon, "Women's New Social Role: Contradictions of the Welfare State," in *Women and the State: The Shifting Boundaries of Public and Private,* ed. Ann Showstack Sassoon (London: Hutchinson, 1987).

[26]Hochschild, *Second Shift*, p. 268; Arlie Hochschild et al., "Beyond the Mommy Track: Giving the Stalled Revolution a Push," panel discussion, February 27, 1990, Berkeley.

[27]"Groupies" is Sheldon Wolin's term for interest group members in "What Revolutionary Action Means Today," p. 21.

[28]See Pitkin, "Justice," p. 347, for a suggestive paragraph about how private interest can be translated into political demands. Here I offer an example of how this kind of transformative process works.

[29]This is a contentious distinction, of course, since pregnancy cannot always be planned or prevented, and since many "unplanned" illnesses and accidents may be due to an individual's choices about drinking, diet, smoking, and exercise, and might therefore be thought of as preventable.

[30]This prospect is not as farfetched as it sounds. Consider current debates about changes in the workplace to accommodate working parents, or courtroom discussions about child custody, or survivor's benefits for fathers as well as mothers.

[31]Dinnerstein, *Mermaid and Minotaur,* is the source of the argument set out in this passage.

[32]Cynthia Perwin Halpern, "Property, Privacy, and Power," paper presented at the American Political Science Association annual meeting, New York, September 1–4, 1994, p. 43.

[33]See Carole Pateman, *The Sexual Contract* (Cambridge: Polity, 1988); Nancy J. Hirschmann, "Freedom, Recognition, and Obligation: A Feminist Approach," *American Political Science Review* 83.4 (December 1989): 1227–44; Seyla Benhabib, "The Generalized and the Concrete Other: The Kohlberg-Gilligan Controversy and Feminist Theory," in *Feminism as*

Critique, ed. Seyla Benhabib and Drucilla Cornell (Minneapolis: University of Minnesota Press, 1987); Okin, *Justice, Gender, and the Family.*

[34] See Okin, *Justice, Gender, and the Family,* pp. 105–7; Gilligan, *In a Different Voice.*

[35] Arendt, *Human Condition,* p. 176.

[36] Wolin, "What Revolutionary Action Means Today," p. 21.

[37] Dietz, "Citizenship with a Feminist Face," pp. 31–32. One could add justice to her list. Dietz also writes: "Without question, Aristotle was wrong to restrict women to the household and render them eternally subject to natural and familial inequalities. But this forms no necessary part of his argument concerning politics and citizenship" (p. 28).

[38] "Maternal virtues cannot be political in the required sense because . . . they are connected to and emerge out of an activity that is special, distinctive, unlike any other. We must conclude, then, that this activity is unlike the activity of citizenship; the two cannot be viewed as somehow encompassing the same attributes, abilities, and ways of knowing." Ibid., pp. 30–31.

[39] Pitkin, "Justice," helped me think about this connection; others have already argued for connecting an ethic of care to justice. See Tronto, *Moral Boundaries;* Iris Young, "Punishment, Treatment, Empowerment: Three Approaches to Policy for Pregnant Addicts," in *Expecting Trouble: Surrogacy, Fetal Abuse, and New Reproductive Technologies,* ed. Patricia Boling (Boulder, Colo.: Westview, 1995), pp. 109–34.

[40] Tronto, *Moral Boundaries,* pp. 175–76.

[41] Ibid., pp. 167–68.

[42] Ibid., pp. 162, 171, 173.

[43] Ibid., pp. 168, 177.

Chapter Six. "The Personal Is Political"

[1] But see Judy Scales-Trent, *Notes of a White Black Woman* (University Park: Pennsylvania State University Press, 1995), for fascinating stories and an analysis of the experiences of a black woman whom many take for white.

[2] Janet E. Halley, "The Politics of the Closet: Towards Equal Protection for Gay, Lesbian, and Bisexual Identity," *UCLA Law Review* 36: (1989): 946–47. I use "gay" or "queer" as shorthand for lesbian, gay, and bisexual to avoid awkward, repetitive phrasing.

[3] Eve Kosofsky Sedgwick, *Epistemology of the Closet* (Berkeley: University of California Press, 1990), p. 68. Others echo Sedgwick's notion that the closet is a fundamental and dreaded institution for most lesbians and gays, though often not with her appreciation for the difficulty of escaping it. For example, although Richard Mohr and Michelangelo Signorile acknowledge that the closet is a social convention that centrally defines the gay community, they argue it must be abandoned at all costs, even by tactics such as outing. See Richard Mohr, *Gay Ideas: Outing and Other Controversies* (Boston: Beacon Press, 1992); Michelangelo Signorile, *Queer in America: Sex, the Media, and the Closets of Power* (New York: Random House, 1993).

[4] See Peter Davies, "The Role of Disclosure in Coming Out among Gay Men," in *Modern Homosexualities: Fragments of Lesbian and Gay Experience,* ed. Ken Plummer (London: Routledge, 1992), p. 75. See also Halley, "Politics of the Closet," p. 947.

[5] Many researchers describe coming out as a process that occurs through a regular, predictable, cycle of stages. See, for example, John Alan Lee, "Going Public: A Study in the Sociology of Homosexual Liberation," *Journal of Homosexuality* 3.1 (Fall 1977): 49–78; Gary J. McDonald, "Individual Differences in the Coming Out Process for Gay Men: Implications

for Theoretical Models," *Journal of Homosexuality* 8.1 (Fall 1982): 47–60; Carmen de Monteflores and Stephen J. Schultz, "Coming Out: Similarities and Differences for Lesbians and Gay Men," *Journal of Social Issues* 14.3 (1978): 59–72.

[6]Davies, "The Role of Disclosure," p. 78. Mark Blasius also conceptualizes coming out as a lifelong process of becoming lesbian or gay, in the sense that it takes ongoing work to create a lesbian or gay self and a gay community in which to come out. For Blasius, coming out is a matter of "working on the self" as an "object of ethico-aesthetic work." Mark Blasius, "An Ethos of Lesbian and Gay Existence," *Political Theory* 20.4 (November 1992): 650, 655. See also his book *A Politics Of Sexuality: The Emergence of a Lesbian and Gay Ethos* (Philadelphia: Temple University Press, 1993).

[7]Monteflores and Schultz, "Coming Out," p. 66. The examples are from Blasius, "An Ethos of Lesbian and Gay Existence," p. 656.

[8]Thus, for example, one would not ordinarily speak of "coming out" as pregnant, even though that is an important and, at first, hidden or unapparent characteristic. The difference may be that pregnancy is not a lasting, lifelong condition, and is not (usually) stigmatized in the same way as being gay or having been a substance abuser. It is interesting to compare this example to Eve Sedgwick's example of "coming out" as fat; see n. 10.

[9]Sedgwick, *Epistemology of the Closet,* p. 72.

[10]By "coming out" as a fat woman, one could be acknowledging that society's messages about being fat have powerfully shaped one's feelings about oneself (self-hatred, shame), while raising as problematic the media and institutions that convey these messages, and their widespread acceptance.

[11]Sedgwick, *Epistemology of the Closet,* pp. 3–4.

[12]Jeffrey Escoffier gets at the change in strategy which occured after the Stonewall riots in 1969: "The gay liberationists, who rarely had much appreciation for traditional gay life, proposed a radical cultural revolution. Instead of protecting the right to privacy, gay-liberation radicals insisted on 'coming out'—the public disclosure of one's homosexuality—which then became the centerpiece of gay political strategy." Jeffrey Escoffier, "Sexual Revolution and the Politics of Gay Identity," *Socialist Review* 15 (July–October 1985): 143. Blasius echoes this: "The contemporary lesbian and gay movement since Stonewall has made living one's life as an openly gay or lesbian person a criterion of 'liberation' " ("An Ethos of Lesbian and Gay Experience," p. 647).

[13]" 'The open avowal of one's sexual identity,' explains John D'Emilio, 'whether at work, at school, at home, or before television cameras, symbolized the shedding of the self-hatred that gay men and women internalized, and consequently it promised an immediate improvement in one's life. To come out of the "closet" quintessentially expressed the fusion of the personal and the political that the radicalism of the late 1960's exalted.' " From *Sexual Politics, Sexual Communities,* quoted in Shane Phelan, *Identity Politics* (Philadelphia: Temple University Press, 1989), p. 103.

[14]"Why should you go to all this trouble [of taking the next step out of the closet,] risking life, limb, and financial security? . . . By increasing gay visibility, we can put a face on the stereotype and make it more difficult for thinking people to accept the caricature that the hate-mongers try to paint of homosexuals. Quite simply, you will be doing yourself a favor in the long run. This is a chance to change the world by changing your little corner of the world." *Dignity/Lafayette* newsletter (September/October 1992): 1. Phelan echoes this: "Coming out makes the possibility and actuality of difference more visible, with the aim of enhancing both the awareness of others and the self-esteem of the one coming out" (*Identity Politics,* p. 103).

[15]Blasius, "An Ethos of Lesbian and Gay Existence," p. 660. "The morale and destiny of that community is at stake in being able to live one's own ethos. Thus, in the formation of an ethos, the earlier posed 'How shall I live?' becomes inextricably connected to 'How shall we live?' The stake that one has in the morale and destiny of the local lesbian and gay community, that makes one's 'self' possible, becomes a stake in civic involvement in wider sociohistorical existence in all aspects of such existence that may affect one's ability to come out and live as a lesbian and gay ethos." Ibid., p. 659.

[16]For a fuller discussion of the politicalness of refusing to assimilate—that is, to adopt values and characteristics that deny and belittle who one really is—see Chapter 3. See also Morris B. Kaplan, "Intimacy and Equality: The Question of Lesbian and Gay Marriage," *Philosophical Forum* 25.4 (1994): 333–60.

[17]In many cities the gay community provides a physical space where visibly out homosexuals live, work, cruise, or frequent businesses owned or run by gays, or aimed at a gay clientele. Such communities are sometimes characterized as "gay ghettos," "ethnic" enclaves, or subcultures. Lesbian separatist communities may exclude men altogether. In some cities the gay community may exercise a degree of political power, may even form a "gay public." See especially Steven Epstein, "Gay Politics, Ethnic Identity: The Limits of Social Constructionism," *Socialist Review* 17 (1987): 9–54.

[18]Epstein, "Gay Politics, Ethnic Identity," p. 21. Epstein persuasively argues for an analogy between gay identity and ethnic identity, drawing on a cogent analysis of the essentialist-constructivist debate to show that, despite being acquired through secondary socialization as an adult, gay identity works very much like ethnic identity, in that neither is completely given nor chosen. "To paraphrase Marx," he writes, "people make their own identities, but they do not make them just as they please. Identities are phenomena that permit people to become acting 'subjects' who define who they are in the world, but at the same time identities 'subject' those people to the controlling power of external categorization" (pp. 29–30). See also Escoffier, "Sexual Revolution and the Politics of Gay Identity."

[19]Epstein, "Gay Politics, Ethnic Identity," p. 45; see also pp. 20, 38.

[20]Ibid., p. 22.

[21]Hanna Pitkin, "Justice: On Relating Private and Public," *Political Theory* 9.3 (August 1981): 347.

[22]Escoffier, "Sexual Revolution and the Politics of Gay Identity," p. 148.

[23]"Straight women are confused by men, don't put women first, they betray Lesbians and in its deepest form, they betray their own selves. You can't build a strong movement if your sisters are out there fucking the oppressor." Rita Mae Brown, "The Shape of Things to Come," quoted in Phelan, *Identity Politics,* p. 46.

[24]Phelan, *Identity Politics,* pp. 45, 49.

[25]Ibid., pp. 101, 130 (quoting Lorna Weir and Leo Casey, "Subverting Power in Sexuality," *Socialist Review* 75–76 [May/August 1984]: 154), 89, 125–26, 112–13.

[26]Ibid., p. 97. One writer suggests that antipathy to bisexuals within the lesbian and gay communities may be connected to unconscious racism in these communities, which kept whites who defined the gay and lesbian communities from seeing that bisexuality was common among people of color. Brenda Marie Blasingame, "The Roots of Biphobia: Racism and Internalized Heterosexism," in *Closer to Home: Bisexuality and Feminism* (Seattle: Seal Press, 1992).

[27]Ibid., pp. 132, 167. Phelan suggests this when she writes: "The result of this knowledge [that sexuality is a means of control] need not be a microscopic examination into the

details of each individual's sexuality. We may draw the conclusion that, in fact, it is precisely this that commands us to respect one another's privacy, to refrain from confessing or demanding confession, and to seriously reconsider demands that we be hetero- or homo-, perverted or normal, marginal or central" (p. 160).

[28]Escoffier, "Sexual Revolution and the Politics of Gay Identity," p. 149. See also Davies, "The Role of Disclosure in Coming Out among Gay Men," p. 83; and Morris B. Kaplan, "Autonomy, Equality, Community: The Question of Lesbian and Gay Rights," *Praxis International* 11.2 (July 1991): 211.

[29]Jeb Rubenfeld, "The Right of Privacy," *Harvard Law Review* 102.4: (1989): 779.

[30]Phelan is scathing in her criticisms of the closed lesbian community; see, for example, *Identity Politics,* pp. 57, 139, 156–57, 160, 170.

[31]Signorile, *Queer in America,* p. 84.

[32]To accept the closet, in Mohr's view, is at best to be "the 'happy slave' . . . committed to the institution of slavery in the way a dog is committed to his food bowl" (*Gay Ideas,* p. 32).

[33]Signorile, *Queer in America,* p. 155. Most advocates of outing argue that only public figures or people in positions of public power should be outed, not ordinary private persons. See ibid., pp. 78, 82.

[34]Gabriel Rotello, "Tactical Considerations," *OutWeek,* May 16, 1990, p. 52. See also Signorile, *Queer in America,* p. 83. Several writers have drawn on the analogy between gays and Jews, to very different ends. Mohr analogizes gay "keepers and bearers of secrets" to Jews and Nazies during the Holocaust: "The openly gay keeper of The Secret is morally *not* like those who, working the fields, simply observed in the distance trains carrying Jews to the East; rather, the keeper is like those who, while not setting the trains in motion, nevertheless voluntarily serviced the trains on their way to the East" (*Gay Ideas,* p. 31). Contrast this with Fran Lebowitz's comments on outing: "To me this is a bunch of Jews lining up other Jews to go to a concentration camp." Rebecca Lewin, "A Few Minutes with Fractious Fran: Writer Fran Lebowitz Chews Up More Than Her Dinner," *The Advocate,* July 3, 1990, p. 63. Perhaps the difference in opinion has to do with how dangerous different writers perceive homophobia to be.

[35]Signorile, *Queer in America,* pp. 81–82.

[36]Ibid., pp. 79–80. See also Mohr, *Gay Ideas,* p. 17.

[37]Mohr, *Gay Ideas,* p. 30. For the general argument that there is no right to secrecy, see pp. 12–23. See p. 14 for the argument that one's marital status is almost never secret, though one's amorous activities are. I discuss this claim at length later in this chapter. And see Rotello, "Tactical Considerations," p. 52.

[38]Signorile defended outing Pentagon official Pete Williams on these grounds (*Queer in America,* chap. titled "Outing, Part II"). The openly gay congressman Barney Frank has advocated outing hypocritical legislators in some cases. Rick Harding, "Outing," *The Advocate,* July 17, 1990, p. 9. See also Blasius, "An Ethos of Lesbian and Gay Existence," p. 661: "If one is currently engaging in or has in the past engaged in homoerotic sex, and wages war against the lesbian and gay community or is actively indifferent to the waging of war by others when one could make a palpable difference, that community has the political right to defend itself by exposing the hypocrisy at the very least. . . . Thus outing is best conceived as a strategy of insuring accountability among policymakers . . . or public figures."

[39]See Mohr, *Gay Ideas,* pp. 20–21, for a statement of this position, with which he disagrees.

[40]See, for example, Signorile, *Queer in America,* pp. xix, 315; Mohr, *Gay Ideas,* p. 47; Rotello, "Tactical Considerations," pp. 52–53.

[41]See, for example, *Paul v. Davis* 424 U.S. 693 (1976) for a case involving a man falsely accused of shoplifting who objected to a flyer being circulated to stores, headed "Accused Shoplifters" and bearing his photograph. There is also a legally recognized interest in preventing strangers from having access to the details of one's life, even when that information is not shameful. For treatment of cases involving an innocent person's interest in avoiding publicity about her private life, see *Time v. Hill* 385 U.S. 374 (1967). For a discussion of this interest, see David M. O'Brien, *Privacy, Law, and Public Policy* (New York: Praeger, 1979).

[42]"Human sexuality is too mysterious and too fluid to be reduced to [simply declaring a person's sexual orientation]. Honesty can destroy relationships, candor in the affairs of the heart is almost always a means to assert some sort of control." Andrew Sullivan, "Washington Diarist: Sleeping with the Enemy," *New Republic,* September 9, 1991, p. 43.

[43]Mohr, *Gay Ideas,* p. 14.

[44]Ibid., p. 19; See also pp. 24, 30, 32–33.

[45]"People have a right to protect themselves from the hatred of others without being accused of hating themselves." C. Carr, "Why Outing Must Stop," *Village Voice,* March 19, 1991, p. 37.

[46]See Mohr, *Gay Ideas,* pp. 29–30.

[47]For example, Carr writes that "it is *never* right for gay people to use homophobia to punish each other" ("Why Outing Must Stop," p. 37). In the same vein, Rick Harding reports that "NGLTF [National Gay and Lesbian Task Force] executive director Urvashi Vaid said her organization opposes outing under any circumstances. 'Outing is counterproductive because it doesn't tackle homophobia,' she said. 'In fact, it relies on homophobia for titillation. If we argue that the government and the church shouldn't have control over people's private lives, then who are we, as gays, to assume that kind of control ourselves?' " Rick Harding, "Outing," *The Advocate,* July 17, 1990, p. 9.

[48]Hunter Madsen, "Tattle Tale Traps," *OutWeek,* May 16, 1990, pp. 41–42.

[49]Carr, "Why Outing Must Stop," p. 37. Mohr also argues that it is homophobia, not outers, that ruins careers (*Gay Ideas,* p. 34).

[50]Blasius, "An Ethos of Lesbian and Gay Existence," p. 661.

[51]Madsen echoes this argument: "Being out is good, but coming out is better. We must cherish the process of coming out. No gay person should deny another the incomparable, irreplaceable, once-in-a-lifetime opportunity to come out of the closet under his or her own steam, as the fruit of deep personal reflection, courage and conviction. . . . For many a closeted homosexual, the moment does eventually arrive when she steps forward to affirm her own character openly, and thereby becomes the author of it. This rite of passage is far too important to the development of a positive gay identity for someone else—some venal or irresponsible blabbermouth—to callously preempt it, to steal it away. . . . Being flushed into the open by others before one is ready . . . can [be crushing] because one has lost forever, at that terrible instant, the single thing that makes coming out socially bearable: the dignity one may claim from having at least *chosen* to come out, chosen to be different" ("Tattle Tale Traps," pp. 41–42).

[52]E. J. Graff, "Outing Cannibalizes Our Community," *Gay Community News,* July 29–August 4, 1990, p. 5. Madsen echoes the point: "A positive role model who has to be outed simply isn't one! . . . The image of homosexuality as a furtive, sick, shameful thing is amply

reinforced by the spectacle of otherwise prominent closet-cases being driven out from their dark places into the blinding light of day, only to suffer (as they usually do) an immediate fall from public grace. Role models, indeed" ("Tattle Tale Traps," p. 42).

[53]Michelangelo Signorile argues that heterosexuals who want to understand the outing debate may try "to get some insight from homosexual friends, but that's another problem: Depending on whom they ask they'll get different answers, all of which are bound to confuse them. Certainly the closeted, as captives, suffer such profound psychological trauma that they develop a relationship to their closets similar to that of hostages to their captors: They defend them—lulled into a false sense of security and blind to the trauma they experience—and are threatened by those who are completely out." In other words, no one can believe gays who defend the closet because they suffer from false consciousness, a position that allows Signorile to discount genuine differences of opinion about the closet and outing (*Queer in America,* p. xviii).

[54]Lewin, "A Few Minutes with Fractious Fran," p. 63.

[55]Carr, "Why Outing Must Stop," p. 37. Her point is echoed by Sullivan, "Washington Diarist," p. 43.

[56]See *Oxford English Dictionary.* This discussion is indebted to Mary Dietz, Hanna Pitkin, Hannah Arendt, and Sheldon Wolin, whose understandings of politics have greatly enriched my own.

[57]Mary Dietz evokes this understanding of politics beautifully in the opening pages of "Citizenship with a Feminist Face: The Problem with Maternal Thinking," *Political Theory* 13.1 (February 1985): 19–37.

[58]Hanna Pitkin writes: "Theirs [the alienated and oppressed who suffer in private] is the sort of transformation to which C. Wright Mills alludes: what had been accepted as personal trouble comes to be seen as an actionable political issue, a matter of justice. Here we find the housewife who learns for the first time that she is not alone in her misery and boredom, that what troubles her is part of a social structure that can be altered." Pitkin, "Justice," pp. 347–48.

[59]Phelan writes that Jean Grimshaw "cites [Mary] Daly's use of phrases such as 'fembots' and 'puppets of Papa' to describe women who are not feminist enough, which does not suggest a willingness to stay and struggle with these women, to spend energy on them." Phelan, *Identity Politics,* p. 107.

[60]Ibid., p. 155.

[61]See especially Bernice Johnson Reagon, "Coalition Politics: Turning the Century," in *Home Girls: A Black Feminist Anthology,* ed. Barbara Smith (New York: Kitchen Table/ Women of Color Press, 1983), pp. 356–68; and Phelan, *Identity Politics,* pp. 167–69.

[62]Epstein, "Gay Politics, Ethnic Identity," pp. 46–47.

[63]Many suggest that identity politics can and should incorporate differences. See Minnie Bruce Pratt, "Identity: Skin Blood Heart," in Elly Bulkin, Minnie Bruce Pratt, and Barbara Smith, *Yours in Struggle: Three Feminist Perspectives on Anti-Semitism and Racism* (New York: Long Haul Press, 1984), pp. 11–63; Phelan, *Identity Politics,* chap. 8; Biddy Martin and Chandra Talpade Monhanty, "Feminist Politics: What's Home Got to Do with It?," in *Feminist Studies/Critical Studies,* ed. Teresa de Lauretis (Bloomington: University of Indiana Press, 1986), esp. pp. 193, 196, 207–9; Reagon, "Coalition Politics." Others point to the diversity within gay and lesbian communities. See, for example, Marilyn Frye, "Lesbian Community: Heterodox Congregation," in *Willful Virgin* (Freedom, Calif.: Crossing Press, 1992), pp. 120–23; Esther Newton, "Just One of the Boys: Lesbians in Cherry Grove, 1960–1988," in

The Lesbian and Gay Studies Reader, ed. Henry Abelove, Michele Barale, and David Halperin (New York: Routledge, 1993), pp. 528–41.

Conclusion. Privacy and Democratic Citizenship

[1]For example, Seyla Benhabib refers to "a radical feminism which can hardly conceal its own political and moral authoritarian undertones." Benhabib, "Feminist Theory and Hannah Arendt's Concept of Public Space," *History of the Human Sciences* 6.2 (1993): 110. See also critics of "outing" discussed in Chapter 6.

[2]For a fine argument about this temptation to avoid judging political issues, see William Greider, *The Education of David Stockman and Other Americans* (New York: New American Library, 1986), pp. 118–31.

[3]Benhabib, "Hannah Arendt's Concept of Public Space," pp. 109–10. See also Sheldon S. Wolin, "Democracy and the Welfare State: The Political and Theoretical Connections between Staatsrason and Wohlfahrtsstaatsrason," *Political Theory* 15.4 (1987): 467–500.

Index